THE ARCHDRUID REPORT
The Ecology of Collapse
Collected Essays, Volume II, 2008

THE ARCHDRUID REPORT

The Ecology of Collapse

Collected Essays, Volume II, 2008

JOHN MICHAEL GREER

FOUNDERS HOUSE PUBLISHING

The Archdruid Report: The Ecology of Collapse
Collected Essays, Volume II, 2008
Copyright © 2017 John Michael Greer
Published by Founders House Publishing, LLC
Cover art copyright © Grandfailure/Dreamstime
Cover and interior design © 2017 Founders House Publishing, LLC

Paperback Edition: October 2017

ISBN-13: 978-1-945810-10-7
ISBN-10: 1-945810-10-6

The contents of this book appeared in a slightly different form on the blog www.thearchdruidreport.blogspot.com during its eleven-year run.

For more information please visit www.foundershousepublishing.com

Published in the United States of America

CONTENTS

THE ARCHDRUID REPORT
The Ecology of Collapse
Collected Essays, Volume II, 2008

INTRODUCTION

2008 was in many ways a banner year for The Archdruid Report, though that had as much to do with external events as it did with anything I did or didn't do in that year's blog posts. Over the course of the year, the price of crude oil soared to previously unimagined heights and then crashed again, confounding both the pundits of the mainstream and many of the writers in the then-burgeoning peak oil scene; the real estate bubble that had been inflating since 2002 or so, to the accompaniment of clueless cheerleading from economists and the media, tipped over into a spectacular bust; the global financial system briefly tottered as the Lehman Brothers brokerage firm imploded and dozens of banks worldwide suffered gargantuan losses; and the words "peak oil" crept out of their long exile to trouble the pages of newspapers of record.

In such a setting it wasn't surprising that a blog that tried to talk sensibly about the shape of history and the future of industrial society would begin to attract serious attention. It helped that in 2008 my first book on the future, The Long Descent, saw print; it also helped that in the fall of that year I attended the Sacramento conference of the US branch of ASPO, the Association for the Study of Peak Oil, and was a featured speaker at the Conference on Peak Oil and Community Solutions in a suburb of Detroit. Behind those highlights was a steady climb in the blog's readership, and an equally steady diffusion of some of the concepts I was trying to discuss into the peak oil scene generally. The Archdruid Report was hitting its stride, and the flurries of sometimes harsh criticism it attracted showed me just how broad an impact it had.

What strikes me, as I read back over the posts from 2008, is the relative optimism so many of them display. That wasn't unique to The Archdruid Report, admittedly. The dizzying spike in oil prices mentioned above had demonstrated clearly — or so many of us thought at the time — that the pundits who insisted the price of oil couldn't possibly spin out of control were quite simply wrong. Politicians, bankers, and businesspeople were starting to notice the widening gap between the bland predictions of prosperity being offered by the economic mainstream and the far harsher realities in play on the ground. It seemed possible, for a while, that something constructive might be done on a collective level about industrial society's increasingly intractable predicament.

Such hopes occupied only a certain fraction of Archdruid Report posts, though. Meanwhile, the broader project of sketching out a view of history and human life that could support sustainable societies over the long term continued, one Wednesday post at a time.

— John Michael Greer

71: THE FUTURE THAT WASN'T
PART ONE: "THE SUNSET-DROWNING OF THE EVENING LANDS"
(Originally published 26 December 2007)

I'd planned to devote this week's Archdruid Report post to the fine and practical art of composting, and for good reason. It's one of the most important and least regarded techniques in the ecotechnic toolkit, and it's also a near-perfect model for the way that today's mindlessly linear conversion of resources to waste can be brought back around in a circle, like the legendary ouroboros-snake that swallows its own tail, to become the sustainable resource flows of the human ecologies of the future.

Still, that profoundly worthwhile topic will have to wait a while. Even the most mercenary writer is now and then at the mercy of his muse, held hostage by some awkwardly timed bit of inspiration that elbows other projects aside, and I think that most of us who write for a living learn sooner or later to put up with the interruption and write out what has to be written. If this sudden veering from the pragmatic issues central to the last few posts needs a justification, that's the only one I have to offer.

Well, maybe not quite the only one. The holiday season now lurching past is not a time I particularly enjoy. Our solstice ceremony a few days back was a bright spot, mind you; midsummer is a more significant occasion in my Druid faith, but it's as pleasant as it is moving to gather with local Druids in the circle of the sacred grove to light the winter solstice fire and celebrate the rebirth of the sun in the depths of winter. Nor do I find anything in the least offensive in the Christian celebrations of the season. As human beings, we're all far enough from the luminous center of

things that we have to take meaning where we can find it; if someone can grasp the eternal renewal of spirit in darkness through
the symbol of the midwinter birth of Jesus of Nazareth, I can't
find it in myself to object. From my perspective, though not from
theirs, of course, we're celebrating the same thing.

Nor, for that matter, do I turn Scroogelike at the thought of
gifts, big dinners, and too much brandy in the egg nog. I can't
think of a human culture in the northern temperate zone that
hasn't found some reason to fling down life's gauntlet in the face
of winter with a grand party. Whether it's the Saturnalia of the
ancient Romans, when cold grim Saturn turns back just for a moment into the generous king of the Golden Age, or the Hamatsa
winter dances of the Kwakiutl nation of Canada's Pacific coast,
when the cannibal giant Baxbakualanooksiwae, "Eater of Men
at the River Mouth," is revealed as the source of mighty spiritual gifts, this sort of celebration reflects a profound set of realities
about our life in the world. Besides, I'm fond of brandy, and egg
nog, and a good party now and then, too.

No, what makes the midwinter holidays a less than raptur-
ous time for me is the spectacle of seeing the things I've just list-
ed redefined as artificial stimulants for a dysfunctional economy
supported by nothing so straightforward as honest smoke and
mirrors. When front page news stories about Christmas center
on whether consumer spending this holiday season will provide
enough of an amphetamine fix to keep our speed-freak economic
system zooming along, I start wishing that Baxbakualanooksiwae
and his four gigantic man-eating birds would consider adding
corporate vice-presidents and media flacks to their holiday menu.

And that, dear readers, is what sent me for refuge to Oswald
Spengler. A mild depression can be treated with Ogden Nash poems and Shakespeare comedies, but when things get really grim
it's time for the hair of the dog. The same effect that leaves the soul
feeling oddly lighter after taking in a Greek tragedy, or listening
to an entire album of really blue blues, hits a history geek like
myself after a chapter or two of Der Untergang des Abendlandes.

I insist on the German title, by the way. The splendor of Germany's literature and the curse on its history come from the same

source, the brilliant but sometimes misleading way the German language naturally expresses abstract ideas in concrete, sensuous terms. Untergang, which gets turned in English into the anemic Latinism "decline," is literally "going under," and calls to mind inevitably the last struggles of the drowning and the irrevocable descent of the sun below the western horizon. Abendland, the German for "the West," is literally "the evening land," the land toward sunset. Put them together and the result could be turned into a crisp line of iambic pentameter by an English poet—"the sunset-drowning of the evening lands"—but there's no way an English language book on the philosophy of history could survive a title like that. In German, by contrast, it's inevitable, and for Oswald Spengler, it's perfect.

Spengler has been poorly treated in recent writings on the decline and fall of civilizations. Joseph Tainter's The Collapse of Compex Societies, for example, takes him to task for not providing a scientific account of the causes of societal collapse, which is a little like berating Michelangelo for not including accurate astrophysics in his frescoes in the Sistine Chapel. Spengler was not a scientist and never pretended to be one. He was a philosopher of history; in some ways, really, he was an artist who took the philosophy of history for his medium in place of paint or music. This does not make his contributions to our understanding of history less relevant. It's only in the imagination of the most fundamentalist kinds of scientific materialism that scientific meaning is the only kind of meaning that there is. In dealing with human behavior, above all, a sonnet, a story, or a philosophical treatise can prove a better anticipation of the flow of events than any scientific analysis—and the decline and fall of our present civilization, or any other, is preeminently a story about human behavior.

Tainter's critique also fails in that Spengler was not even talking about the fall of civilizations. What interested him was the origin and fate of cultures, and he didn't mean this term in the anthropological sense. In his view, a culture is a overall way of looking at the world with its own distinct expressions in religious, philosophical, artistic, and social terms. For him, all the societies of the "evening lands"—that is, all of western Europe from roughly 1000

CE on, and the nations of the European diaspora in the Americas and Australasia—comprise a single culture, which he terms the Faustian. Ancestral to the Faustian culture in one sense, and its polar opposite in another, is the Apollonian culture of the classic Mediterranean world, from Homeric Greece to the early Roman empire; ancestral to the Faustian culture in a different sense, and parallell to it in another, is the Magian culture, which had its origins in Zoroastrian Persia, absorbed the Roman Empire during its later phases, and survives to this day as the Muslim civilization of the Middle East. Other Spenglerian cultures are the Egyptian, the Chinese, the Mesopotamian, the Indian, and the Mexican.

Talking about the rise and fall of a culture in Spengler's sense, then, isn't a matter of tracing shifts in political or economic arrangements. It's about the birth, flowering, and death of a distinctive way of grasping the nature of human existence, and everything that unfolds from that—which, in human terms, is just about everything that matters. The Apollonian culture, for example, rose out of the chaotic aftermath of the Minoan-Mycenean collapse with a unique vision of humanity and the world rooted in the experience of the Greek polis, the independent self-governing community in which everything important was decided by social process. Greek theology envisioned a polis of gods, Greek physics a polis of fundamental elements, Greek ethics a polis of virtues, and so on down the list of cultural creations. Projected around the Mediterranean basin first by Greek colonialism, then by Alexander's conquests, and finally by the expansion of Rome, it became the worldview and the cultural inspiration of one of the world's great civilizations.

That, according to Spengler, was also its epitaph. A culture, any culture, embodies a particular range of human possibility, and like everything else, it suffers from the law of diminishing returns. Sooner or later, everything that can be done from within the worldview of a culture—everything religious, philosophical, intellectual, artistic, social, political, you name it—has basically been done, and the culture fossilizes into a civilization. Thereafter the same things get repeated over and over again in endless combinations; disaffected intellectuals no longer capable of creativity settle for mere novelty or, worse still, simple shock value; artistic and intellectual traditions from other cultures get imported to fill the widening void; technology progresses in a kind of mechanical forward lurch until the social structures capable of supporting it fall away from underneath it. Sooner or later, the civilization falls apart, basically, because nobody actually believes in it any more.

What made this prophecy a live issue in Spengler's time was that he placed the twilight of Western culture and the beginning of its mummification into Western civilization in the decades right after 1800. Around then, he argued, the vitality of the cultural forms that took shape in western Europe around 1000 began trickling away in earnest. By then, in his view, the Western world's religions had already begun to mummify into the empty repetition of older forms; its art, music, and literature lost their way in the decades that followed; its political forms launched into the fatal march toward gigantism that leads to empire and, in time, to empire's fall; only its science and technology, like the sciences and technologies of previous cultures, continued blindly on its way, placing ever more gargantuan means in the service of ever more impoverished ends.

Exactly how the Faustian culture would metastasize into a future Faustian civilization he did not try to predict, but one element of the transition seemed certain enough to find its way into his book. The society that would play Rome to Europe's Greece, he suggested, was none other than the United States of America. In the brash architecture of American skyscrapers and the casual gesture that flung an army across the Atlantic to save France and England from defeat in the last years of the First World War, he thought he saw the swagger of incipient Caesarism, the rise of the empire that would become Faustian culture's final achievement and its tomb.

It was a common belief at that time. Interestingly enough, it also shaped the thought of Spengler's counterpart and rival, the British historian Arnold Toynbee, whose ten-volume A Study of History stands like hoplites in a Greek phalanx not far from the couch where Spengler and multiple cups of good oolong offered some consolation for the wretched orgy of economic excess and hallucinated well-being playing itself out outside my windows. For Toynbee, who shared Spengler's cyclical theory of history but rejected all his philosophy and most of his conclusions, the natural next step in the unfolding of history was the transition from a time of troubles to a planetary empire, and like many English intellectuals in the twilight of the British Empire, he expected an alliance between the United States and the British Commonwealth to become the seed of that empire-to-be.

As it turns out, though, this plausible and widely held belief was quite incorrect, and the actions taken by three generations of politicians and intellectuals in response to that belief are all too likely to play out with disastrous results in the fairly near future. We'll discuss that in next week's post.

PART TWO: THE PHANTOM OF EMPIRE
(Originally published 2 January 2008)

Perhaps it's just an outward projection of the jaundiced attitude toward the holidays I expressed in last week's Archdruid Report post, but it seems to me that this year's New Year celebrations were a bit more restrained than usual, or more than a bit. Most of the people I know chose to stay at home on the last night of 2007, and while many of them claimed they were planning to toast in the new year with something more or less festive, my best guess is that most of them did some equivalent of hiding under their beds. One friend's emailed New Year message expressed the bright hope that 2008 wouldn't suck as much as 2007.

Nor has the opening of the year failed to live up, or down, to expectations; the news from 2008's first business day is not precisely encouraging. As I write these words, the US stock market is doing its best to prove Isaac Newton right by dropping like a stone, on news that US manufacturing output has slumped unexpectedly. Gold has soared to a new record and oil is back above $97 a barrel; one-quarter of all US subprime mortgages are now in some stage of the foreclosure process, and default rates in the rest of the mortgage market, not to mention car loans and credit card debt, are climbing steadily.

My favorite story of the day so far, though, is the Australian real estate holding company that bought no fewer than 700 American shopping malls—I have a hard time imagining a better image of speculative excess than that one fact—using funds from the commercial paper market. They've got $3.4 billion in loans due for repayment on February 15, and their chance of finding a lender to roll those loans over just now ranks down there with the proverbial snowball in Beelzebub's back yard. So the entire company is up for sale. I don't imagine any of my readers cherish a lifelong ambition to own 700 shopping malls, but if I'm wrong, here's your chance.

All this, for reasons that go beyond the obvious, makes an excellent backdrop for the subject of today's post. My regular readers will recall that last week I introduced the redoubtable Oswald Spengler, whose theory of the decline and fall of Western culture got so much attention between the two world wars and has been dismissed so patronizingly since that time. Spengler argued that the cultural possibilities of Western society reached the point of diminishing returns around the beginning of the nineteenth century and run out completely by the dawn of the twentieth. The future of the West, in his view, was the same fate that overtakes every great culture: the fossilization of cultural forms and the rise of a gargantuan empire propped up by brute force.

He was far from the only thinker to envision the future in those terms. Not all of the others put the same negative spin on it, and one of those who saw the upside of empire had far more influence than Spengler ever did. This was Arnold Toynbee, whose ideas have appeared on this blog more than once already. Toynbee was by no means a mindless fan of empire, and much of his sprawling A Study of History focuses on the ways that empires inevitably destroy themselves. Still, like Spengler, he argued that societies go through predictable stages in their life cycle; like Spengler, he saw the rise of a Universal State as the next stage in the history of the Western world; unlike Spengler, he was in a position to help that stage come about.

Toynbee spent most of his working life at the helm of the Royal Institute for International Affairs (RIIA), and published A Study of History under its auspices. The RIIA is the British counterpart of the Council on Foreign Relations (CFR), an influential association of prominent politicians and businessmen that has been a bugbear of the American conspiracy scene for decades now. The two organizations emerged right after the First World War out of the same network of business interests, and Toynbee was in some sense the pet historical theorist of both; in the early days of the Second World War, for example, all the notes and drafts for his not-yet-written volumes were stored for safekeeping at CFR headquarters in New York City.

What makes this relevant is that Toynbee's work has been a template for public policy in Britain and America since the 1920s. Point for point, the mainstream in both countries has embraced all the things Toynbee considered good for empires and rejected those he labeled bad. According to Toynbee, for example, when an imperial power borders a poorer and less advanced society, it's a fatal mistake to allow that border to degenerate into a guarded frontier. In case after case in history, this kickstarts a struggle that the imperial power will ultimately lose. The US policy of an open border with Mexico, maintained in the face of mass migration that has seen something like a tenth of Mexico's population cross the Rio Grande, is hard to understand unless some overriding concern requires it; Toynbee may well be the source of that concern.

None of this is any sort of secret. Anybody with internet access or a decent library can get the membership list of the CFR, request copies of CFR position papers, and subscribe to Foreign Affairs, the journal published by the CFR, in which public policy issues come up for debate well before they find their way into politics and the media. The irony, and it's not a small one, is that conspiracy theorists could have gotten plenty of ammunition from Toynbee, or for that matter from the pages of Foreign Affairs, if they had bothered to do a bit of research. Toynbee, remember, believed that the coming American empire would be a good thing. His reasons are unpopular in today's political climate, but in the context of their own time they were by no means completely empty.

In Toynbee's vision of history, every civilization is born when a people facing a serious challenge responds to it by achieving a new level of integration as a society, and develops exactly as long as its leadership can meet new challenges with responses that inspire the respect and loyalty of the rest of the population. Once the leadership starts trying to force new problems to fit old solutions, its power to inspire breaks down, and the civilization enters a time of troubles from which only the rise of a universal state can save it. In Toynbee's eyes, the time of troubles for Western civilization arrived in 1914, and the rise of an American empire was the only thing that could prevent Europe from sliding further down a death spiral of internecine war.

Behind this interpretation of history, and its equivalents in Spengler and many other thinkers of the same time, lay a belief that Western history was locked into a parallel with a specific period of the past. Every schoolchild in Spengler's Germany and Toynbee's Britin learned about the quarreling city-states of ancient Greece, which created most of classical culture and then nearly destroyed it and themselves in an age of fratricidal warfare. In the wake of 1914, people across Europe decided that their own society had reached the equivalent of 431 BCE, the beginning of the Peloponnesian War and ancient Greece's time of troubles. To many of them, the comparison between Greece and Europe made a comparison between Rome and America inescapable, and no small number came to hope for an American equivalent of Augustus Caesar — someone who would rein in the unruly nation-states and impose peace on the world.

This was Toynbee's view. It also seems to have been the view of the CFR, the RIIA, and those sectors of the American and British political classes who shared their agenda. It's popular these days to assume that this was simply window dressing over a desire for power, but that says at least as much about our contemporary habit of demonizing political enemies as anything else. Doubtless the people who backed the project of American empire thought about how they might benefit from it, but then such motives are anything but absent from many of those who denounce American empire today. In a world reeling from the effects of two catastrophic wars, the idea of a global Pax Americana had an appeal that was by no means wholly imaginary.

What neither Spengler nor Toynbee realized, though, was that the American ascendancy in the twentieth century rested on foundations far more fleeting than Rome's. The basis of American power was geological, rooted in the accidents of paleoecology that left immense deposits of crude oil in half a dozen American states, and can be measured by the fact that in 1950 the United States produced more crude oil than the rest of the world put together. Winston Churchill famously remarked that the Allies had floated to victory in the First World War on an ocean of American oil, and the Second depended even more dramatically on oil production, with oil-poor Germany and Japan overwhelmed by the tanks, ships, and planes of oil-rich America and Russia.

By the first wave of energy crises in the 1970s, however, the geological basis for American ascendancy no longer existed, because most of it had been pumped out of the ground and burnt. I've argued elsewhere that the American political class in the Seventies faced a difficult choice between a transition to sustainability and a high-tech, high risk nuclear society, and ended up choosing neither because the costs on both sides were too high. Since then, political and economic gimmicks and a willingness to burn through our remaining resources with reckless abandon have papered over the hard reality of American decline.

It's in this context, I've suggested, that the neoconservative adventures of the last decade needs to be interpreted. By the end of the 1990s, it was very likely clear even to the most recalcitrant members of America's political class that trusting the free market to find a long-term solution to America's energy dependence had failed. It's a matter of public knowledge that investment banker Matthew Simmons, one of the first voices to raise an alarm over peak oil in the 1990s, was brought in as a consultant to Vice President Cheney immediately after the 2000 election. The march to war that followed can best be understood as a desperate attempt to keep the dream of empire from collapsing completely by giving America control over Iraq's petroleum reserves.

It was a bad plan, pragmatically as well as ethically, and the incompetence with which it was put into effect has not exactly helped the situation. Still, I'm far from sure that those Americans who talk about their eagerness to see the troops come home from the Middle East have quite grasped what they are asking for. For the last sixty years the American way of life has depended on wildly unequal international relationships that guarantee the 5% of the human race that lives in the United States access to more than 30% of the world's energy and other resources. The collapse of American empire, when it occurs, will see that state of affairs come to an end. It remains to be seen how enthusiastic the critics of empire will be when their own standard of living drops to one-sixth of its current level.

It's hard to ignore the likelihood that some such discontinuity waits in America's near future. Our political class, chasing after the phantom of empire, has followed it right over the edge of a cliff. Exactly how the results will play out is anybody's guess right now. Equally uncertain is how the political classes in America and elsewhere will respond when a vision that has guided public policy for most of a century turns out to be as insubstantial as air. One way or another, though, we are likely in for a wild ride.

72: BACK UP THE RABBIT HOLE
(Originally published 6 February 2008)

One of this blog's central purposes, the attempt to glimpse the future's patterns in the Rohrshach inkblots of the present, poses a notoriously difficult challenge. Perhaps the worst of the difficulties involved in that attempt, as I've suggested here more than once, is the pervasive influence of mythic narratives so deeply ingrained in our culture that few people even notice them. In a retrospective essay on his own work, historian Arnold Toynbee offered a useful warning in this regard: "If one cannot think without mental patterns—and, in my belief, one cannot—it is better to know what they are; for a pattern of which one is unconscious is a pattern that holds one at its mercy."

Toynbee was critiquing historians of his own period who treated the idea of progress as a simple fact, rather than the richly imaginative secular mythology it actually is. Still, his caution can be applied far outside the limits of the academic study of history. Nearly every dimension of contemporary culture, today just as in Toynbee's time, embraces the unthinking assumption that the wave of history inevitably leads onward and upward through the present to a future that will look pretty much like the present, but more so.

This very widespread article of faith begs any number of questions. It seems to me, however, that one of them deserves special attention. The notion of history implicit in the modern mythology of progress is a straight line without branches or swerves, much less dead ends from which we might have to be retrace our steps. That idea of history, if it's embraced unthinkingly, leaves us with desperately few options if adaptations to some temporary set of conditions turn out to be counterproductive when those conditions go away.

This is anything but an abstract concern just now. As the world closes in on the end of the 21st century's first decade, its industrial societies are leaving behind a period in which just such a temporary set of conditions held sway. Until we recognize the blind alley down which those conditions led the developed world, we will be hard put to respond to a future that has begun to move in a very different direction.

A glance back three decades or so offers a necessary perspective. In the last years of the 1970s, conventional wisdom had it that the energy crises of that decade were the first waves of an "Age of Scarcity" that would demand either a massive conversion to nuclear power or an equally daunting and costly transition to a conserver economy in which relatively modest renewable energy inputs would be used with maximum efficiency. Both possibilities involved serious challenges and huge price tags, but in the face of the inevitable depletion of finite fossil fuel resources, those were the only rational options.

Unfortunately human affairs are not always governed by rational options. At the beginning of the 1980s, the political leadership of most Western countries—with the United States well in the lead under Ronald Reagan's myopic guidance—rejected both these possibilities in favor of short-term gimmicks that papered over the symptoms of the energy crisis while doing nothing to address its causes. The improved energy efficiencies bought so dearly during the Seventies made it possible for reckless overproduction in the North Slope and North Sea oil fields to send the price of oil plunging lower, in constant dollars, than ever before in human history. All through the Eighties and Nineties, political manipulation of the oil markets kept petroleum not too far from $10 a barrel: around 24 cents a gallon, in other words, for the industrial world's most precious natural resource.

The results of this disastrous collective choice have not, I think, been adequately measured even by most thinkers in the peak oil community. For a quarter of a century, from 1980 to 2005, petroleum could be had throughout the industrial world at prices so low it might as well have been free. Other energy costs dropped accordingly, as cheap oil competed with other resources for market share while simultaneously cutting the production and distribution costs of its competitors. The economic, infrastructural, and cultural initiatives that emerged during those years all embodied the assumption that "can we afford the energy cost?" was not a question anybody in the industrial world ever needed to ask.

One result was the movement toward economic globalization that spawned so much media chatter and devastated so many communities during those years. Propagandists for the private-sector socialism that passes for capitalism these days have insisted that this reflects the natural emergence of a global free market from which everybody would allegedly prosper someday, while their opponents have argued that it reflects a deliberate plot to force down wages and working conditions worldwide for the benefit of the rich. What has rarely been recognized is that perhaps the most important of all the forces driving globalization in those years was artificially low energy prices.

During the quarter century of ultracheap energy, transportation costs were so low that they became a negligible fraction of the cost of goods. This allowed manufacturers to arbitrage the difference in labor costs between industrial and nonindustrial countries without having to take shipping costs into account. The sort of predatory trade relationships pursued by European colonial empires in the 19th century could be replicated without the ferocious trade barriers and imperial misadventures of that earlier time; local industries could be flattened by overseas production without any need for naval bombardments or colonial administrations, because distance had no economic meaning.

Another result, at least as dramatic as globalization though less ballyhooed then or now, was the rise of a throwaway economy all through the industrial world. Not all that long ago, one business you could readily find in most American towns and urban neighborhoods was the small appliance repair shop, where toasters, clocks, radios, hair dryers, and a hundred other consumer goods could be taken for repair when they stopped working. An entire industry of small-scale entrepreneurs, and the support businesses that kept them stocked with spare parts, tools, and materials, survived on the economic realities that made it worthwhile to pay a repairman to fix small appliances instead of throwing them out and buying new ones.

That industry was already faltering by 1980 as the economic consequences of American empire distorted currency exchange rates and allowed other countries to export goods to the United States at a fraction of the cost of domestic production. The plunge in energy costs after 1980, though, finished the job. Once the cost of energy no longer mattered, consumer goods could be manufactured and shipped for a fraction of what they had previously cost, and repairing them made no economic sense when the repair might cost twice as much as a new model.

The explosive spread of the internet, finally, was also a product of the era of ultracheap energy. The hardware of the internet, with its worldwide connections, its vast server farms, and its billions of interlinked home and business computers, probably counts as the largest infrastructure project ever created and deployed in a two-decade period in human history. The sheer amount of energy that has had to be invested to create and sustain today's internet, along with its economic and cultural support systems, beggars the imagination.

Could it have been done at all if energy stayed as expensive as it was in the 1970s? It's hard to see how such a question could be answered, but the growth of the internet certainly would have been a much slower process; it might have moved in directions involving much less energy use; and some of the more energy-intensive aspects of the internet might never have emerged at all. It remains to be seen whether a system adapted to a hothouse climate of nearly free energy can cope with the harsher weather of rising energy costs in a postpeak world.

These examples could be multiplied almost endlessly, from our extravagant and dysfunctional health care system right up to the delusional economics that helped millions of Americans convince themselves that it made sense to buy poorly insulated, shoddily built new houses a three-hour drive from jobs and shopping. For a quarter century, people throughout the industrial world have become accustomed to economic, social, and personal arrangements that only work if energy is basically free. Just as with every previous economic shift in modern history, too, proponents of these arrangements wrapped them in the rhetoric of progress. Globalization was progress, we were told, and therefore as inevitable as it was irreversible; so was the internet; so, when it was noticed at all, was the throwaway economy.

Yet describing these changes as progress, in the sense given that word by our contemporary mythic narratives, dramatically misstates the situation. For a 25-year interval, by reckless overproduction of rapidly depleting resources and purblind manipulations pursued for short term political gain, the cost of energy was driven down to artificially low levels that had never been seen before—and, barring a whole concatenation of miracles, will never be seen again. The resulting glut of energy fostered ways of doing things that make no sense at all under any other conditions.

In hindsight, I suspect, the entire period from 1980 to 2005 will be seen as one of history's supreme blind alleys. A great many of the economic arrangements, infrastructure, and personal and collective habits that grew up in response to that age of distorted priorities will have to be reworked in a hurry, no matter what the cost, as energy prices rise to more realistic levels. At the same time, the grip of the myth of progress on the industrial world's imagination remains unshaken.

The possibility that the only way forward out of the present blind alley may require going back to less convenient and more costly ways of doing things is nowhere on our collective radar screens just now. It's easy to understand why. After all, most people living in the industrial world today have spent a majority of their lives in settings in which cheap abundant energy was the unquestioned birthright of anyone outside the poverty class, and those less than thirty years old never had the chance to experience anything else.

Those who borrow Lewis Carroll's metaphor and talk about the need to go down the rabbit hole have thus, I think, missed an important point. For the last quarter century, that's exactly where we've been. The challenge before us now—a challenge many upcoming Archdruid Report posts will grapple with in different ways — is to climb back out of the rabbit hole and deal with the world we will have to face when the extravagant Wonderland of the brief era of ultracheap energy dissolves into windblown leaves and the shreds of a departed dream.

73: THE LITTLE STEPS THAT MATTER

(Originally published 13 February 2008)

Over the last few months, the uncomfortable phrase "peak oil" has started to appear more and more frequently in the mainstream media, and the usual denunciations by the usual suspects are starting to wear noticeably thin. It's been more than half a century since M. King Hubbert first started trying to sound the alarm, granted, but better late than never.

Still, as I suggested in an earlier post, the process of coming to terms with peak oil has more than a little in common with the five stages of grief famously outlined some years back by Dr. Elisabeth Kubler-Ross. We've already seen two of those stages displayed in living color in recent years, and of course both are still very much with us.

The poster child for denial just now is Cambridge Energy Research Associates (CERA), a petroleum industry-funded think tank that has nonchalantly churned out predictions of soaring oil production and declining oil prices for years now, while production and prices in the real world have been headed the other way. For anger, you can hardly do better than watching the current US administration, brandishing its gargantuan war machine and bellowing its rage at Arabs, Venezuelans, and anybody else arrogant enough to think that they have some sort of right to the oil underneath their own territories.

At this point, though, we're beginning to see the next stage in the process, which is bargaining. The recent rush to pour our food supply into our gas tanks via ethanol and various flavors of biodiesel is one example; another is the belated attempt to launch a crash program of nuclear power plant construction. These and others partake of the basic logic of bargaining: we promise to mend our ways in some sufficiently large, loud, and colorful fashion that the wolf at the door will be satisfied with the puppy biscuit we throw its way, and let us go on with our lives.

It doesn't work for the dying, and it won't work for modern industrial society, either, but it's not hard to see this logic in the two examples I've already cited, and many other grandiose proposals of the same sort. The results of this distorting factor have not been good. The rush to ethanol and biodiesel has already played a significant role in sending grain prices to record levels and, as Stuart Saniford pointed out in a recent post on The Oil Drum, will quite probably cause mass starvation in the Third World within a decade or so if it continues at its present pace.

Attempting to revive the nuclear industry on a large scale is, if anything, a more misguided proposition. Even aside from the highly dubious economics of nuclear power, the severe and ongoing depletion of fissionable uranium reserves, the risks of nuclear weapons proliferation, and the far from minor point that nuclear reactors produce wastes so lethal that they have to be isolated from the environment for geologic time scales, the sheer cost of building enough nuclear plants to matter in the relatively narrow window of opportunity left to us could easily bankrupt any industrial society that attempted it.

What makes these and similar projects as destructive as they are futile is precisely that they are meant to allow us to continue living our lives in something like their present form. That fantasy, it seems to me, is the single largest obstacle in the path of a reasoned response to the predicament of peak oil. The hard reality we have to face is the fact that the extravagant, energy-wasting lifestyles of the recent past cannot be sustained by any amount of bargaining or any number of grand projects. Accept that reality, on the other hand, and redefine the situation in terms of managing a controlled descent from the giddy heights of the late industrial age, and the range of technological options widens out dramatically.

I want to talk about one of those less dramatic options here, partly because it's among the simplest and most accessible technologies in the toolkit of the ecotechnic age, partly because it could relatively easily become part of an effective response to one of the most pressing challenges the coming of peak oil poses us, and partly because it makes a good introduction to principles that will likely be central to many, perhaps most, of the key technologies of the future. The option I have in mind is the homely art of composting.

So far I've been unable to find an even remotely plausible figure for the total amount of compostable food, garden, and farm waste generated annually in the United States, or any other industrial country for that matter. It's certainly a very large volume, and the amount of it that goes into landfills rather than being recycled into fertile soil through composting is not much smaller. Those of my readers who have compost bins know how much of their own kitchen, garden, and yard waste goes into them; my wife and I generate between two and four cubic feet of compostable waste in an average week.

All of it goes into a compost bin of black recycled plastic in the back yard. So does another cubic foot or so per week from a friend's kitchen; his living situation doesn't permit him to have his own compost bin, so he contributes to ours. All the peelings and scraps and moldy bits from the produce that passes through our kitchen and his go into the compost pile, along with garden weeds, plants that have passed their season, and other forms of yard and garden waste, leavened with double handfuls of dried leaves saved from last autumn. Those are the only inputs, other than a little labor with a shovel once a month or so to keep the pile turned and working. Once a year, the hatch at the bottom of the compost bin disgorges the output—black, damp, sweet-smelling compost, ready to be worked into our garden beds.

This output is potent stuff. The first garden my wife and I planted started out as a patch of bare dirt on the north side of an urban apartment building, so poor and barren that even the most rugged of the local weeds made only half-hearted forays into it. Two years of double-digging beds with homebrewed compost turned it into a lush cottage garden that yielded shade-tolerant vegetables and medicinal herbs three seasons of the year, and supported some of the biggest earthworms I've ever had the pleasure of encountering. Given a reasonably good mix of raw materials—which an ordinary kitchen and garden provide quite well—compost is a balanced soil amendment that works over the long term, improving fertility, tilth, and pH balance while providing a good mix of soil nutrients.

Properly handled, the composting process also takes out unwanted seeds and pathogens. Decomposition generates heat—150° to 160°F is a fairly common temperature for the core of a good compost pile—and that sort of heat over weeks or months will kill anything in your compost you don't want there. If you live in a warm climate, in fact, it's usually wise to put your compost bin where the summer sun won't shine on it, and you may have to wet it down on hot days; compost heaps have been known to burst into flames when the heat of decomposition rose past the ignition temperature of the pile's more flammable ingredients. (The possibility that this heat could be used in other ways seems to have gotten little notice, even from the appropriate technology crowd; we'll discuss it, and other uses for "waste" heat, in a later post.)

Is compost a replacement for fossil fuel-based fertilizers? In the straightforward sense of this question, of course not. It's possible to make compost on an industrial scale—and there are businesses and public utilities that do this—but compost is not well suited to the industrial model of agriculture. It works best when applied in intensive small-scale truck gardening, where it can be combined with other low-energy but labor-intensive techniques for maximizing soil fertility and productivity. Composting is not, in other words, an effective way to maintain business as usual.

Instead, it's a bridge—or part of a bridge—that reaches beyond the end of the industrial age. The industrial model of agriculture, for reasons rooted primarily in current economic and political arrangements, has established a stranglehold on food production in the developed world. Barring drastic political intervention—a new Homestead Act, say, meant to repopulate the abandoned farm country of the Great Plains—that situation is unlikely to change suddenly or soon.

At the same time, this doesn't mean that the industrial model of agriculture will actually work well in a postpeak world. Far more likely is a situation in which soaring fossil fuel prices cascade down the food chain, turning industrial farms and their far-flung distribution networks into economic basket cases propped up by government subsidies, sky-high food prices, and trade barriers that keep other options out of the existing marketplace. In such a context, local microfarms and market gardens, and the co-operatives, farmers markets, and community-supported agriculture schemes that give them a market outside the existing system, are guaranteed steady and dramatic growth.

In a decade or so, in fact, American agriculture may well resemble nothing so much as the agricultural system of the Soviet Union in its last years, with huge and dysfunctional corporate farms filling the role of the sprawling industrialized kolkhozii while a large proportion of the food people actually eat comes from backyard garden plots. It's in that secondary economy of small gardens and microfarms that composting has its place — and just as the collapse of the Soviet Union would have been far more devastating in human terms without the underground economy that kept people fed, the downward arc of the industrial age can be made less traumatic if technologies such as composting, relevant to an underground food economy already being born, become widely distributed and practiced in the near future.

Thus the homely, humdrum, and vital art of composting offers a model for the kinds of adaptive, flexible, and scalable responses to the predicament of industrial society we need to locate and deploy. It's not a total solution, and it makes a very poor bargaining chip in the sort of haggling with fate I discussed earlier in this post. Rather, if the twilight of the industrial age is going to be anything but an uncontrolled crash, it's one of the little steps that could actually make a difference. In the months to come I plan on talking about more of these. In next week's post, however, I want to talk a little more about composting, because it offers several crucial insights to the ground rules that will very likely define the successful technologies of the deindustrial age.

74: A THEOLOGY OF COMPOST

(Originally published 20 February 2008)

The Druid order I head hosts an email list for its members and friends, and the conversations there cover a dizzying range of topics. Some months ago, as I recall, composting became the subject du jour. In the course of the discussion, one listmember reminisced about the day she decided to marry the man who is now her husband. It was Valentine's Day, romantically enough, and he arrived with a very special gift: a new compost bin. Anyone might have brought flowers or chocolates, she explained, but the fact that he realized how much a compost bin would mean to her defined him, in her eyes, as Mr. Right.

Nobody on the list laughed, because it made perfect sense to the rest of us, too. Composting is a curious thing; people get very passionate about it. In one of its dimensions, of course, it's a simple, practical, and ecologically elegant way of boosting and maintaining soil fertility. Still, as I suggested toward the end of last week's Archdruid Report post, it has other dimensions that go well beyond that comfortably pragmatic focus. I'd like to explore a few of those in this week's post, because they offer a useful guide to some of the core elements of the ecotechnic society that could well be our species' best bet in the postpetroleum future.

What makes composting such a useful template for an ecotechnic society is precisely that it highlights the ways such a society would have to differ from the way things are done in today's industrial civilization. Some of the crucial points of difference that come to mind are these:

First, where industrial civilization converts resources into waste, composting converts waste into resources. The core dynamic of today's industrial economies is a one-way process in which fossil fuels, other energy sources, mineral deposits, soil, water, air, and human beings, among many other things, are transformed into waste products — directly, in the form of pollution, or indirectly, in the form of goods and services that go into the waste stream after the briefest possible useful life. This same dynamic drives the emerging crisis of industrial civilization; no matter how much lipstick you put on this particular pig, a society that burns through its supply of necessary resources while heaping up progressively larger volumes of toxic wastes is going to run into trouble sooner or later. Composting reverses the equation by turning waste into a resource and meeting crucial needs — and there are few needs more crucial to a human society than food production — using wastes that would otherwise be part of the problem.

Second, where industrial civilization works against natural processes, composting works with them. At the center of contemporary Western ideology is the vision of progress as the conquest of nature, and this way of thinking has backed industrial societies into an approach to natural processes that sees them as obstacles to be overcome — or even enemies to be crushed. The result is the sort of massive misuse of resources visible in, say, modern agriculture, where conventional farming methods convert soil into something approaching a sterile mineral medium, and farmers then have to buy and apply an ever-increasing volume of fertilizers and soil additives to make up for the fertility that natural cycles in healthy soil provide all by themselves. Composting, by contrast, works because it fosters the natural processes that break down organic matter into healthy humus. There's no need to add anything extra, or to go shopping for the lively mix of bacteria, fungi, and soil fauna that makes the miracle of compost happen. To borrow a Hollywood slogan, if you build it, they will come.

Third, where industrial civilization requires complex, delicate, and expensive technologies to function at all, composting — because it relies on natural processes that have evolved over countless millions of years — thrives on a much simpler and sturdier technological basis. Once again, industrial agriculture is the poster child for this comparison. Set the factory complexes, energy inputs, and resource flows needed to manufacture NPK fertilizer using conventional methods with the simple bin and shovel needed to produce compost from kitchen and garden waste, and the difference is hard to miss. Imagine that your small town or urban neighborhood had to build and provide energy and raw materials for one or the other from scratch, using the resources available locally right now, and the difference becomes even more noticeable.

Fourth, where industrial civilization is inherently centralized, and thus can only function on a geographic and political scale large enough to make its infrastructure economically viable, composting is inherently decentralized and can function on any scale from a backyard to a continent. Among the many reasons why a small town or an urban neighborhood would be stark staring nuts to try to build a factory to produce NPK fertilizer is that the investment demanded by the factory equipment, energy supply, and raw materials would be far greater than the return. A backyard fertilizer factory for every home would be even more absurd, but a backyard compost bin for every home is arguably the most efficient way to put composting technology to use.

Fifth, where industrial civilization degrades exactly those factors in its environment that support its existence, composting increases the factors in its environment that support its existence. In a finite environment, the more of a nonrenewable resource you extract, the more energy and raw materials you have to invest in order to extract the remaining resource, and the more of a persistant pollutant you dump into the environment, the more energy and raw materials you have to invest in order to keep the pollutant from interfering with economic activities. Thus industrial civilization, in the course of its history, has to climb a steepening slope of its own making, until it finally falls off and crashes back to earth. By contrast, the closed loop that runs from composting bin to garden plot to kitchen and back around to composting bin again becomes more effective, not less, as the cycle turns: rising nutrient levels and soil biota in the garden plot lead to increased harvest, and thus to increased input to the compost bin.

Finally, all these factors mean that where industrial civilization is brittle, composting—and future ecotechnic societies modeled on the composting process—are resilient. One of the lessons of deep time opened up by geologists and paleontologists over the last decade or two is that the Earth is not a safe place. One of the lessons that historians have been pointing out for centuries, usually in vain, is that history is not particularly safe, either. It's a common lesson taught by all these fields of study, and more, that the intricate arrangements made possible by periods of stability tend to shred like cobwebs in a gale once stability breaks down and the environment (natural, social, or both) lurches its way unsteadily to a new equilibrium. In a time of turbulence, systems that are dependent on uninterrupted access to concentrated resources, unimpeded maintenance of intricate technologies, and undisturbed control over geographical areas of the necessary scale to make them economical face a much higher risk of collapse than systems that have none of these vulnerabilities.

Now of course many other sustainable technologies embrace one or more of these same factors. As yet, however, not many of them embrace all of them. Even technologies as promising as metal recycling—a crucial ingredient in any ecotechnic society, especially now that current industrial societies have extracted most of the world's easily accessible metal ores from within the Earth—have a long way to go before they become as scalable, self-sustaining, and resilient as composting. Comparisons of this sort point up the way that such highly sustainable techniques as composting can be used as touchstones and sources of inspiration for a much wider range of approaches. Equally, of course, other technologies that achieve particular types of ecological harmony composting can't yet manage—and some of those will be explored here later on—can become a resource for refining the composting process as well.

Still, as ecotechnic methods go, composting deserves a distinguished place, and as a source of inspiration and fruitful comparison, its uses are by no means limited to the purely technical. In Druid circles, at least, talk about composting almost always seems to blend practicalities with deeper issues. So far, at least, the romantic dimension of composting seems to be limited to stories like the one with which I began this post, but the philosophical dimension is always close by—as is the theological.

From the contrast between the monumental absurdity of industrial society's linear transformation of resource to waste, on the one hand, and the elegant cycle of resource to resource manifested in the humble compost bin on the other, it's hard to avoid moving on to challenging questions about the nature of human existence, the shape of history, the meaning of the cycles of life and death, and the relationship of humanity to the source of its existence, however that may be defined. The practicalities of composting can't be neglected in any sense—nor, of course, should the romantic dimension, when that shows up!—but the insights made available by a philosophy and a theology of compost may yet turn out to be at least as valuable as either.

75: IN THE DARK WITH BOTH HANDS
(*Originally published 27 February 2008*)

Composting, the theme of the last two Archdruid Report posts, has turned out to be unusually timely as the current winter draws toward its end. The prospects for this year's wheat crop, a topic of discussion until recently relegated to Grange halls and local newspapers in small western towns, have recently become the focus of news stories and punditry in business media worldwide.

There's good reason for this unexpected shift of attention. A sequence of jarring upward leaps in the commodity markets have brought wheat prices up to levels never before seen in modern times, with no visible end in sight. Other grains and, for that matter, a wide range of other agricultural commodities, have posted vertiginous price hikes of their own. Unlike so many of the booms and busts that have enlivened recent economic history, the current surge in grain prices isn't insulated from the real economy of goods and services, and has already begun to play out in rising food costs worldwide.

The boom in grain prices is the product of many factors. At the top of the list belongs the simple if awkward fact that the world's capacity to produce grain in recent years has failed to keep up with increasing demand. Despite all the handwaving of cornucopian economists, it turns out, the world really is finite, and rising demand for grain-fed livestock in newly prosperous India and China turned out to be the proverbial one straw too many for the world's agricultural system. Add to that the impact of climate instability on grain harvests, the activities of speculators, and the bizarre spectacle of the current biofuel boom, in which large portions of the industrial world are attempting to cope with rising petroleum prices by pouring their food supply into their gas tanks, and you have a fine recipe for chaos in the grain market.

Still, there's another factor at work, one that will likely play a major role in the agricultural history of the next century or so. The fertilizers that make modern industrial agriculture work derive almost entirely from nonrenewable sources. Nitrate and ammonia fertilizers are manufactured from natural gas; phosphates come from rock phosphate, and potassium from mineral potash deposits — and global supplies of the first two of these, at least, are beginning to run short.

It's been argued that this isn't a problem, because improvements in technology make it possible to extract economically useful amounts of minerals from ever more dilute source materials. In theory, this is quite true. In practice, though, a crucial ingredient usually gets left out of the mix: the more dilute the source material, the more energy needs to be invested per unit of refined product. During the last two decades of the 20th century, when energy prices reached their lowest levels in human history, nobody needed to pay attention to the energy side of the equation, and this fostered a climate of thought in which futurists could picture future industrial societies that met all their material needs by extracting dissolved minerals from seawater.

As the age of cheap abundant energy comes to an end, though, this sort of thinking makes bad science fiction and worse propaganda. As energy supplies dwindle, using ever increasing among energy to extract ever smaller fractions of minerals from the ground quickly becomes a losing bet. At the same time, without significant inputs of nitrogen, phosphorus, and other minerals, it becomes impossible to maintain soil fertility at levels high enough to matter. Unless the world can find some other abundant, concentrated source of plant nutrients in time to matter, it may not be much of an exaggeration to suggest that large parts of the world may face a Hobson's choice between starving to death and freezing in the dark.

This is where the perspectives of the last few Archdruid Report posts become relevant, because such an abundant, concentrated source of plant nutrients already exists. The methods needed to obtain the raw material and process it into high-grade fertilizer are mature technologies, readily available and thoroughly tested. The only reason the source in question is not already being exploited on a large scale in the industrial world is that most people nowadays don't seem to be able to distinguish it from a hole in the ground.

We are talking, of course, about human feces — or, as one book on the subject has usefully labeled it, "humanure." The average human being in the industrial world produces between 2.5 and 3 pounds of fecal matter a day, along with about a third of a gallon of urine. Over one year, that works out to approximately half a ton of feces and a hundred gallons of urine per person; multiply this by the 300 million residents of the United States, and then factor in the equally massive waste streams generated by domestic animals and livestock, and you may get some sense of the scale of the resource that we are, quite literally, flushing down the toilet.

The technology that converts this resource into fertilizer happens to be the one we've been examining in the last few posts. Composting uses natural biological processes to break down fecal material and other wastes, converting them into a concentrated, odorless source of plant nutrients. In the process, composting kills pathogenic bacteria by sheer biological competition — a compost pile is a fiercely Darwinian environment in which organisms bred in the sheltered setting of a human body's insides don't last long. Study after study has shown that fecal matter, after it has been competently composted, contains no more human pathogens than ordinary soil.

So why haven't we been able to get our fertilizer together on this issue? What keeps composted humanure from being an obvious resource to help replace dwindling inorganic sources of plant nutrients? Part of the reason reaches deep into the crawlspaces of the industrial world's collective imagination. People who object to composting humanure quite often cite concerns about pathogens or odors, but it rarely takes more than a short discussion to get down to the level of a five-year-old clenching his eyes shut and squealing "Ewww, ick!"

This invites satire, but beneath it lies a set of very widespread attitudes far less appealing than simple human waste. C.S. Lewis pointed out quite a while ago in The Abolition of Man, and with far more power in his fantasy novel That Hideous Strength, that a great many modern attitudes have their source in what might as well be called biophobia—a pathological fear and hatred of the realities of biological life, coupled with an obsessive fascination with the sterile, the mechanical and the lifeless.

Biophobia guides the creation of human environments so biologically sterile that, according to recent research, many currently widespread illnesses may be caused by understimulated immune systems; it also inspires the absurd fantasies of so-called "transhumanists" who look forward to the day when they can put their personalities into robots and do away with biological existence altogether. (Back in the Sixties, Ira Levin crafted a smart horror novel, The Stepford Wives, about the replacement of human beings by robots programmed with imitations of their personalities, but not even he seems to have imagined that people might set out to do that to themselves.) The same attitude, I'm convinced, drives the horror many people feel when faced with the prospect of eating food fertilized with composted humanure.

The same aversion to biological realities, it may be, has shaped another factor that makes the commonsense use of human waste as plant food difficult for many people to contemplate. The economic thinking that guides the industrial world has long been stuck in a linear rut, imposing patterns of one-way flow on a universe that consistently moves in circles. Our economists sort out the tangled exchanges, multiple roles, and mixed motives of real market economies into neat flowcharts that move matter from suppliers to producers, to distributors, and then to consumers, before vanishing into thin air.

Food systems built on the same pattern take nutrients from natural deposits, put them into soil, haul the resulting crops into a baroque system of manufacturing and distribution before they get to people, and then dump the resulting waste into the world's fresh water supply. That sort of straight-line pattern is the way most people in the industrial world think; it's a measure of how pervasive such thinking is that following nature's patterns, and cycling "waste" back around to become a resource, seems so unthinkable to most people.

Now it deserves to be said that there are valid reasons why composting, with or without humanure, would be difficult to apply to the kind of industrial farming that produces most bulk agricultural commodities in the western world these days. The infrastructure necessary to collect 150 million tons of humanure a year, plus an amount of compostable animal manure that may well be larger still, and convert it en masse into fertilizer for Iowa corn and North Dakota winter wheat simply doesn't exist; it would be extremely expensive to construct, and resources put into that project would have to be diverted from many other pressing needs.

Still, the kind of industrial farming we have nowadays is a creation of the age of cheap abundant energy. As fossil fuels deplete, that kind of farming will become less and less economically viable, until it finally ceases altogether. It's quite true, as some writers on peak oil have argued recently, that the current agricultural economy won't simply revert to the agriculture of an earlier time; that's not how change happens in the real world of economics—or ecology. What will happen instead, of course, is that new patterns will evolve in the interstices of the old.

In ecological terms, these new patterns will fill available niches the old system no longer occupies; in economic terms, they will use resources and fill marketable needs outside the scope of existing economic activity. Arguably, these patterns have already started taking shape, in the form of the thriving economy of small organic farms and truck gardens that sprang up around most cities in the western half of North America beginning in the 1970s. As I hope to show in next week's post, this new farming economy offers a glimpse at the agriculture of the future—if, that is, we can get our heads out of our fertilizer supply long enough to notice.

76: THE NEXT AGRICULTURE
(Originally published 5 March 2008)

Archdruids take breaks from time to time, but the peak oil debate does not, and during my recent vacation a lively discussion sprang up on The Oil Drum about the future of agriculture in a postpetroleum world. The point at issue was whether today's mechanized agriculture will remain in place, or be replaced by a new rural economy of small farms using human and animal labor, as the world skids down the far side of Hubbert's peak.

Summarizing a vigorous discussion of a complex topic in a few paragraphs is a risky proposition, so I'll focus here on the two essays that defined the debate, Stuart Saniford's "The Fallacy of Reversibility and Sharon Astyk's "Is Localization Doomed?" Saniford argued that those who expected a nonmechanized, small-farm economy in the wake of peak oil were claiming that the history of agriculture over the last century would simply run in reverse, tracking the decline in fossil fuel availability in the same way it tracked the growth in fossil fuel production.

If this view was correct, he claimed, rising fuel prices would have already begun to push American agriculture in the direction of smaller, less energy-intensive farms, and this would show in currently available statistics about profitability, labor costs, farm size and the like. He then demonstrated that no such changes could be found in the statistics, and on this basis claimed that what he called the "reversalist" position had no merit.

Astyk, responding to Saniford, made two major points. First, she noted that nobody claimed that the transition from today's agribusiness to tomorrow's rural landscape of small farms would simply run history in reverse, and Saniford was therefore kicking a straw man. Second, she suggested that the emergence of a non-mechanized, small-farm economy in the postpetroleum future was not an inevitability, but a policy choice that Saniford's so-called "reversalists" considered the best option in the face of peak oil.

Like many readers of the debate, I found neither of these positions really satisfactory. By the time I finished reading the comments, though, it was getting late, and I decided to round out the evening by pouring myself a glass of scotch and reading a few pages of a Gary Larson Far Side anthology. Somewhere toward the bottom of the glass I dozed off; I must have been reading one of Larson's dinosaur cartoons in my last waking moments, because I slipped into a dream in which a conference of dinosaurs pondered the approaching end of the Mesozoic era.

Quite a few dinosaurs had already given speeches about the threat of global cooling. Several of them had mentioned that mammals, with their warm blood and furry coats, might be better off in a post-Mesozoic world. At this point in the debate, however, another dinosaur lumbered up to the podium to speak.

"This talk of mammals taking over the world is nonsense," it said. "It's true, of course, that the ancestors of mammals—the therapsids—ruled the earth back before dinosaurs came along, in the Permian period, before the earth's climate shifted to its long Mesozoic warm spell." This sparked a good deal of discussion among the audience, and the Tyrannosaurus rex who presided over the meeting had to display its foot-long teeth and growl to quiet things down.

"Nonetheless," the speaker went on, "this claim that evolution will run in reverse can readily be refuted. If that were true, the global cooling we've seen already would have made dinosaurs become smaller and furrier, and that hasn't happened. In fact"—at this point it nodded toward the Tyrannosaurus rex—"it's clear that we're getting larger and scalier all the time. There's every reason to think that as the climate cools, and selection pressures become more extreme, big scaly dinosaurs will have even greater competitive advantages than they do now."

At this point the buzz of conversation in the audience could not be restrained, even when the Tyrannosaurus rex killed and ate one of the loudest talkers. A few moments later, though, a bright light flashed through the sky. "Did you see that?" said the Triceratops sitting next to me, pointing toward the sky with the horn on its nose. "I've never seen a shooting star that big." A moment later I was jolted awake by what felt like the shockwave from an asteroid impact, but was actually the Gary Larson anthology sliding from my lap and hitting the floor.

The parallels between Saniford's argument and that of his saurian equivalent, as it happens, go well beyond the obvious. Both, strictly speaking, are quite correct in their core assertions. As the Mesozoic era drew toward its close, dinosaurs did not retrace the process that led up to the monster reptiles of the Cretaceous. In fact, important branches of the dinosaur clan—the carnosaurs that led to Tyrannosaurus rex, the ceratopsians that ended with Triceratops, and others—got progressively larger as the Cretaceous drew on.

These successful evolutionary lineages continued to follow their established trajectory as long as it remained viable. When it stopped being viable, they didn't shift into reverse and shrink back down to the size of their Permian ancestors; they died out, and other organisms better suited to the new conditions took over. In the same way, Saniford's assertion that today's industrial agriculture will not throw the gearshifts of its combines into reverse, and gradually retrace its tracks into the 19th century, is almost certainly correct.

Saniford is also correct to point out that in a world intent on pouring its food supply into its fuel tanks, rising energy prices mean that industrial farming is becoming more profitable, not less. As a member of the Grange, I've had the chance to watch this from an angle that may be rare in the peak oil scene. Where the rest of the media bemoans rising grain prices, the Grange News is full of satisfied comments by family farmers who can finally make ends meet, now that their grain sells for more than it cost to grow.

Yet Saniford's overall argument fails, for the same reason that his imaginary Mesozoic equivalent missed seeing the future in plain sight -- both rely on linear models to predict a nonlinear situation. In his essay, Staniford used the distinction between reversible and irreversible processes as a model for historical change in agriculture. The difference between linear and nonlinear change, however, is at least as relevant.

Watch a frozen lake melt and you have a seasonally timely example of nonlinear change. The transition from ice to liquid water doesn't happen gradually as temperature rises; it happens at a specific point in the temperature spectrum, 32°F, and only then once the ice has absorbed enough energy to overcome its thermal inertia and provide the heat of fusion. A five-degree warming can be irrelevant to the process, if it's from 15°F to 20°F, or for that matter from 40°F to 45°F. The same rise between 30°F and 35°F, on the other hand, can cause drastic change.

Nonlinear change happens most often in systems that have negative feedback loops which balance out pressures for change. In the case of the frozen lake, the main sources of negative feedback are the stability of water's solid state and its capacity as a heat sink. Only when enough heat has entered the situation to overcome these factors does change happen, and when it does, the lake shifts from one relatively stable state to another.

The modern agricultural economy is a classic candidate for nonlinear change. The feedback loops resisting agricultural change in the modern world are at least as potent as the ones that keep a lake from melting at 20°F. The food production and distribution system is oriented toward business as usual, and the psychology of previous investment and the very real costs of retooling to fit a different model both raise obstacles to change. Monopolistic practices and the government subsidies and price supports that make most of today's "capitalist" agriculture a case study in corporate socialism also give the status quo impressive inertia.

At the same time, if something is unsustainable, it's a given that sooner or later it won't be sustained. Today's industrial agriculture, with its far-flung supply and distribution chains, its dependence on huge inputs of nonrenewable resources, and its severe impact on topsoil, water quality, and environmental health, is a case in point. As transport costs rise, fossil fuel and mineral reserves deplete, and the burden of coping with ecological damage climbs, industrial agriculture will sooner or later reach the point of negative returns — and as Joseph Tainter pointed out in a different context, that's the point at which collapse becomes the most likely outcome.

Saniford has argued elsewhere that the energy crisis caused by the end of cheap oil will be temporary. He proposes that nuclear power and other technologies will sooner or later make energy cheap and abundant again. If he's right, it's possible that new energy sources will come on line soon enough to keep industrial agriculture from hitting the wall. None of the theorists he critiques in his essay agree that the approaching crisis will be temporary, though, and this latter assessment gives their argument compelling force: as energy supplies dwindle and a social fabric predicated on cheap energy comes apart, the pressures on the agricultural status quo will eventually reach a level high enough to force nonlinear change.

This is where the second half of Sharon Astyk's argument comes in. She points out that many of the writers critiqued in Saniford's essay see a nonmechanized small-farm agricultural economy not as the inevitable result of economic forces, but as a deliberate policy choice. If our existing agriculture could fold out from under us, they suggest, getting plan B in place is a good idea.

Now this may well be true, but history teaches that when ideology collides with economics, it's inevitably ideology that comes off worst. The same trap that has blocked most proposals for lifeboat communities so far — how do you make them economically viable in the world we inhabit today? — lies in wait for schemes to relocalize agriculture that don't take the actual economics of farming in today's world into account.

Fortunately, there's reason to think that economic factors will favor the rise of a nonmechanized small-farm economy in the industrial world in the decades to come. The best evidence for this suggestion comes, ironically enough, from Stuart Saniford. In his posts about the agricultural side of peak oil — notably "Fermenting the Food Supply" — Saniford pointed out that the use of grain as a feedstock for ethanol is likely to drive up the price of basic foodstuffs so far that many people will no longer be able to afford to eat.

This is potentially a serious crisis, but it also represents an opportunity. Sharp increases in the price of food mean that food production methods that may not be economical under current conditions could well pass the breakeven point and begin turning a profit. To thrive in the economic climate of the near future, of course, such methods would have to meet certain requirements, but most of these can be anticipated easily enough.

These alternative farming projects would have to use minimal fossil fuel inputs, since fuel costs will likely be very high by past standards for much of the foreseeable future. They would need to focus on local distribution, since those same fuel costs will put long-distance transport out of reach. They would have to focus on intensive production from very small plots, since acreage large enough for industrial farming will likely increase in price. They would also benefit greatly by relying on human labor with hand tools, since the economic consequences of peak oil will likely send unemployment rates soaring while making capital hard to come by.

All of these criteria are met, as it happens, by the small organic farms and truck gardens that many relocalization theorists hold up as models for future agriculture. Already a growing presence, especially around West Coast cities, these agricultural alternatives have evolved their own distribution system, relying on farmers markets, co-op groceries, local restauranteurs and communi- ty-supported agriculture schemes to carry out an end run around food distribution systems geared toward corporate monopolies.

As more grains and other fermentable bulk commodities get turned into ethanol, and food prices rise in response, such ar- rangements may well become a significant source of food for a sizeable fraction of Americans — and in the process, of course, the economics of small-scale alternative farms are likely to improve a great deal. The result may well resemble nothing so much as the agricultural system of the former Soviet Union in its last years, featuring vast farms that had become almost irrelevant to the na- tional food supply, while little market gardens in backyards pro- duced most of the food people actually ate.

If Saniford is correct and the postpeak energy crisis turns out to be a passing phase, that bimodal system might endure for quite some time, as it did in the Soviet Union. If more pessimistic assessments of our energy future are closer to the mark, as I suspect they are, the industrial half of the system can be counted on to collapse at some point down the road once energy and resource availability drop to levels insufficient to sustain a continental economy. If this turns out to be the case, the small intensive farms around the urban fringes — mammals amid agribusiness dinosaurs — may well become the nucleus of the next agriculture.

77: PIECES OF THE PUZZLE
(Originally published 12 March 2008)

One of the more interesting things highlighted by recent debates about the future of agriculture after peak oil is the pervasive modern tendency to seek single solutions for complex problems. We had an example here on The Archdruid Report a few weeks back, when a reader responded to a discussion of composting by putting up a comment saying, in effect, that composting was a waste of time and we ought to be talking about sheet mulching instead.

For those who don't keep up with the state of the art in organic growing, sheet mulching means spreading a thin layer of uncomposted organic material — leaves, straw, or what have you — over the top of the soil. This keeps moisture in the soil, keeps weeds down, and cycles organic matter back into humus to improve soil tilth and fertility. In dryland bioregions, in particular, it's a key technique for intensive organic food production.

On the other hand, it's not a panacea, and there are other bioregions where it doesn't work anything like so well. In the part of the Pacific Northwest where I live, for example, slugs are serious garden pests, and sheet mulch is a slug magnet; if you use mulch early in the growing season, in particular, you can expect to lose much of your crop to slugs. Like many local organic growers, therefore, I use sheet mulching to overwinter the garden, from harvest's end to planting time, and then dig the mulch under when it's time to prepare the beds for the new crops.

Like many local organic growers, too, I also compost, and so organic material enters the soil by both routes. Different materials follow their own trajectories: kitchen scraps go into the compost bin, for example, while autumn leaves get raked up into heaps for use as sheet mulching, then finish rotting into humus once they're turned under in spring. The two methods don't conflict with one another at all, and the same springtime digging that turns the mulch under also works in the year's dose of compost from the bin.

Nor are these the only options for closing the loop and cycling organic matter back into the soil. You can use green manure — this, for the organically uneducated, means planting a cover crop of clover or some other nitrogen-fixing plant in the fall, letting it grow all winter, and then turning it under in the spring. You can feed your kitchen scraps to chickens, rabbits, or some other live-stock and turn their manure into plant food. You can use a worm bin instead of the usual composting methods, using redworms to break down the organic matter in place of bacteria. You can even borrow a lick from the appropriate technology movement of the Seventies, set up an aquaculture system, feed some of your spare organic matter to tilapia or some other tasty fish, and use the waste water, with its load of fish feces, to irrigate your crops.

Which of these is the answer to the challenge of post-peak food production? Put that way, the answer is obvious: none of them is the answer. All of them, and all their various combinations, can be workable responses to some of the needs people will have as they try to keep themselves and their families fed as our society skids down the far side of Hubbert's peak. Put another way, they are pieces of a puzzle; each has its place, but no one piece completes the puzzle by itself.

This same logic can be applied more generally. One of the con-tinuing disputes on the end of the peak oil community concerned with agriculture is whether farming will continue to use tractors and the like, or whether draft horses will prove to be more via-ble. Both sides have good arguments. On the one hand, a large farm running tractors on homegrown biodiesel can keep them fu-eled by devoting 10% or so of its acreage to oilseed crops, while it takes around 30% of acreage to produce fodder for draft horses to provide the same amount of power. On the other, you don't need a factory or its substantial inputs of energy and resources to manufacture horses — they do it themselves, with noticeable enthusiasm and no tools other than the ones nature gave them — and a properly fed horse also produces large amounts of excellent organic fertilizer, a significant value that tractors don't provide.

Which is the best option? That depends on a galaxy of factors, few of which can be predicted on the basis of abstract arguments. If enough of today's industrial economy survives long enough into the post-peak era that factories are still around to produce tractors and transport networks can still get them to farmers, that makes tractors more viable; if the industrial economy goes to pieces, chalk one up for draft horses. Issues of scale, crop, and climate are also crucial; the option that would work best for a 16,000-acre wheat farm on the Great Plains might prove disastrous for a 25-acre truck farm growing vegetables on the outskirts of a West Coast city.

For that matter, neither horses nor tractors have any place in the sort of backyard mixed gardens that had so crucial a role in helping people in the old Soviet Union survive its collapse, and may well play the same role in getting Americans through a similar experience in the not too distant future. The form of intensive organic gardening that, as David Duhon documented some years back in One Circle (Ecology Action, 1985), can produce a spare but adequate diet for one person on 1000 square feet of soil, requires only hand tools and human labor. Intensive gardening and extensive field agriculture are not the same thing, but both will likely have important roles to play in feeding people in the post-peak era.

I suggest that this same logic can be extended much further. Consider the ongoing debates about potential replacements for petroleum and other fossil fuels. To some extent, of course, this sort of talk is whistling past the graveyard. None of the proposed alternatives seem at all likely to provide the same combination of vast abundance, low extraction and processing cost, and protean flexibility as fossil fuels — nor is there any good reason to think they could.

The earth's supply of fossil fuels, after all, represent hundreds of millions of years of stored solar energy. Only sheer human egotism justifies the presumption that, after burning through that huge and thermodynamically improbable stockpile in a few extravagant centuries, we can expect the universe to hand us an equivalent in some other form. Much more likely, as I have argued here and elsewhere, is a centuries-long period of contraction and decline, in which we as a species must struggle to get by on much less energy than recent history has taught us to expect.

Whether or not this turns out to be the case, though, the mismatch between a civilization built on abundant, concentrated fossil fuels and the relatively sparse and diffuse energy sources available to replace them makes today's bickering about which energy source is "the answer" an exercise in futility. Even today, coal, oil, natural gas, and other energy sources fill different roles in the overall energy economy; the future promises much more diversity of the same kind. Far more likely than not, the future of energy lies in a crazy-quilt patchwork in which each of the available energy sources is matched with its most appropriate uses by a process of trial and error.

The point that has to be recognized, it seems to me, is that nobody alive today has the least idea how an ecotechnic civilization—a society that can maintain relatively advanced technology on the basis of sustainable resources—might best be constructed. All the experience of the last three centuries has focused on the opposite end of the possible spectrum of technic societies, where you'll find the civilizations that burn through nonrenewable resources at the fastest pace they can manage. We've followed that road just about as far as it can go, far enough that the dead end at its terminus should be visible to anyone who is willing to notice it.

Nor can we turn to the past for conclusive answers. The societies that existed before the industrial revolution offer hints about how sustainability can be woven into the fabric of human life, and warnings about the results when this fails to happen, but it's only the most simpleminded or polemical analyses that define the task of our future as a return to the past. The resources available to us and the limits imposed on us by history and environment are different enough from those of past cultures that we don't have that option. Rather, the challenge imposed on us by the predicament of our time is that of moving into uncharted territory.

In energy, just as in agriculture and in many other fields, all we have are pieces of the puzzle. It will likely take ruthless sorting and a great deal of trial and error to make those pieces fit together in any sort of meaningful way. This makes the habit of fixating on a single response more than usually useless just now, and makes it imperative that any option in harmony with the wider project of building a sustainable civilization in harmony with the biosphere needs to be taken into account.

78: A MILESTONE IN THE DUST

(Originally published 19 March 2008)

Earlier this month, according to several peak oil bloggers, the world passed a milestone worth noting: the point at which oil, in constant dollars, became more expensive than ever before in history. Plenty of us in the peak oil community have been expecting that milestone any time now, and the surge that pushed one widely watched price marker past $112 a barrel last week turned the expectation into reality.

Profit-taking and a flurry of margin calls driven by the wider economic crisis brought oil prices back down at the beginning of this week, at least for the moment. Meanwhile, though, the higher cost of oil is already starting to trickle down to the consumer level. Diesel fuel is up over $4 a gallon in many US markets, while gasoline, heating oil, and other petroleum products are following the same curve. Speculation, in several senses of the word, has begun to focus on the upcoming summer driving season and the likelihood of soaring prices at the pump.

Just now, however, it may be worth taking the long view. When Goldman Sachs suggested, not so long ago, that oil prices might rise above $110 a barrel, their analysts thought that it would take a crisis threatening some significant fraction of world oil production to drive such a "superspike." (That warning was widely and, I think, correctly interpreted as an attempt by New York financial interests to talk the cowboys in Washington D.C. out of launching a war with Iran.) The crisis has so far failed to materialize, but the superspike showed up anyway.

Like any other economic phenomenon in the real world, that unexpected event had numerous causes. One factor not often given sufficient weight, at least in the peak oil community, is the role of speculation. The global economy these days is dominated by flows of speculative money that pour into any investment promising an above average rate of return. Just now, commodities—fossil fuels, grains, metals, and the like—yield better returns than most other investments, and so that's where the money goes.

Monday's events demonstrated that. The drastic declines in most stock markets that day resulted in a bumper crop of margin calls. For those of my readers who don't follow the markets, a margin call is what happens when investments bought with borrowed money lose enough value that the lender demands more collateral for the loan. Since few speculators keep large amounts of ready cash on hand, that usually means that other investments have to be turned into cash in a hurry; this is one of the ways financial panics spread from market to market.

Hit with margin calls in the stock market, speculators unwound positions in the commodities market, and most commodities dropped sharply in Monday's trading. Oil slumped from $111 to $106 in a matter of hours. They rallied after that, but today's ticker shows another dive, with oil futures down near $104 a barrel as I write these words. With stock markets sliding again, further declines are tolerably likely. None of this ought to come as any kind of surprise; the role of speculation as a source of whipsaw motions in energy prices has been discussed here on The Archdruid Report, and elsewhere across the peak oil blogosphere.

Still, speculation is only one part of the picture. Another part, hard to miss just now, is the plunging value of the dollar. Since oil, like most commodities, is priced in US dollars—a circumstance that has given the United States some notable advantages—a portion of the price increases that have roiled commodities markets and startled American consumers in recent months are simply readjustments by which commodities retain their value against the measure of a weakening currency.

There are good reasons for the dollar to shed value just now, of course, but I sometimes wonder if deliberate policy may play a role as well. After a quarter century of reckless deficit spending, the United States is insolvent by any reasonable measure, saddled with debts it will never be able to pay off. Unlike other countries that have recently landed in the same bind, though, it has a notable advantage—all those debts are payable in a currency it controls. The other day, US Treasury Secretary Henry Paulson made the usual ritual noises about upholding a strong dollar policy, but I suspect it has crossed his mind that the national debt would be a good deal less intimidating if the dollar were to slide to 5% of its current value over the next ten years or so. It's hard to think of another policy, in fact, that will keep the United States from having to default on its sovereign debt sooner or later.

Whether or not this is on the official agenda, though, some such readjustment is inevitable. The imperial economics that enabled the five percent of the world's population who are Americans to monopolize a third of the world's resources have begun to unravel, with predictable results. Pundits who denounce "resource nationalism" and laud the alleged benefits of free trade have conveniently forgotten that America built the largest industrial economy in the world in the shelter of protective tariffs, and used its own natural resources as a political weapon whenever it had the chance—for example, against Japan in the years before the Second World War. We may not enjoy seeing the tables turned, but it's not as though we have grounds for complaint.

Behind the wild swings of speculative excess and the tidal forces set in motion by a collapsing US dollar, in turn, lies a third factor—from a peak oil perspective, the signal half-hidden by a great deal of economic noise. This is the failure of world petroleum production to break out of the plateau it has occupied since 2004. Those who have been following the peak oil scene for more than a year or so will recall any number of confident predictions concerning improved secondary recovery, new discoveries, or alternative fuels, that would enable oil production to continue on its upward path once prices rose enough to make them economical.

That hasn't happened. Instead, world oil production has continued to bump along at roughly the same level, while prices have soared through the skylight. The latest news from the International Energy Agency (IEA) shows that with ethanol, biodiesel, and every other source of liquid fuels added in, world production of petroleum and equivalents nudged just slightly over the records set in 2006, while production of conventional petroleum continues to wobble downward from its May 2005 peak. Demand remains strong and prices have soared, but supply has barely budged — and plenty of technologies and energy sources supposedly poised to surge onto the market once oil broke $30, or $40, or $50 a barrel are still pie in the sky.

What this implies is that for all practical purposes, peak oil has arrived. Pinpointing the peak precisely in time quickly becomes an exercise in quibbling over definitions; petroleum is not a single thing but a diverse assemblage of chemically related resources, extracted in many ways and traded in a baroque diversity of markets. Should tar sand extractives, which require huge energy inputs to bring to market, be counted alongside light sweet crude, which requires little? What about ethanol from American corn, cultivated by energy-intensive methods that burn more fuel than the corn itself yields? Should the ethanol and the oil used to produce it both be included in total production, even though this amounts to counting the same energy twice?

Still, there's another way to think about peak oil that's less difficult to define: the point along the curve of petroleum production at which geology trumps market forces, and all the price adjustments in the world can't make supply increase to meet the potential demand. Set aside the whipsaw motions of speculative excess and the impact of a disintegrating currency, and this is what the rising price of petroleum seems to be telling us. Unless events in the very near future offer a different message, it's fair to suggest that the milestone of record oil prices fading into the dust behind us may mark the end of the age of cheap abundant energy, and the coming of a new world of limits and scarcities for which most of us are hopelessly unprepared.

79: THE PARADOX OF PRODUCTION
(Originally published 26 March 2008)

One of the things that makes the challenge of peak oil so insidious, and so resistant to quick fixes, is the way in which many things that seem like ingredients of a solution are actually part of the problem. Petroleum provides so much of the energy and so many of the raw materials we take for granted today that the impacts of declining oil production extend much further than a first glance would suggest.

Read through discussions of the energy future of industrial society from a few years back, for example, and you'll find that many of them treat the price of coal and the price of oil as independent variables, linked only by the market forces that turn price increases in one into an excuse for bidding up the price of the other. What these analyses missed, of course, is that the machinery used to mine coal and the trains used to transport it are powered by diesel oil. When the price of diesel goes up, the cost of coal mining goes up; when supplies of diesel run short in coal-producing countries — as they have in China in recent months — the supply of coal runs into unexpected hiccups as well.

I've pointed out in previous posts here that every other energy source currently used in modern societies gets a substantial "energy subsidy" from oil. Thus, to continue the example, oil contains about three times as much useful energy per unit weight as coal does, and oil also takes a lot less energy to extract from the ground, process, and transport to the end user than coal does. Modern coal production benefits from these efficiencies. If coal had to be mined, processed, and shipped using coal-burning equipment, those efficiencies would be lost, and a sizeable fraction of total coal production would have to go to meet the energy costs of the coal industry.

The same thing, of course, is true of every other alternative energy source to a greater or lesser degree: the energy used in uranium mining and reactor construction, for example, comes from diesel rather than nuclear power, just as sunlight doesn't make solar panels. What rarely seems to have been noticed, however, is the way these "energy subsidies" intersect with the challenges of declining petroleum production to boobytrap the future of energy production in industrial societies. The boobytrap in question is an effect I've named the paradox of production.

It's crucial to understand that the problem with our society's reliance on petroleum is not simply that petroleum will become scarce in the future, and will have to be replaced by less concentrated or less abundant fuels. It's that a huge proportion of industrial society's capital plant—the collection of tools, artifacts, trained personnel, social structures, information resources, and human geography that provide the productive basis for society — was designed and built to use petroleum-derived fuels, and only petroleum-derived fuels. Converting that capital plant to anything else involves much more than just providing another energy source.

Consider the difficulties that would be involved in building the sort of hydrogen economy so often touted as the solution to our approaching energy crisis. We'll grant for the moment that the massive amounts of electricity needed to turn seawater into hydrogen gas in sufficient volume to matter turn out to be available somehow, despite the severe challenges facing every option proposed so far. Getting the electricity to make the hydrogen, though, is only the first of a series of tasks with huge price tags in money, energy, raw materials, labor, and time.

Hydrogen, after all, can't be poured into the gas tank of a gasoline-powered car. For that matter, it can't be dispensed from today's gas pumps, or stored in the tanks at today's filling stations, or shipped there by the pipelines and tanker trucks currently used to get gasoline and diesel fuel to the point of sale. Every motor vehicle on the roads, along with the vast infrastructure built up over a century to fuel them with petroleum products, would have to be replaced in order to use hydrogen as a transport fuel.

The same challenge, in one form or another, faces nearly every other energy source proposed as a replacement for petroleum. It's not enough to come up with a new source of energy. Unless that new source can be used just like petroleum, the petroleum-powered machines we use today will have to be replaced by machines using the new energy source. Furthermore, unless the new energy source can be distributed through existing channels — whether that amounts to the pipelines and tanker trucks used to transport petroleum fuels today, or some other established infrastructure, such as the electric power grid — a new distribution infrastructure will have to be built. Either task would add massive costs to the price tag for a new energy source; put both of them together — as in the case of hydrogen — and the costs of the new infrastructure could easily dwarf the cost of bringing the new energy source online in the first place.

Factor the impact of declining oil production into this equation and the true scale of the challenge before us becomes a little clearer. Building a hydrogen infrastructure — from power plants and hydrogen generation facilities, through pipelines and distribution systems, to hydrogen filling stations and hundreds of millions of hydrogen-powered cars and trucks — will, among many other things, take a very large amount of oil. Some of the oil will be used directly, by construction equipment, trucks hauling parts to the new plants, and the like; much more will be used indirectly, since nearly every commodity and service for sale in the industrial world today relies on petroleum in one way or another. Until a substantial portion of the hydrogen system is in place, it won't be possible to use hydrogen to supplement dwindling petroleum production, which is already coming under worldwide strain as demand pushes up against the limits of supply. Instead, the fuel costs of building the hydrogen economy add an additional source of demand, pushing fuel prices higher and making scarce fuel even less available for other uses.

The same thing is true of any other alternative energy system that attempts to replace petroleum in its current uses. The costs differ, depending on how much of the existing infrastructure has to be replaced, but there's always a price tag—and a large portion of the energy needed will have to come from petroleum, because that's the energy source our society uses for a great many of its crucial needs. If the new energy source can be produced and used by existing infrastructure with minimal modification, this effect may well be small enough to discount, but it is always there.

The advantage of energy sources that can use existing infrastructure is one of the reasons why ethanol and biodiesel have entered the energy stream in amounts large enough to affect total liquid fuel numbers, and have helped drive grain prices to stratospheric levels into the bargain, while so many other alternative fuels languish on the drawing boards and the imaginations of peak oil optimists. Both of these can be distributed and used as though they were petroleum products. Neither one is a viable response to the broader problem, of course; stark limits get in the way of fueling an industrial economy by pouring our food supply into our fuel tanks. All the arable land on the planet is not enough to produce more than a small fraction of the liquid fuels we get from petroleum today, and long before even that inadequate point was reached, mass starvation or violent revolution would cut the process short.

All other proposed replacements for petroleum, however, require much larger investments of money, energy, and raw materials for new infrastructure. The production of energy and raw materials depends on petroleum nowadays; so does the global economy which gives money its value—and conventional petroleum production worldwide is almost three years into what is most likely an irreversible decline.

At this point the paradox of production can be easily defined. If energy prices are high because supplies are limited, the obvious solution is to increase the supply by producing more energy. If this requires replacing one energy resource with another that cannot be produced, distributed or consumed using the identical infrastructure, though, the immediate impact of such a replacement will be to raise energy prices, not lower them. The direct and indirect energy costs of building the new energy system become a source of additional demand that, intersecting with limited supply, drive prices up even further than they otherwise would rise.

If the new energy source turns out to be more abundant, more concentrated, and more easily extracted than the source that it's replacing, this effect is temporary; if the new source can be distributed and used, at least at first, via old technology, the effect is minimized; if the new source is introduced a little at a time, in an economy reliant on many other sources of energy, the effect can easily be lost in the static of ordinary price fluctuations. All three of these were true of petroleum in its early days. It started as a replacement for whale oil in lamps, and was distributed and consumed in existing technology; decades later, it found a niche as a transportation fuel, and relied on the old lamp-oil distribution system until a new one could be constructed on the basis of existing revenues; its other uses evolved gradually from there over more than half a century, until by 1950 it was the world's dominant energy source

None of the proposed replacements for petroleum, though, have those advantages. None of them yield as much net energy as crude oil under natural pressure, and none combine petroleum's unique mix of abundance, concentration, ease of production and distribution, and fitness for a world of machinery designed and built for petroleum-based fuels. The fuel they need to replace remains by far the most important energy source in the world today. Nor do we have half a century to ramp up a new energy system for the industrial economy; conventional petroleum production is already declining steadily, and the most reasonable projections of future production show it dropping off a cliff within the next decade or so.

At the very least, then, trying to solve the energy crisis on the downside of Hubbert's peak by bringing new energy sources online will drive up the cost of petroleum further than it would rise on its own, since the direct and indirect energy costs of the new source and its infrastructure have to be met from existing sources. That poses the same political test faced, and failed, by the nations of the industrial world in the late 1970s, when promising steps toward sustainability went into the dumpster because their immediate costs had more political impact than their long-term benefits.

It also risks potentially fatal damage to the industrial economy itself, which will face severe strains already as the age of cheap abundant energy comes to an end. Pursued with enough misplaced enthusiasm, a crash program to bring some new energy source online in a hurry could drain enough energy, raw materials, labor, and money out of an already fragile system to drive it over the edge into economic and political collapse.

Fortunately, this is not the whole story. There is at least one proven way to counter the paradox of production, exert downward pressure on energy prices, and free up resources and time that can be used to respond constructively to our predicament. I'll discuss it in next week's post.

80: NET ENERGY AND JEVONS' PARADOX

(Originally published 2 April 2008)

As last week's Archdruid Report post suggested, a difficult paradox lies in wait for attempts to bail industrial society out of its peak oil predicament by bringing new energy sources online. To build the infrastructure to produce a new energy source in meaningful quantities, a great deal of energy will be needed. If the new source can't be shipped via existing distribution networks, or used in existing end-use technology, more energy will have to be invested to provide these as well.

Until much of the new infrastructure is in place, though, the energy needed to develop it will have to come from existing sources. This is where the jaws of the trap open wide, because in a world already on the far side of Hubbert's peak, existing energy resources are fully committed. Thus the immediate effect of launching a project to make energy more available will be to make energy less available, driving up prices even faster than they would rise under the pressure of resource depletion.

One conclusion worth drawing from what I've called the "paradox of production" is that some recent debates over net energy may need reassessment. Net energy or EROEI (energy return on energy invested), for those who haven't been following these debates, is the energy that can be obtained from a given resource, minus the energy that has to go into providing that resource to users. Just as net receipts, rather than gross receipts, determine whether a business prospers or goes bankrupt, it's the net energy available to our society, rather than the total amount of energy it consumes, that determines whether something like today's industrial civilization can survive.

At the same time, as the paradox of production points out, the energy costs that have to be factored into net energy are not limited to those needed to produce energy from a given source in the first place. The energy cost to get it to the end user and to convert it into useful work at that point also have to be taken into account. Thus it's important to distinguish production costs—the direct and indirect energy inputs needed to turn a natural resource into useful energy ready for distribution—from system costs—the direct and indirect energy inputs needed to apply that energy to its end use, whatever that happens to be. Both have to be accounted for, but each has its own distinctive features.

In particular, the production costs of a given energy resource depend almost entirely on the nature of the energy resource itself. The system costs of a given resource, on the other hand, depend partly on the resource and partly on the nature of the end use, and the same energy source can have dramatically different system costs depending on the form in which it's distributed and the use to which it's put.

Compare the net energy of photovoltaic cells used to power computers, for example, with the net energy of photovoltaic cells used to power automobiles. The production costs are the same in either case, but the system costs are totally different. The data center makes use of an existing distribution network (the electric power grid) and a mature technology (electronic computers), so its system costs are identical to those involved in powering any other computer. Putting the same energy to work powering automobiles requires the manufacture of millions of new cars (if the electricity is used directly in electric cars), or a network of fuel plants, pipelines, and filling stations, in addition to millions of new cars (if the electricity is used indirectly, in a form such as hydrogen).

Discussions of net energy in the peak oil community have generally tended to focus on production costs, to the neglect of system costs. There's an interesting irony here, because market forces and political pressures in the real world tend to focus on system costs, to the neglect of production costs. The recent ethanol boom in America is the poster child for this oddity of contemporary economics.

In terms of production costs, ethanol made from American corn is a losing proposition. It takes more energy to provide the fertilizers, pesticides, tractor fuel, and other energy inputs to grow the corn, and to ferment and distill it into fuel ethanol, than you get back from burning the ethanol. The system costs of ethanol, on the other hand, are negligible: the US already has an extensive transportation system for getting bulk grains from farms to factories, and existing liquid fuel distribution networks are perfectly capable of handling fuel ethanol. All that has to be added to the mix are factories to turn corn into fuel, and misguided government grants and tax writeoffs seem to be taking care of that nicely.

This same effect shapes less embarrassingly self-defeating choices as well. Look at the suite of alternative energy sources that are getting significant funding these days—windpower comes to mind—and you'll find that all of them use existing infrastructure to distribute and use the resulting energy. Meanwhile, those alternatives that pose high system costs—the much-ballyhooed hydrogen economy is the classic example—wither on the vine.

This is part of the blowback from the paradox of production, because system costs have another feature that sets them apart from production costs: if an energy resource requires new distribution networks or end-use technologies, all the new items have to be in place before the energy resource can be used at all. If you don't have every piece of a hydrogen transport economy in place, for example—the electric power plants, the hydrogen factories, the pipelines, the filling stations, the hydrogen-powered cars, and everything else associated with them—you can't use any of it.

The more existing infrastructure you can use, by contrast, the more flexibility you have. Since windpower can use the existing electric grid to power existing electric appliances, for example, you can add windpower capacity one windmill at a time, and upgrade as you go. In a world of depleted energy reserves and rising prices, this is a viable option; sinking huge sums into new infrastructure for distributing and using a new energy resource probably won't be.

There's another dimension to system costs, though, that opens up an unexpected window of opportunity. Since total net energy includes system costs as well as production costs, cutting system costs boosts net energy. One of the largest components of system costs for any energy resource is inefficiency, and in many cases this can be reduced significantly without impacting the flow of energy through the system. When this is done, the effective net energy of the resource goes up.

This is the logic behind Jevons' paradox, first propounded by British economist William Stanley Jevons in his 1866 book The Coal Question. Jevons pointed out that when improvements in technology make it possible to use an energy resource more efficiently, getting more output from less input, the use of the resource tends to go up, not down. His argument is impeccable: as the use of the resource becomes more efficient, the cost per unit of the end result tends to go down, and so people can afford to use more of it; as efficiency goes up, it also becomes economically feasible to apply the energy resource to new uses, and so people have reason to use more of it.

Jevons' paradox has been used more than once to argue against conservation, on the grounds that using energy more efficiently will simply lower the cost of energy and encourage people to use more of it. The problem with this logic is that it assumes that the only thing constraining energy supply is price—and in a world already starting to skid down the far side of Hubbert's peak, this is no longer true. Now that geological realities rather than market forces are placing hard limits on the upper end of petroleum production, Jevons' paradox becomes a counterweight to rising energy prices.

Now it's sometimes been suggested that all the easy gains from conservation were made in the 1970s, and that further gains will come at much higher cost. This would be true if the achievements of the Seventies had been kept in place, as they should have been—but were not. Compare the poorly insulated McMansions and gas-guzzling SUVs that define the recent American lifestyle with the snug homes and efficient compacts so common in 1979, and it takes an effort of will to avoid seeing the ground that has been lost.

This offers a bitter commentary on the missed opportunities

of the last quarter century. From another perspective, though, this provides a certain amount of qualified hope, because it allows life-style changes and simple upgrades perfected decades ago to be dusted off and put back to work. Those of my readers who recall the Seventies will remember just how simple and cost-effective many of these changes were. They played a crucial part in drop-ping petroleum consumption worldwide by 15% between 1972 and 1985. That decrease could have been used to free up resources for the transition to sustainability, instead of being blown off in a final 25-year orgy of conspicuous overconsumption. That didn't happen, and the arrival of petroleum production declines means that it won't happen again, but the same effect could be used now to help cushion the otherwise rocky descent into the deindustrial age ahead of us.

The same insight can be put in another way. One crucial mea-sure of our predicament is the steady decline in net energy avail-able to industrial society, from the 200-to-1 surplus of light sweet crude flowing under natural pressure to the single digits avail-able from those renewable sources that manage to rise above the breakeven point at all. As we've seen, though, the whole picture of net energy includes systems costs as well as production costs, and rising production costs can be countered to some extent by conser-vation and efficiency improvements that lower system costs. This won't bring back the age of cheap abundant energy, but it could make things easier for many people in the near future.

If governments in the industrial world want to launch a crash program to do something about soaring energy prices and spi-ralling energy shortages, then, the obvious choice is the one that worked in the 1970s — conservation. Just now, given the ideol-ogies that dominate the political classes of the major industrial nations, this seems about as likely as a resumption of the Punic Wars, but attitudes and political climates can change abruptly. In the meantime, the more people who learn, practice and prepare to teach the homely but valuable conservation skills that were part of everyday life in the Seventies, the easier the transition will be when it arrives. Where the people lead, at least in this case, the leaders will eventually be obliged to follow.

81: MASTER CONSERVERS
(Originally published 9 April 2008)

For those of us who have been watching the energy scene for the last few decades, there's a certain wry amusement to be gained from the daily fare on the peak oil newsblogs. Once the conservation and appropriate tech movements of the 1970s collapsed beneath the weight of the falling oil prices of the 1980s, it became highly unfashionable to question the theory that the market economy could extract infinite resources from a finite planet.

During the quarter century of extravagant waste that followed, the conventional wisdom across the industrial world's political and cultural spectrum insisted that turning sow's ears into silk purses was not merely possible, but a great investment opportunity that would drive a bigger and shinier global economy than the one we already had. A very short time ago, it bears remembering, the suggestion that crude oil might cost more than $60 a barrel within this decade was roundly dismissed as preposterous alarmism, while the grim prospects of economic decline and global famine raised by concerned voices in the Seventies were so far off the radar screens that nobody even bothered to denounce them.

A glance down the leading stories on Energy Bulletin or The Oil Drum makes a tolerably good indicator of how far we've come from that comfortable consensus. Today a widely used measure of crude oil prices broke $111, after recovering from a sharp selloff a few weeks back that took it down all the way to the upper $90s. Meanwhile the energy sources and technological breakthroughs that were supposed to come on line once oil hit $30, or $40, or $50 a barrel are still nowhere to be seen.

The wider picture is no more encouraging. Crippling electricity shortages outside the industrial world are starting to play hob with a global economy that depends on Third World factories to produce First World amenities. Likewise, the blowback from US energy policies that poured a fifth of the American corn harvest into ethanol is sending grain prices soaring worldwide, raising the unwelcome prospect that millions of the poor around the planet may not be able to buy enough food to survive the coming months. Barring some improbable deus ex machina that comes along in time to bail us out of the mess we've made for ourselves, it's fair to say, the limits to growth are back.

Up to this point the political leaders of the world's industrial nations have had very little to offer in response to all this. Most seem to think that the advice allegedly given to Victorian brides on their wedding nights—"Close your eyes and think of England"—counts as a proactive energy policy. Eventually they will have to think of a better response, if only because political survival does have its appeal. Food riots in Haiti and Egypt are one thing, but when the price of food and gasoline starts putting serious pressure on the American and European middle classes, expect politicians to trip over one another in the rush to respond to the crisis.

Many of the resulting policies and programs will be counterproductive, and even more of them will be useless. In most of the nations of the industrial world, politics has long since devolved into a spoils system whereby different factions of the political class buy the loyalty of pressure groups among the electorate by a combination of ideological handwaving and unearned largesse. As long as that remains in place—and it has proven enormously durable, surviving wars, revolutions, and massive economic changes—a very large fraction of the responses proposed to this or any other crisis will be aimed at pushing ideological agendas or rewarding voting blocs rather than actually doing anything about the crisis.

Still, it's by no means impossible that some constructive changes might come out of the approaching mess. We have, after all, a resource at hand that, while rarely recognized, has a great deal to offer: we have been here before, during the energy crises and resource shortages of the Seventies. Some of the projects launched in those days turned out to be expensive flops, but others have more to offer. I'd like to talk a bit about one of these.

I have no idea how common this is outside the West Coast, but out here state and county agricultural extension services launched Master Gardener programs some years ago. Staffed by volunteers, many of them retirees with a lifetime of gardening experience, and run on a shoestring budget, these programs train and certify people to field gardening questions that would otherwise clutter up the ag extension phone lines. In the small Oregon town where I live, you can find a Master Gardener's booth at the local farmers market every Tuesday, staffed by a brace of volunteers who will happily help you figure out what's chewing on your cabbages or what soil amendments your blueberries need.

Soaring garbage disposal costs a while back led to the birth of a second project on the same lines, the Master Composter program. Less visible than the Master Gardeners, the Master Composters have mostly concentrated on teaching people how to set up backyard compost bins and take their yard waste and kitchen scraps out of the waste stream. When I lived in Seattle in the years right around the turn of the millennium, the city government helped the Master Composters out to the extent of giving away free compost bins to anybody who attended their classes; the reduction in garbage disposal costs was substantial enough that this made economic sense.

The late Seventies and early Eighties, though, saw the birth and abandonment of another project of the same sort: the Master Conserver program. I was one of some hundreds of people, ranging from teenagers to retirees, who attended weekly classes in the auditorium of the old downtown branch of the Seattle Public Library. We studied everything from basic thermodynamics to the fine details of storm window installation. Those who completed the curriculum took an exam, then put in at least a minimum number of hours of volunteer work helping schools, churches, nonprofits, and elderly and poor homeowners retrofit for energy conservation, to receive their Master Conserver certificate. I still have mine, tucked away in a drawer, much the way old soldiers I've known kept medals from the wars of their youth.

Could such a program be put back to work by local governments in the face of the approaching energy crisis? You bet. A quarter century of further experience with the Master Gardener and Master Composter programs on county and state levels would make it child's play to organize; the information isn't hard to find, and the dismal level of energy efficiency common in recently built houses and the like could make a Master Conserver program a very useful asset as energy prices climb and the human cost rises accordingly.

For that matter, I can't be the only Master Conserver from those days who still has all the class handouts from the program in a battered three-ring binder, or who keeps part of a bookshelf weighed down with classic conservation books — The Integral Urban House, The Book of the New Alchemists, Rainbook, and the like. I don't quite remember anybody in the last days of the program saying "Keep your Whole Earth catalogs, boys, the price of oil will rise again!" Still, the sentiment was there.

More generally, of course, the experiences of any of the 20th century's more difficult periods can be put to work constructively as we move deeper into the 21st century's first major crisis. The victory gardens and ingenious substitutions that kept the home front functioning during the Second World War are another potential source of ideas and inspiration well worth a sustained look. Still, the experiences of the Seventies offer a particularly rich resource in this regard. Close enough to the present to be part of living memory for many people, and faced with the same basic challenge of too little energy, too few resources, and too much economic instability for an overheated and overextended industrial world, it parallels our present predicament too closely to be neglected.

One crucial lessson from that decade may be particularly worth keeping in mind. In the depths of the Seventies energy crisis, the conventional wisdom had it that energy would just keep on getting more costly as a lasting Age of Scarcity dawned over the industrial world. That didn't happen, of course. I've suggested elsewhere, based on the way other civilizations have fallen in the past, that the end of the industrial age will trace out a stairstep decline, with periods of crisis and breakdown punctuated by periods of partial recovery.

This has its drawbacks, but it also offers the hope of breathing spaces in which the lessons of each time of crisis can be assessed and put to use in dealing with the next. By the time we start on the downward arc following the one we're approaching just now, with any luck, the Master Conservers of that time will have the accumulated knowledge of a second round of crises to draw on, and may be able to make the transition to lower energy use a little less rough than the one that looms before us today.

82: THE SPECIALIZATION TRAP
(Originally published 16 April 2008)

Few ideas are quite as unpopular nowadays as the suggestion that the fate of past civilizations has something to teach us about the likely destiny of our own. This lack of enthusiasm for the lessons of history pervades contemporary culture; what makes this interesting is that it is also among the most fruitful sources of disaster in the modern world. The ongoing implosion of real estate prices around the industrial world is simply one example out of many.

Long before the phrase "condo flipper" entered common usage, one thing should have been obvious: anybody who claims that an asset class can keep on increasing in value forever is shoveling smoke. From the 17th century Dutch tulip mania to the internet bubble of the late 1990s, financial history is littered with the blackened ruins of speculative booms that crashed and burned while in hot pursuit of the fantasy of endless appreciation. None of this kept investors in the last few years from betting the future on the belief that this time was different, and real estate prices would keep rising forever — or from lambasting those few spoilsports who suggested that what went up would inevitably, in due time, come down.

Those of us who insist on reading today's headlines about peak oil in the light of history risk a similar reaction. Still, it's a risk worth taking. The logic that insists that while all other civilizations have risen and fallen, ours will just keep rising forever, differs not a whit from the logic underlying the late real estate bubble; the only difference is one of scale. It's for this reason among others that I try to keep up with scholarship on the decline and fall of past civilizations, and that was what brought me to Bryan Ward-Perkins' valuable book The Fall of Rome and the End of Civilization (Oxford UP, 2005).

Those of my readers who don't keep track of current fashions in historiography may not know that for several decades now, such phrases as "the Dark Ages" and "the fall of Rome" have been nomina non grata in scholarly circles. The transition that turned western Europe from the crowded, cosmopolitan Roman world into the depopulated, impoverished patchwork of barbarian chiefdoms that succeeded it has been recast by several influential writers as a process of positive cultural evolution that just happened to feature such awkward incidents as, say, the sack of Rome by the Visigoths.

Now it's only fair to say that, like most revisionist histories, this one made a necessary point. An older generation of historians had gone so far in the other direction—demonizing the barbarians, ignoring the real cultural achievements of the centuries following Rome's fall, and paying too little attention to the survival of the eastern Roman Empire during the years when its western twin imploded—that a reaction was overdue. Like most revisionist histories, however, the reaction pushed itself to the point of absurdity, and Ward-Perkins' book is a useful corrective.

One of the tools he uses to document the real scale and impact of the western empire's collapse is the humble but eloquent voice of pottery. The Roman pottery industry was huge, capable, and highly centralized, churning out fine tableware, storage vessels, roof tiles, and many other goods in such vast quantities that archeologists across Roman Europe struggle to cope with the fragments today. The pottery works at La Graufesenque in what is now southern France and was then the province of Gallia Narbonensis, for instance, shipped exquisite products throughout the western empire, and beyond it—goods bearing the La Graufesenque stamp have been found in Denmark and eastern Germany. Good pottery was so cheap and widely available that even rural farm families could afford elegant tableware, sturdy cooking pots, and watertight roof tiles.

Rome's fall changed all this. When archeologists uncovered

the grave of a sixth-century Saxon king at Sutton Hoo in eastern Britain, for example, the pottery found among the grave goods told an astonishing tale of technical collapse. Had it been made in fourth century Britain, the Sutton Hoo pottery would have been unusually crude for a peasant farmhouse; two centuries later, it sat on the table of a king. What's more, much of it had to be imported, because so simple a tool as a potter's wheel dropped entirely out of use in post-Roman Britain, as part of a cascading collapse that took Britain down to levels of economic and social complexity not seen there since the subsistence crises of the middle Bronze Age more than a thousand years before.

Ward-Perkins' book contains many other illustrations of the human cost of the Roman collapse — the demographic traces of massive depopulation, the way that trends in graffiti track the end of widespread literacy, the decline in the size of post-Roman cattle as a marker of agricultural contraction, and much more — but I want to focus on the pottery here, because it tells a tale with more than a little relevance to our own time. Cooking vessels, food containers, and roofing that keeps the rain out, after all, are basic to any form of settled life. An agricultural society that cannot produce them is impoverished by any definition; an agricultural society that had the ability to produce them, and loses it, has clearly undergone an appalling decline.

What happened to put such obviously useful items out of the reach of the survivors of Rome's collapse? As Ward-Perkins shows, the post-Roman economic collapse had its roots in the very sophistication and specialization that made the Roman economy so efficient. Pottery, again, makes an excellent example of the wider process. Huge pottery factories like the one at La Graufesenque, which used specialist labor to turn out quality goods in immense volume, could make a profit only by marketing their wares on a nearly continental scale, using sophisticated networks of transport and exchange to reach consumers all over the western empire who wanted pottery and had denarii to spend on it. The Roman world was rich, complex, and stable enough to support such networks — but the post-Roman world was not.

The implosion of the western empire thus turned what had

been a massive economic advantage into a fatal vulnerability. As the networks of transport and exchange came apart, the Roman economy went down with it, and that economy had relied on centralized production and specialized labor for so long that there was nothing in place to take up the slack. During the Roman Empire's heyday, people in the towns and villas near Sutton Hoo could buy their pottery from local merchants, who shipped them in from southern Britain, Gaul, and points further off. They didn't need local pottery factories, and so didn't have them, and that meant their descendants very nearly ended up with no pottery at all.

Even where Roman pottery factories existed, they were geared toward mass production of specialized types, not to small-scale manufacture of the whole range of pottery products needed by local communities. Worse, as population levels declined and the economy contracted, the pottery on hand would have been more than adequate for immediate needs, removing any market for new production. A single generation of social chaos and demographic contraction thus could easily have been enough to break the transmission of the complex craft traditions of Roman pottery-making, leaving the survivors with only the dimmest idea of how to make good pottery.

Trace any other economic specialty through the trajectory of the post-Roman world and the same pattern appears. Economic specialization and centralized production, the core strategies of Roman economic success, left Rome's successor states with few choices and fewer resources in a world where local needs had to be met by local production. Caught in the trap of their own specialization, most parts of the western empire came out the other end of the process of decline far more impoverished and fragmented than they had been before the centralized Roman economy evolved in the first place.

Map this same process onto the most likely future of industrial society, in turn, and the parallels have daunting implications. In modern industrial nations, the production and distribution of goods are far more centralized than anything Rome ever achieved. Nearly all workers at every level of the economy perform highly specialized niche jobs, most of which only function within the structure of a highly centralized, mechanized, and energy-intensive global economy, and many of which have no meaning or value at all outside that structure. If the structure falters, access to even the most basic goods and services could become a challenge very quickly.

Food is the obvious example—a very small number of people in any industrial nation have the skills necessary to grow their own food, and even fewer could count on access to the land, tools, and seed stock to give it a try—but the same principle holds for every other necessity of life, not to mention countless other things that would be good to have in the deindustrial dark age that looms up ahead of us in most of our possible futures. Consider the suite of skills needed, for example, to locate and process suitable fibers, spin and weave them into cloth, and make the cloth into clothing. Not many people these days have any of those skills, much less all of them; the tools needed to do most of them are not exactly household items in most homes these days, and the ability to build and repair those tools are even more specialized.

Our situation is thus far more precarious than Rome's was. On the other hand, we have an advantage that the Roman world apparently lacked—if we choose to use it. The possibility of a future dark age apparently never entered the cultural dialogue in Roman times, but it has been raised repeatedly in ours. Preventive action—the deliberate revival of nonindustrial ways of providing necessary goods and services—is well within the reach of individuals and local communities, and indeed some of this work has already been done by hobbyists and people involved in historical reenactment societies of various kinds.

A great deal more of the same thing will be needed, though, to keep the decline of industrial society from leaving the same sort of economic vacuum in its wake that Rome's fall left behind. I am coming to think that one of the most useful things anyone concerned about the future can do is to adopt some practical craft that produces goods or services useful in a deindustrializing world, and get skilled at it. If we are to get much of anything out from between the jaws of the specialization trap, projects such as this are a crucial step.

83: THE END OF BUSINESS AS USUAL
(Originally published 23 April 2008)

Those of us who are watching the crisis of industrial society arrive on schedule take our omens where we find them, and one appeared yesterday morning in the unlikely form of an internet ad riding shotgun on a peak oil blog. The header was striking enough — "Oil Will Hit $100!" — or it would have been, except that one of the main benchmark grades of crude oil closed not far below $120 a barrel this evening. When the ads on your computer screen have already been left in the dust by the headlines, it's fair to say, yesterday's assumptions are in serious need of revision.

Meanwhile, rolling blackouts and food shortages are making life more difficult for people in many of the world's poorer nations. Even in the United States, where instant availability of consumer products is generally considered an inalienable right, the first spot shortages of grain products have made ripples in the media. I won't even get into the plunging real estate prices and financial implosions along the route of the slow-motion train wreck the global economy resembles so much these days. One way or another, it's turning into a bad week for believers in an imminent return to what most people nowadays consider business as usual.

Yet there's an irony, a rich one, in the chorus of reassurances still rising from the mainstream media across the industrial world. Like the frogs in Aesop's fable, they praised the replacement of the boring King Log of New Deal economic regulations and Seventies energy-efficiency standards by the far more exciting King Stork of the unfettered market, only to find that too much excitement in the economic sphere has its downside; their attempt to return to a free market succeeded mostly in kickstarting a recurrence of the cycle of disastrous depressions that reached its crescendo in 1929 and bringing about a recurrence of the energy crises of the 1970s, but on a larger scale. Before you decide to return to business as usual, in other words, it's useful to have some sense of what business as usual actually is.

We are arguably facing a much more threatening example of the same phenomenon right now, as the fuel gauge on the world's oil, coal, and natural gas supplies moves visibly in the direction of that unwelcome letter E. For the last three centuries or so, a steadily increasing flow of cheap abundant fossil fuel energy has driven the growth of industrial societies across much of the world. For the last century, since petroleum replaced coal as industrial civilization's prime mover, and widespread electrification made it possible to apply fossil fuels at second hand to most business and domestic energy needs, most of the work done in the industrial world has been done by machines powered directly or indirectly by fossil fuels.

This seems perfectly normal to most of us who have grown up in the industrial world. Up until very recently, essentially all the talk about the disparity between the world's industrial societies and the rest of the planet focused on how to bring the Third World "into the twenty-first century." The phrase itself betrays the huge burden of ideology that shaped that discussion—the belief, as potent and devoutly held as any other religion, that history progresses straight to us, that any different social arrangement is simply some version of our own outmoded past, and that our peculiar and extravagant way of managing human communities is thus as inevitable as it is inevitably beneficent.

Yet the whole debate was also an exercise in futility. We are seeing right now what happens when an appreciable number of people in the world's nonindustrial societies do exactly what so many decades of rhetoric insisted they ought to, and claim a share of the world's fossil fuels and industrial output. The limits to growth were always there; it was merely the political arrangements that restricted the benefits of industrialism to a small portion of the human species that made it look as though unlimited growth was even an option.

What we most need to realize at this juncture is that the way things have been in the world's industrial societies over the last century or so is in no way normal. It's precisely equivalent to the new lifestyle adopted by winners of a lottery whose very modest income has suddenly leapt upward by $1 million a year or so. After a few years, the lottery winners might well become accustomed to the privileges and possessions that influx of wealth made possible, and children growing up in such a family might never realize that life could be any other way. The hard fact remains, though, that when the lottery money runs out, it runs out, and if no provision has been made for the future, the transition from a million dollars a year to the much more modest income available from an ordinary job can be very, very rough.

The huge distortions imposed on the modern industrial nations by the flood of cheap abundant energy that washed over them in the 20th century can be measured readily enough by a simple statistic. In America today, our current energy use works out to around 1000 megajoules per capita, or the rough equivalent of 100 human laborers working 24-hour days for each man, woman, and child in the country. The total direct cost for all this energy came to around $500 billion a year in 2005, the last year for which I was able to find statistics, or about $1667 per person per year.

Now consider how much it would cost to hire human laborers to perform the same amount of work. At the current federal minimum wage of $5.75 an hour, hiring 100 workers in three shifts to provide the equivalent amount of energy would cost each American $512,811 a year, or about 308 times as much as the energy costs—and this doesn't count payroll taxes, health insurance, paid vacations and the like. Mind you, it would also require the US to find food, housing, and basic services for an additional workforce of 30 billion people, but we can let the metaphor go before tackling issues on that scale.

What makes this huge disparity relevant is that as recently as a hundred years ago, the majority of work done even in the most advanced industrial societies was done by human beings using hand tools. Kitchens had servants instead of appliances; factories and shops had workbenches instead of industrial robots; the functions now carried out by computers were performed instead by legions of clerks wielding pen and ink. Go back a little further in history, to the time when fossil fuels hadn't yet become a significant energy source, and human muscles and minds did the vast majority of work of all kinds, with modest supplements from animal muscle, sun, wind, and water power.

The familiarity of our current arrangements, and the rhetoric of progress we use to justify those arrangements, make it easy to dismiss such a human-powered economy as some sort of primitive oddity that existed only because people didn't yet know any better. Look at the disparity in economic terms and a different picture emerges. In a society without access to cheap abundant energy resources, it makes much more economic sense to train and employ a human worker than to develop a machine to fill the same niche; except in special circumstances, the additional cost of building, powering, maintaining, and operating the machine more than outweighed the additional benefits of mechanical speed and regularity.

This was why ancient Rome and imperial China, both of which had a solid understanding of mechanical principles and sophisticated technical traditions, never had industrial revolutions of their own. Lacking massive energy supplies of the sort that made modern industrial society possible, it simply made more economic sense to invest the available resources into the labor force. The Romans did this the cheap, crude, and ultimately ineffective way, by expanding a slave economy to the breaking point; the Chinese did it far more sustainably and effectively by evolving an extraordinarily robust system of small-scale capitalism, on the one hand, and equally durable traditions of specialized craftsmanship on the other.

All this has a pressing relevance to the present situation, because we're running out of the energy resources that make it possible for every man, woman and child in America to dispose of the equivalent of $512,811 in labor every year. It's as though the 30 billion invisible guest workers whose sweat powers the American economy are quitting their jobs one by one, and moving back to their homes in the Paleozoic. When the process completes itself, and the long curve of depletion finally sinks low enough that it's no longer economically worthwhile to extract the remaining dregs of fossil fuel from the ground, the amount of labor each of us will have at our disposal will be much, much less than it is today.

With any luck, it'll be more than 1/308th as much—we know more about collecting and using energy than the Romans or the Chinese did, and may well be able to get enough renewable energy sources up and running in time to matter. Still, it's mere wishful thinking to assume that the universe is obliged to give us another vast windfall of cheap abundant energy to replace the one we've wasted so enthusiastically over the last few centuries, and none of the proposed replacements for fossil fuels seem likely to live up to their billing. On a finite planet subject to the laws of thermodynamics, claims that the trajectory of industrialism must inevitably continue into the future are statements of faith, not of fact.

Far more likely is the reemergence of an economy in which the work of human hands and minds is once again the main source of economic value—and with luck and hard work, it may be a good deal closer to the Chinese than the Roman model. In a low-energy economy, after all, human beings have huge economic advantages over machines. Machines do not develop their own energy sources and find their own raw materials, much less manufacture their own replacements, and the products of a given machine do not improve over time all by themselves, as the products of a farmer or a craftsperson so often do.

The farmers of the future may well use intensive organic methods rather than the field agriculture of an earlier day, just as the craftspeople of the future may well spend some of their time crafting solar hot water heaters and shortwave radios. Still, this sort of handicraft economy is a mature and effective social technology, and far and away the most common way societies provide for the needs of their members. It is, one might say, business as usual.

84: NOT THE END OF THE WORLD

(Originally published 30 April 2008)

You know that things are beginning to heat up when both sides of a controversy declare victory at the same time. Over the last week or so, that's happened in the peak oil scene. On the one hand, quite a number of cornucopians—those enthusiastic souls who believe that we can get ourselves out of the hole we're in by digging faster and paying less attention to where the dirt lands—have trumpeted the discovery of a few new oil fields as proof that peak oil is a myth.

The Bakken shale, a geological formation down in the basement of the northern Great Plains, has attracted the bulk of this cheerleading. Mind you, the Bakken's a significant discovery; there's apparently a fair amount of oil down there, though the technical challenges involved in extracting more than a tiny fraction of it are immense, and nobody's yet sure if the energy that can be extracted from it will be more or less than the energy cost needed to extract it. Even if it turns out to be the oil find of the decade, though, and North Dakota oil millionaires start showing up as a recognized type in American popular culture, the most the Bakken can do is make up some of the production losses from older oil fields and slow, for a time, our descent from Hubbert's peak.

Meanwhile, on the other side of the spectrum, the number of voices proclaiming the imminence of total collapse has skyrocketed. Typical is a recent post in Sharon Astyk's useful peak oil blog. Astyk claims that recent events have decisively settled the debate between the fast-crash and slow-grind models of post-peak oil reality, in favor of the fast crash—and we're already in it. Her argument is basically that the drastic spikes in food and energy costs over the last few months have outrun the limits of the slow-grind scenario; ergo, the fast crash is here.

I've commented several times in these essays about the way that linear thinking distorts our view of the future, and Astyk's prediction makes a good example. The drastic price spikes in many commodities over the last few months offer a warning that shouldn't be ignored, but treating them as evidence that industrial society is about to implode imposes a linear model onto the complex realities of socioeconomic change. The fact that change is happening quickly right now does not mean that it will continue to happen at the same pace, or even in the same direction.

Human societies are complex homeostatic systems that respond to changes in their environments by trying to maintain their equilibrium. Both the cornucopians and the fast-collapse theorists too often lose track of this basic rule of human ecology, but it's interesting to note that they do so in different ways. In the face of faltering oil production, industrial societies intensify the search for new oil fields and exploit fields that would have been considered uneconomical in the halcyon days of cheap oil; that's how they try to maintain equilibrium. These are responses to crisis, however, not evidence that the crisis is over. When an oil reservoir as geologically challenging as the Bakken looks like a good place to drill, that in itself provides a good measure of how serious the drawdown of existing reserves has become.

At the same time, soaring costs of energy and food are among the ways that a market-based society attempts to maintain equilibrium when supply fails to keep up with potential demand. Rationing by price is a profoundly inequitable way to sort out who gets food and energy in a time of shortages, and who does not, but unless the industrial world goes through drastic political changes in the very near future, it's the way we're stuck with, and it does have at least one pragmatic advantage: the ration coupons (we call them "money") and the entire system of rationing are already in place, ready to use, without massive social engineering.

As prices go up, a great many of the poor and disenfranchised worldwide are sliding closer to the edge where destitution turns into starvation. That's a tragedy, and a moral crisis of no small magnitude. Still, those who think that it announces the imminent collapse of industrial society need to revisit the history of the nineteenth century, when famines racked the Third World with appalling frequency and a good half of the population in many industrial nations lived in desperate poverty. Most people in the industrial world nowadays, I suspect, have forgotten just how much routine deprivation was a part of ordinary life before the brief twentieth-century heyday of cheap abundant energy.

At the same time, rising prices in a market society also help drive responses to crisis. Here in Oregon, much of the farmland in the long and fertile Willamette valley has been used for years to grow grass seed for the lawn-improvement market. This year, though, a good many of the grass-seed farmers are planting wheat instead — the grass seed market is weak, while the price they can expect for wheat is higher than it's been in generations. Similar responses are beginning to show up in other agricultural and economic sectors; that's the sort of response that can be expected, after all, from a complex homeostatic system.

That's also why the collapse of previous civilizations follows a stairstep process that combines periods of severe crisis with periods of partial recovery. Knocked out of one state of equilibrium by the pressures driving it toward collapse, a society in decline finds a new balance lower down the scale of socioeconomic complexity; when that balance becomes unsustainable, another transition follows, and then another point of equilibrium lower still; that's the underlying logic of the theory of catabolic collapse, the basis for most of what appears on this blog. It's hard to argue against the suggestion that we're entering such a period of crisis just now, and if this is the case, we can expect hard choices and troubled times in the years immediately ahead.

In the case of today's soaring food prices, likely results include increased starvation in the world's poorest countries, and a sharp increase in the world's roster of failed states. Meanwhile, drastic economic, political, and cultural readjustments will hit the industrial world as income redistributes itself from urban centers to farm country. Further down the road, expect prices of many agricultural commodities to come crashing back to earth as steep increases in production intersect with the boom-and-bust cycle of commodities speculation. They'll head back up thereafter — many centuries will likely pass before food is ever again as cheap compared to incomes as it was in the second half of the twentieth century — but the wild swings in commodity prices will place added pressure on economic systems already creaking under existing strains.

Perhaps the most likely result of the current wave of crises, however, is the twilight of the much-ballyhooed global market of the twentieth century's last decades. That was never the wave of the future its cheerleaders labeled it; it was a temporary artifact of a world in which energy costs had been forced so low, and economic disparities between nations raised so high, that distance apparently didn't matter and arbitraging labor costs across continents seemed to make economic sense. As energy costs have risen in recent years, nations with energy resources have done the sensible thing and recognized the political dimensions of economic exchange. Free-market fundamentalists who denounce this "resource nationalism" seem to have forgotten that the government of Russia, for example, was not elected by the citizens of America, and gains no conceivable benefit by embracing policies that benefit American consumers or politicians while disadvantaging their Russian equivalents.

The food crisis has pushed this same transformation into overdrive. Governments around the world that once made their nations' ability to feed their own people a sacrosanct element of national policy, and were talked out of this sensible strategy during the heyday of cheap energy, have suddenly realized that the lukewarm gratitude of foreign politicians and the plaudits of economists snugly sheltered in their ivory towers don't count for much when a hungry mob heads for the presidential palace. Most of the Asian countries that produce rice, the grain that has soared most in price, have accordingly limited rice exports to ensure that their own people get enough to eat. Where fossil fuels and food crops go, other resources will follow; my guess is that potash for fertilizer, an essential resource for industrial agriculture, will be next in line.

The "free market," for that matter, was never that free in the first place; a slanted playing board designed to maximize the flow of wealth to the world's industrial nations and minimize flows in the other direction, it replaced more straightforward forms of colonialism while maintaining unequal patterns of exchange that allow the 5% of the world's population who live in the United States to dispose of about 30% of the world's natural resources. It's not surprising that countries assigned the short end of the stick by these arrangements would throw them off as soon as they could get away with it, and the resource crunch now underway offers them a perfect opportunity to do so.

The end of the global economy may make life a good deal harder for those of us in the United States and those other industrial nations, such as Canada and Australia, that have become used to the absurdly lavish energy and resource expenditures of the recent past. It bears remembering, though, that people in Europe maintain a standard of living in many ways higher ours on roughly one-third the energy per capita Americans seem to think is necessary for civilized life. We can get by, and get by tolerably well, on much less energy and many fewer resources than we think.

This is likely to be a crucial point to keep in mind as the present crisis unfolds. It's not the end of the world, or even the end of industrial civilization, but if history is anything to go by, we could be in for a couple of very rough decades. A crisis phase in the downward arc of catabolic collapse is not a pleasant thing to live through, and we can expect it to have social, economic, political, and (unless we're extraordinarily lucky) military dimensions that will transform most people's lives for the worse, temporarily or forever. That need not stop us from facing the emerging crisis with as much grace and humanity as we can muster, while doing our part to lay the foundations for the ecotechnic societies of the future—unless, that is, we allow premature proclamations of triumph or catastrophe to distract us from the work that must be done.

85: PREPARING FOR WHAT FUTURE?

(Originally published 7 May 2008)

Last week's Archdruid Report post, as my regular readers will recall, tried to point out that the current round of price spikes in food and petroleum prices does not justify claims that industrial civilization was on the brink of a rapid and total collapse. Predictably enough, this suggestion brought down a flurry of criticism.

Some of that was simply another helping of the standard arguments for the progressive and apocalyptic fantasies that play so large a role in today's collective consciousness. Fortunately, not all fell into that reflexive category. My essay cited a recent post by relocalization blogger Sharon Astyk suggesting that a fast crash was imminent, and she responded the next day with a thoughtful rebuttal. I won't try to summarize her arguments here; those interested should certainly read her response in full.

One point, though, deserves a response in detail. My essay last week ended with what I thought was a fairly straightforward comment: "...unless, that is, we allow premature proclamations of triumph or catastrophe to distract us from the work that must be done." Sharon took exception to this and suggested, if I follow her correctly, that the phrase was simply a rhetorical flourish. That it certainly was not. It could doubtless have been expressed more clearly, but it points to what, as I see it, is one of the most crucial factors in discussing the future of industrial society.

The actions we take to prepare for the future, after all, should be shaped by the future we expect. If we can reasonably expect the future promised us by the modern myth of progress—a future of constant improvement toward a destiny among the stars—then it makes sense to plan on business as usual, to treat each ephemeral new technology as the wave of the future, and to treat nature as a sort of green decor worth saving solely for esthetic and sentimental reasons. If, on the other hand, we can reasonably expect the future promised us by the modern myth of apocalypse—a future of sudden chaos and mass death that will leave, at most, a handful of survivors huddled in isolated hideouts—then it makes sense to abandon any hope of improving the status quo and eschew any plan for the future that doesn't involve firearms, canned food, and subsistence skills basic enough to be practiced in the desolate silence of a mostly empty world.

The problem with either of these decisions is obvious enough. If our plans rely on the arrival of some particular future, and that future does not come about, whatever money, effort, resources, and time have been invested in our imagined future has gone down a rathole. If the future we get turns out different enough from the one we expect, in turn, our actions may have closed doors and wasted opportunities that could have spared us major difficulties. The textbook example in recent times is the decision taken around 1980, by nations across the industrial world, to discard the promising steps toward sustainability made in the previous decade. If those steps had been followed up, the transition to a postpetroleum world could probably have been made without massive disruption. At this point, after a quarter century of wasted opportunities, the chance of doing that is slim at best.

Seeing this catastrophic error as a matter of choosing the wrong future to prepare for, though, rather begs the question. There's at some reason to think that the decisions that turned the industrial world away from sustainability in the early 1980s were not the result of a conscious decision that a future of infinite economic growth on a finite planet was possible and desirable. Rather, it seems all too likely that people wished to take certain actions—for example, scrapping expensive and inconvenient conservation programs—and justified those actions by imagining a future in which those actions seemed to make sense. Certainly the same thing has happened in a big way in the alternative scene.

Look for proposals for responding to the crisis of industrial society these days and you'll find that nearly all of them fall into three groups. First are those who want to organize a political movement to throw the current rascals out of office and put a new set of rascals in. Second are those who talk about building ecovillages in the countryside, to provide a postapocalyptic version of suburban living to today's smart investors. Third are those who plan on holing up in a cabin in the mountains with guns and canned beans, and waiting until the rubble stops bouncing. I've argued elsewhere that none of these is a viable response to the future we're most likely to face, but there's another point worth noting: each of them is also something many people in today's American middle class want to do anyway. Quite a few people nowadays think they ought to have more political power; an equally large number like to daydream about moving to a new exurban development far out in the countryside; and of course, the appeal of firearms collections and fantasies of self-reliance remains strong in an age that has problematized traditional images of masculinity. To a great extent, peak oil has simply become another excuse for the pursuit of activities, real or imagined, that many people find desirable for other reasons.

Amplifying this is one of the most enduring habits in the American tradition of public rhetoric—the attempt to scare the bejesus out of people in the hope that this will motivate them to follow a desirable course of action. Colonial preacher Jonathan Edwards' famous sermon "Sinners in the Hands of an Angry God" set a cultural fashion that remains alive to this day. Choose any cause you care to think of, and if it's attracted anything like a mass movement, odds are that its prophets are announcing the imminent arrival of some variety of doom—closely modeled on the Book of Revelations, far more often than not—unless people change their wicked ways. If it's not a mass movement, the odds are even better that its prophets will be proclaiming some inevitable doom which will sweep away the unbelieving multitudes and leave the earth to the righteous remnant—that is, the prophets in question and those who agree with them. In either case, the catastrophe is simply rhetorical ammunition meant to back the claim that whatever action you're supposed to take is the only alternative to doom. Peak oil, of course, has attracted a sizeable number of would-be prophets of both kinds.

I should hasten to say at this point that I'm not assigning Sharon Astyk to either camp. Mind you, I suspect she would propose relocalization as a good idea — as, indeed, many people have been doing, for a variety of good reasons, since the early decades of the 20th century — even if nothing like peak oil were in the offing. Still, retooling lifestyles to rely more on local resources and one's own efforts, and less on a far-flung and increasingly fragile global economic system, is likely to prove a very useful strategy during the cascading series of crises unfolding around us right now. In that, I think, we're very much in agreement. Going beyond that, however, requires a clearer sense of what kind of future we are facing — and not just on a global basis.

Local and personal scales also count; everyone shares the same future only when "the future" has been reduced to an ideological abstraction. The same problem afflicts current talk about the possibility of a crash, fast or otherwise: exactly what is crashing, and how far, and how uniformly? I've done my best to be clear about such issues here and elsewhere, but it's probably worth repeating myself. My take is that modern industrial civilization is on the downslope of its history, headed for the compost heap of fallen empires alongside all the dead civilizations of the past. Peak oil and the other elements of the crisis of the contemporary world, in this analysis, are simply the current manifestations of patterns that shaped the fall of other civilizations, and our future will most likely follow a similar course — an extended, uneven decline extending over more than a century, including repeated periods of crisis followed by partial recoveries, ending in a dark age in which much of the technology, knowledge base, and cultural heritage of today will survive in fragments or be completely lost.

Those parts of the world peripheral to today's industrial civilization will follow trajectories of their own — it's worth remembering that the Muslim world and T'ang dynasty China reached the zeniths of their own cultural arcs while the western world was scraping the bottom of the last round of dark ages — and new cultures will arise from the ruins of the modern industrial world in time. The global reach of industrial civilization, though, makes it unlikely that any part of the world will escape the approaching troubles entirely, and the equally global drawdown of resources erases the possibility that societies of the future will be able to duplicate the industrial model; their technics, while potentially even more sophisticated than ours, will have to work with much less concentrated and abundant energy sources.

The current round of global troubles—the peak of conventional petroleum production worldwide, soaring prices and incipient shortages in other commodities, spiraling breakdowns in the international debt market, and the fraying of America's global empire—marks, in this analysis, the onset of one of the periods of crisis mentioned above. If this is the case, we face several decades of serious social, economic, and political turmoil, with a high likelihood that many of these troubles will spill over onto the battlefield. As I've suggested elsewhere, the period between 1929 and 1945, with its economic crises, political horrors, and global power struggles ending in a brutal world war, may make a tolerably good model for the period now dawning around us.

If I'm right—and every discussion of the future needs to start with those unpopular words—the future for which we have to prepare has two aspects, one overarching, one immediate. The overarching aspect is the slow curve of decline I've called the Long Descent, the final trajectory of industrial civilization toward its death. The immediate aspect is the need to deal with the particular round of crises breaking over us just now. Those two aspects are related but they're not the same, and the resources and skills needed to deal with them are also not the same.

These, ultimately, are the reflections that lie behind my suggestion that fixating on the short term, and overstating the implications of short-term trends, may well get in the way of a constructive response to the broader picture. This is why it's problematic to insist, as a number of internet bloggers did recently, that the discovery of a new oil resource in North Dakota means that peak oil is no longer a problem. On a global scale, with most of the world's oil producing countries and most of its supergiant fields already in decline, the Bakken shale simply doesn't make that much difference, and planning for a future that will allow us to keep up the extravagant energy-wasting lifestyles of the recent past will likely have disastrous results.

Yet it's just as problematic to insist that the current wave of crises will inevitably spin out of control into a fast crash that will bring industrial civilization to its knees. That claim carries its own agenda of actions for the future, and if the claim turns out to be inaccurate, many elements of that agenda could all too easily prove to be dysfunctional. Moving to an isolated rural area and making a go of subsistence farming is not a viable strategy for everyone, for example, and even those who are well suited to that life might turn out to have made a dysfunctional choice if the fast crash fails to arrive on schedule.

If the end of the industrial age turns out to be a longer and more complex process than fast-crash advocates suggest, in fact, isolated rural areas may not be the best places to start small farms at all. Truck gardens and organic food production on the outskirts of small and mid-sized cities will be much better positioned to thrive in a world where markets still exist but transport costs are a major limiting factor. In some areas this is already happening; the explosive growth of farmers markets, community-supported agriculture schemes, and direct sales of local produce to local restaurants have put down the foundations on which local and regional food production networks could easily grow. Fostering the emergence of such networks could contribute much to the future. So could the evolution of many other economic specialties that are irrelevant in the context of a fast crash, but not in the more complex terrain I suspect the future holds for us.

Of course there's a broader context to all this. My vision of the future is very much a minority view these days. So many people believe in the fast crash scenario that there's unlikely to be anything like a shortage of people preparing for it, but the Long Descent is another matter. It doesn't echo any of the narratives our culture and media circulate about the future, and it doesn't feed the widely held and wildly popular sense of our own uniqueness that underlies so much of today's supposedly innovative thought, so its mass appeal is pretty minimal.

Thus you won't find many people preparing to make the transition from today's high-tech economy to the less complex, more impoverished, more fragmented, but still industrial economies that I expect to emerge from the Great Recession and global troubles of 2010-2030 or thereabouts. Nor will you find many people seriously taking on the role of cultural conserver that will be desperately needed if many things of value are to get through the deindustrial dark ages of 2200-2600 or thereabouts, and reach the successor cultures that will emerge beyond it. As I see it, these are among the crucial tasks before us; they could make the long road to the deindustrial future more bearable, and pass on important gifts to the future; but as I tried to suggest last week, they will not happen if the people who could make them happen get caught up in premature proclamations of triumph or catastrophe.

86: THE SAME NEW IDEAS

(Originally published 14 May 2008)

As I write these words, a week before their publication, The Archdruid Report is starting its third year. It's been a long strange trip, to borrow a phrase from the Grateful Dead. Perhaps the strangest thing about it, and certainly the most interesting, has been the chance to watch the way that ideas rise and sink through the collective imagination of the modern world.

This isn't simply entertainment, though it certainly has its entertaining aspects. Behind the obvious challenges posed by peak oil lies a struggle among basic assumptions about the nature of reality. Underlying the cornucopian position, for example, is a worldview in which all meaning and value center on humanity's upward climb to a modern society, and nature is merely a source of raw materials and a place to dump waste. Go to the apocalyptic true believers at the other end of the spectrum and you enter a worldview in which humanity has fallen from grace by usurping nature's power, and only the purifying force of total catastrophe can admit a righteous remnant back into its proper subservience.

These worldviews, like others in the peak oil debate, have ancient roots, and the belief systems that cluster around them faithfully copy equivalents from past centuries. One of the interesting things about the play of ideas around peak oil is the way that an unfamiliar predicament has been redefined in such familiar terms. What adds irony to the interest, though, is the consistency with which those who present these common notions insist on describing them as new and innovative ideas unlike anything anyone has thought before.

Circumstances give me something of a front row seat to this

odd spectacle. It happens that, as a function of my training and temperament alike, my ideas about the future of industrial society differ sharply from many of the popular views on the subject. I hasten to say that my ideas are no more original than those of the other sides in the debate. Everything I've said about the future here and elsewhere comes out of one thread of what Mortimer Adler used to call the Great Conversation, the play of ideas down the years that traces the cultural history of our world, and they root down into a worldview at least as archaic as those I mentioned a moment ago. What interests me is the number of people who are just as dependent on secondhand ideas as I am, but have apparently never noticed that fact.

Consider the widely circulated theories that the end of industrial society will be sudden, total, and imminent. There's nothing particularly new about this claim, which has been being made regularly since the mid-19th century. There's rarely anything new in the arguments supporting modern versions of the claim, either; most of them were well aged before such durable classics as Roberto Vacca's The Coming Dark Age dusted them off for a new audience in the 1970s. For that matter, the shark-fin theory of history, in which societies rise over time to a peak of wealth, power, and corruption, and then suffer total destruction, can be found in the Old Testament, and underlies the religious rhetoric of apocalypse that coined most of the ideas now being retailed by today's prophets of fast collapse.

The persistence of the shark-fin theory in apocalyptic rhetoric, it has to be said, is not matched by a similar presence in actual history. It's vanishingly rare for a society to collapse at the peak of its wealth and power, for the simple reason that wealth and power are two of the most effective means for staving off collapse. As a rhetorical reality, however, the sudden collapse of unjust power has immense cultural resonance throughout the western world, and people are duly lining up for the chance to say "How art the mighty fallen!" over the corpse of industrialism. What fascinates me most, though, is that each of them seems to think they thought of those words by themselves, and for the very first time.

For amother example, take the confident announcements that

the current troubles of industrial society are the harbingers of an evolutionary breakthrough to a higher mode of being, where the problems that beset us today will have lost their relevance. Few claims about the future are so insistently described by their proponents as new and innovative thinking; even fewer have less right to that title. Glance through the pages of such classics of Victorian thought as Joseph Le Conte's Evolution, published in 1888, and you'll find the same claims of imminent evolutionary transformation that fill so many popular books today.

The idea of an evolutionary breakthrough was necessarily a bit of a latecomer on the cultural scene, since a theory of evolution had to be invented first. Once Charles Darwin took care of this detail, each subsequent generation has duly identified whatever crisis made the headlines as the birth-pangs of the new humanity. Their equivalents today insist that this time, it's for real, since the current crisis is so much more dire than those of the past. In making that argument, they're on familiar ground, since the same thing has been claimed about many crises in the past, and doubtless it will be claimed just as fervently about many crises in the future. The most intriguing detail about all this, again, is the way in which an idea that's been rehashed more often than the average sitcom plot has been trotted out again under the label of new and innovative thinking.

A third example is the profusion of claims that everything will be all right if only the right people are given political power. David Korten's widely touted The Great Turning is a case in point. Korten argues that certain people, who have reached a higher "developmental stage" than the rest of us, are uniquely qualified to hold positions of leadership as the ideology of Earth Community vanquishes Empire, the Satan-surrogate of his intensely dualistic secular mythology. His arguments differ only in details from those Plato uses to justify elite rule in his totalitarian Utopia The Republic or, for that matter, the equivalent arguments used by defenders of aristocratic privilege in 18th and 19th century Europe. Since few of Korten's readers are apparently familiar with these latter, though, his profoundly antidemocratic and illiberal treatise has been hailed as a breakthrough work full of new and innovative thinking.

As these examples suggest, the reappearance of the same new ideas over and over again has a troubling side. Many of those ideas have been tried repeatedly in the past, and have worked very, very poorly. Despite their appeal, there's no good reason to think that they'll work any better in their latest incarnations. Thus it may be worth looking into the immense failure of cultural memory that stands in the way of tracing the histories of our own ideas.

In his scathing 1986 study of the ideologies of gender in late 19th century art, Idols of Perversity, Bram Dijkstra commented:

"In a world which stresses the value of individualism above all else, it is a primary requirement for the 'self-confident' mind, to remain blind to the logical conjunction of personal ideas and the assumptions held by the 'mass' of one's contemporaries. The ideas of 'individual' thinkers, more often than not, are largely constructed from contemporary clichés. These clichés have merely been stripped of their baser trappings, of their rhetorical conventionality, in accordance with whatever happen to be the prevailing guidelines for the 'individualistic' ego" (p.146).

Step past Dijkstra's irritable prose and the point he makes is worth following up. The mythology of progress that provides modern industrial culture with its unacknowledged established religion devalues the cultural legacy of older epochs and the experience of the past; it's symptomatic that one of the more crushing phrases of devaluation in modern teen slang is "Oh, that's all history." Without the depth perception that only an awareness of the past can bring, though, all we have to work with are the two-dimensional surfaces of contemporary popular culture, with all its baggage of unacknowledged borrowings from the past. Santayana's famous dictum, it turns out, needs revision; those who do not remember their history are condemned to rehash it, under the delusion that they are being original.

There's a way out of the paradox of unoriginal originality that besets so much of modern thought, though it's at least as paradoxical: the way to get genuinely new ideas is to learn and value old ones. Partially that's a matter of avoiding old mistakes, as suggested above, but it has other dimensions. Creativity, as Arthur Koestler pointed out many years ago, comes from the collision of incommensurable realities; to put that in less lapidary prose, it's when the mind encounters two or more sharply different ways of making sense of the same thing that it can leap to a new level of understanding and come up with something authentically new.

Just as the 19th century collision between Western painting and the visual arts of other cultures enabled the Impressionists to break through to a new way of seeing light and color, and the cultural flowering of Heian Japan unfolded from the collision between the traditional forms of Japanese society and the arrival of cultural imports from China, our chance of finding the new ideas we so desperately need will go up sharply if the unstated assumptions and easy beliefs of contemporary culture are highlighted by contrast with radically different ways of looking at the world—and the past provides plenty of those.

Put this in the context of industrial civilization's decline and fall, and an unexpected significance emerges. One of the great challenges faced by every dying civilization is the need to pass on as much as possible of its cultural, intellectual, and technical heritage to the future. Most readers of this blog are probably familiar with the role that Christian monks played in safeguarding the heritage of the Classical world during and after the collapse of Rome. The same thing has happened at other times, and in other ways—and there have also been times when it did not happen, and bare enigmatic ruins became the sole legacy of a civilization.

The extraordinary collection and transmission of information made possible by modern industrial society's energy-intensive technological infrastructure raises the prospect that our civilization could leave a far richer legacy to the future than any before it. Still, the vulnerability of that technological infrastructure to the impacts of decline means that we can't count on such a positive outcome. Whatever is to be saved has to be valued highly enough to be preserved, copied, and passed on from generation to generation. In a society that habitually devalues its past, it's by no means guaranteed that anything of the sort will happen.

For this reason among others. I've come to think that a crucial role in shaping the future will be played by cultural conservers—individuals who choose to take on the task of learning and preserving some part of the cultural legacy of the past, and passing it on to the future. That's not a highly valued role these days; our society glorifies the innovator and derides the conserver of tradition. Still, it's a role that can contribute hugely to a better future. Over the weeks to come, I plan on discussing how cultural conservers might practice their craft, what resources might be useful to them, and how the gifts they preserve might benefit the world on the downside of Hubbert's peak.

87: CULTURAL CONSERVERS

(Originally published 21 May 2008)

A few years back the American middle class indulged in another of the periodic orgies of self-congratulation in which it proclaims its opinion of its own historical importance. The inspiration for this particular outburst was a 2000 book entitled Cultural Creatives by Paul H. Ray and Sherry Ruth Anderson, which announced that the spread of certain fashionable ideas through the middle class meant nothing less than the imminent transformation of American society.

Apparently none of its more enthusiastic reviewers remembered that the same imminent transformation had been announced just as confidently in the pages of Marilyn Ferguson's The Aquarian Conspiracy (1980), Charles Reich's The Greening of America (1970), and a long line of predecessors reaching back well into the nineteenth century. Like so many of today's new ideas, in other words, this one has been around for a good long time, just as the "new" attitudes Ray and Anderson identified as hallmarks of their "cultural creatives" have been widely accepted among a sizeable sector of the American intelligentsia since the heyday of the Transcendentalists in the 1820s.

Yet there's more going on here than the simple failure of memory discussed in last week's Archdruid Report post. What is at issue here touches on the meaning and value of culture itself.

Mind you, it's difficult to talk meaningfully about that topic in America today, after decades of "culture wars" in which all sides redefined the very concept of culture to fit their own Utopian fantasies and political objectives. It's doubly difficult because the last half century or so has witnessed the systematic destruction of

America's own national and regional cultures, their replacement with a manufactured pseudoculture based on the values of the American urban intelligentsia, and the consequent revolt of many working class Americans against the concept of culture altogether.

Culture is memory. An authentic culture roots into the collective experience of a community's past, and from this source draws meaning for the present and tools for the future. Thus culture, like memory, is a constant negotiation between the living and the dead, as new conditions call for reinterpretation of past experience and redefine the meanings that are relevant and the tools that are useful. When a society gives up on these negotiations and abandons the link with its past, as last week's post suggested, what remains is not originality but stasis, in which a persistent set of common assumptions and popular narratives are rediscovered and rehashed endlessly under a veneer of apparent novelty.

Woven into this process is the social schism Arnold Toynbee traced in his magisterial A Study of History. As each civilization enters its imperial stage, he showed, a split opens up between its privileged classes and the rest of the population. The latter becomes what Toynbee called an "internal proletariat," expected to perform the work that maintains the civilization but deprived of participation in its benefits and, as the schism in society unfolds, increasingly alienated from its values. The internal proletariat is deprived of its folk cultures by the destruction of the economic basis of traditional lifeways, and barred from participation in elite culture by class and income barriers that grow steadily higher as the imperial stage proceeds.

In the bare ground that results, any number of strange seeds can sprout. Eventually, Toynbee suggests, what fills the cultural vacuum is religion—not the traditional religion of the imperial culture, but some exotic faith dissonant enough from the values of that culture to express the alienation felt by the internal proletariat. As the imperial stage ends in collapse and the privileged classes find themselves stripped of wealth and power by the upwardly mobile warlords of the ensuing dark age, the imperial society's own cultural resources generally hit the scrap heap. The result is a curious feedback loop amplifying the process of cata-bolic collapse; pious hands tore down the temples of the Roman gods and recycled the mathematical papers of Archimedes to pro-vide parchment for Christian homilies, for example, because most people in the postclassical world no longer felt any loyalty to the culture of their ancestors.

We are already well into that process in modern America. The schism in society outlined by Toynbee was clearly visible in his lifetime, and has widened since then. A parallel chasm now gapes down the center of American culture, and most other industrial cultures as well. It bears remembering that in the nineteenth cen-tury, opera counted as popular entertainment, and women in the privileged classes practiced most of the same handicrafts as their poorer sisters; nowadays very few such common factors connect, say, the university-educated middle classes of an east coast sub-urb with the rural poor of a Midwestern farm state. Folk cultures have guttered out or survive only as museum pieces, while elite culture withdraws behind walls of obscurantism—compare the accessible and deservedly popular fine art of the late nineteenth century with the deliberately unwelcoming and often offensive product served up by today's art scene.

In a world lurching through economic crisis and the first wave of impacts from peak oil, it's easy to dismiss the continuing implo-sion of American culture as a minor issue, but such a dismissal is as much a symptom of cultural collapse as anything I've cited al-ready. Again, culture is memory, and among the things it holds in store are the tools, insights, and lifeways that served people well in the days before our civilization started chasing the suicidally addictive rush of empire. Again, Rome offers a useful example; by the time the Roman empire began coming apart at the seams and the grain ships no longer sailed from North African wheat fields to Ostia's wharves, nobody remembered how things had worked in the days when the classical world consisted of independent city-states producing most of their own necessities at home.

Still, the Roman world lacked the extraordinary sense of his-torical time and change that, as John Lukacz has pointed out, is one of modern industrial civilization's most distinctive traits. Roman writers in the declining phase of the empire apparently never noticed that their experiences mirrored, say, the implosion of the Mycenean world in the 13th century BCE, nor did such Roman historians as Livy treat Rome's own past as a guide to the future. Thus it seems never to have occurred to the Romans of the late Empire that their civilization might need to be handed on to a very different future. The task of salvage was left to Irish monks some centuries later, and by the time they got to work, a huge amount of material had already vanished forever. Nor did the monasteries preserve everything that came to them; the immense musical heritage of ancient Rome, for example, was not of interest to monastic scribes, and as a result, all that survives of it is one fragment of a single haunting melody, taking some 25 seconds to play.

Our situation differs from theirs only because the contemporary sense of history makes it possible to place our own experience beside that of the Romans, and any number of other fallen civilizations as well, and draw conclusions about the likely shape of our own future. We are arguably in much the same case as the Romans of the late Empire; we have, as they had, an immense cultural heritage, nearly all of which is disastrously vulnerable to the impacts of collapse; we have done our level best to abandon the heritage of local folk cultures at home and elsewhere in our empire, just as they did, and thus risk losing precious knowledge that might make it easier to weather the descent from today's vertiginous imperial heights. The one difference is that it's possible to talk in these terms today, and to propose concrete responses to what will be one of the most challenging features of the decline and fall of the industrial world.

In an ironic way, the "cultural creatives" whose specter I evoked at the beginning of this essay offer a glimpse at one of the most promising of these potential responses. Behind the inevitable rhetoric of innovation and originality was a very different reality: a sector of America's middle-class intelligentsia discovered a set of ideas their parents, grandparents, and great-great-grandparents had valued in their time, and applied those ideas to the present day. True, most of the people involved in this rediscovery had no idea that this was what they were doing, and thus never made use of the rich heritage of the Transcendentalists, the Theosophists, the Beat generation, or any other expression of the same current of thought. Still, what they did half-unconsciously can be done in a more deliberate and conscious way.

Thus I'd like to suggest that one crucial need of our present predicament is the rise of a movement of cultural conservers — individuals who choose, for one reason or another, to take personal responsibility for the preservation of some part of the modern world's cultural heritage. That's a tall order, not least because the crises inseparable from the decline and fall of a civilization will leave many of us scrambling for bare survival in the face of soaring death rates and increasingly harsh conditions. Still, it's not an insurmountable challenge.

Three themes, it seems to me, sketch out a basic frame on which cultural conservers can weave the individual patterns of their own work:

Focus. The cultural heritage of the modern world is far too vast for any one person even to encounter it all, much less to know enough about it to preserve significant elements of it in any meaningful way. Thus each cultural conserver will need to choose a handful of traditions at most, and focus his or her efforts on those. Since a consensus on what is worth saving is almost certainly impossible to reach, and might not even be a good idea, it seems to me that the best guide to the prospective cultural conserver in choosing a focus is sheer personal passion. The tradition that speaks to you most deeply — be it tablet weaving or Wordsworth's poetry, mountain dulcimers or handbuilt radio technology, classical philosophy or the great American novels — is the one that will inspire you to the efforts necessary to pass it on to the future.

Simplicity. As the requirements needed to maintain a cultural tradition go up, the likelihood of its survival in a time of scarcity go down. Musical forms you can play yourself on an instrument of your own construction are thus more likely to survive as living traditions than musical forms that require a symphony orchestra and an opera company trained to today's exacting vocal standards. More complex traditions can sometimes be stored

in easily maintained forms; the intricate reasonings of Greek philosophers, for example, made it to the Renaissance because they
were written down on durable parchment and left to gather dust
in monastic libraries through the intervening centuries. In many
cases, though, it's possible to choose between simple and complex
options for preserving a technology; if you want to preserve the
technology of printing, for example, a hand-operated letterpress
is much simpler to use, maintain, and build with hand tools and
locally available resources than a computer and a laser printer.
Technologies that are less efficient in the abstract, as this example
suggests, may be more durable in the deindustrial future ahead
of us.

Transmission. It takes more than one lifetime for a civilization
to decline and fall, and so the flip side of preserving some bit of
cultural heritage is the challenge of passing it on to a younger generation. Those traditions that will have obvious economic value in
an age of decline and disintegration have a huge head start here;
it's unlikely in the extreme, for example, that today's advances in
intensive organic food production will be lost anytime soon, since
the skills in question grant a huge survival advantage to those
who know them and have the opportunity to put them to use.
Still, cultural transmission does not always follow the economic line of least resistance. Those who know must be prepared to
teach, and also to use their knowledge in ways that meet community needs.

These three themes sketch out only the first rough lines on
a very broad canvas. In posts to come, I hope to develop these
ideas in more detail. It's worth noting that a significant number of
people have already taken on some elements of the sort of project I am outlining here, some quite consciously, and I propose to
draw on their experience as much as I can. Just as the "cultural
creatives" could have benefited by placing their own projects in a
historical context, too, I intend to offer some historical context to
the mission of the cultural conservers, in the hope that a sense of
what worked (and what didn't work) in the past will help shape
constructive responses to the immense challenges of our future.

88: WHY DECLINE MATTERS
(Originally published 28 May 2008)

One of the most curious blind spots in the contemporary imagination, as I have suggested more than once in these essays, can be traced in the way that the concept of decline has vanished from our collective discourse about the future. What makes this blindness even more curious is that it is a very recent thing.

A century ago the possibility that the modern western world might reach a peak, and then retrace history's familiar path down to the common fate of civilizations, was on many minds. The art of Aubrey Beardsley and the novels of Joséphin Péladan, to name only two leading figures of the Decadent movement announced, and at times wallowed in, the approaching decline that Oswald Spengler detailed a few years later in his magisterial prose. The belief in decline was never universally held, or even a majority view—those who prophesied the imminence of Utopia through progress or violent revolution had at least as large an audience, and apocalyptic fantasies were never hard to find—but the idea was there, and commanded attention from serious thinkers.

Somewhere between the 1920s and the end of the Second World War, however, the entire concept of decline dropped out of the modern world's collective imagination. Except for a brief reprise in the wake of the converging crises of the 1970s, and a few manifestations on the far edges of today's fringe culture, it has yet to return. This odd shift in the shapes of our imagined futures demands attention from those of us who try to sense the shape of the future in advance, because if the future we get is one of decline, the results could be far more challenging than anything the more simplistic notion of sudden collapse can offer

Decline, after all, is not a linear process. Trace the decline of the dead civilizations of the past along the dimension of time, and much more often than not it follows a complex, stairstep curve that alternates periods of crisis with respites and partial recoveries. Compare the process to the sort of sudden apocalyptic collapse that occupies so much space in the collective imagination today, and a striking result emerges: the amount of population decline and cultural loss in any given generation may be much less than would result from a single sudden catastrophe, but the overall impact of decline is much greater, and the capacity for swift recovery much less.

This seems counterintuitive, but it can easily be demonstrated by historical evidence and logic alike. Consider the Black Death in Europe. As an example of dieoff, it's hard to beat—the first terrible epidemic of 1346-1351 killed close to a third of the population of Europe, and recurring outbreaks that followed every decade or so took up to ten per cent of the survivors each time—and, in the form of the peasant revolts of the late 14th century, it even managed to produce some semblance of the marauding hordes that play so large a part in contemporary survivalist fantasies. Despite the horrific death rate, the widespread social disorder, and the huge cultural impacts of the Black Death, European civilization did not collapse, or lose cultural continuity. The survivors simply picked themselves up and went on with things much as before.

Imagine a similar dieoff, or even a much more extreme one, in America today and it's not hard to see why. Let's say the most extreme versions of the peak oil survivalist thesis turn out to be correct; some crisis or other causes petroleum markets to freeze up completely, and gasoline and diesel fuel become completely unavailable; panic and looting set in, governments somehow fail to do anything about the crisis, and society unravels in a general war of all against all, with marauding hordes spilling out of the cities into nearby rural regions in a desperate quest for food. Five horrific years later, the US population has plummeted by 95%. What happens next?

The single largest resource base available to the survivors, in such a case, would be the material culture and knowledge base of pre-collapse society. All over rural America, in areas more than a few hundred miles from big urban centers, small towns and villages would remain, and those in agricultural areas with steady water supplies would likely flourish; lacking gas for their cars, after all, refugees from Chicago or Los Angeles will not make it to North Dakota, or even Iowa. Libraries, schools, and local governments would either still exist, or could be readily rebuilt; abandoned buildings and technology could be dusted off and put back to use; where renewable energy sources exist, those could be reactivated if they stopped running in the first place. Almost everyone alive after the collapse will have grown up in the pre-collapse world, and a great many of them will have learned some of the skills needed to operate a modern society. Before very long, something very like today's rural American culture would have reestablished itself, just as late medieval cultures across Europe reestablished themselves after the Black Death.

What makes so swift a recovery possible, though, is the short time span between collapse and aftermath. Consider the possibility of decline and a much less promising picture emerges. First, and most obviously, decline takes much longer. By the time the process is finished, the people who remember how an advanced civilization used to function are long in their graves, and anything perishable in the material culture they knew has long since perished. It's one thing to break into an abandoned library five years after a sudden collapse, when most of the books will be dusty but readable; it's another thing to do the same thing two hundred years after the beginning of decline, when those books not looted long ago have crumbled into sawdust because they were printed on high-acid paper, or rotted after the roof collapsed and the rains got in.

The stairstep process found in most historical examples of decline, though, is a far more potent force. Periods of crisis, in which urgent needs absorb all available resources, can go on for decades. During that time, anything not immediately relevant to the needs of the moment will likely go begging for maintenance and upkeep, if it isn't stripped for spare parts, burned as heating fuel, or destroyed in war, rioting, or any of the other common disasters that punctuate the downward arc of a civilization's lifespan. Periods of respite offer some recovery time, but then another period of crisis comes and another sorting process hits the surviving legacy of the civilization. Each period of crisis thus becomes a bottleneck through which only a fraction of a civilization's material culture and knowledge base will survive. Repeat the process often enough and very little remains. Thus, if we admit the possibility of decline, we face the possibility of a future more difficult and impoverished than a future of sudden collapse, not less so.

The cultural conserver concept I have proposed in recent weeks on this blog attempts to address that possibility. Alongside the dismal record of cultural loss during ages of decline, history also shows that a motivated minority concerned with the long view can have a disproportionate impact on the survival of cultural heritage in hard times.

Consider the survival of the Jewish people and their cultural heritage after the destruction of the Third Temple in 70 CE, and the obliteration of most of the Jewish presence in Israel over the following century. Faced with the very real risk of cultural extinction, surviving religious leaders drew on memories of the Babylonian captivity to launch one of history's most magnificently successful programs of cultural conservation. As rabbinic Judaism took shape, a very large percentage of its traditions focused explicitly on preserving Jewish religious and cultural continuity. "Why is this night different from all other nights?" asks the Passover ritual; the answer, freely interpreted, is that it embodies one of the distinctive historical experiences of the Jewish people, using potent tools of symbol and ceremony to counter the pressures toward assimilation and absorption.

Equally, the Catholic church after Rome's fall set in motion a massive salvage program that kept much of classical culture alive right through the Dark Ages. Its motives differed from those that drove the founders of rabbinic Judaism; an expanding church needed clergy literate enough to know their way around scripture, the church fathers, canon law, and the philosophical theology the Church had borrowed from Greek Neoplatonism, and this mandated the survival of the Latin literary culture that informed so much early Christian literature in the West. Thus generations of Christian schoolboys learned Latin prosody from Vergil, and acquired a taste for learning that blossomed in the great age of Christian monasticism and preserved countless cultural treasures for the future.

There are plenty of other examples, from the Sanskrit academies of India to the bardic schools of early modern Scotland, but they share a crucial feature in common with these. For a cultural tradition to survive in an age of decline, it needs to find a constituency that values it enough to put the survival of the tradition ahead of more immediate needs. In traditional Judaism, keeping the commandments isn't something to file away for future reference whenever times get hard; it comes first, even ahead of personal survival. Similarly, the Benedictine monks who spent their time copying manuscripts by hand in unheated scriptoria through the worst years of the Dark Ages could have led much easier lives outside the bare walls of their monasteries, if the glory of God had not, in their eyes, outshone all the treasures of the world.

Thus the survival of cultural heritage must draw on emotional drives potent enough to override the tyranny of immediate needs and drive the modest but unremitting daily efforts needed to keep cultural heritage intact. This is especially true of the traditions of elite culture, which typically lack any short term survival value and often require a sizeable investment of time and resources. It is above all true of modern elite culture, which has specialized in the mass production of information to such a degree that the ability to maintain adequate storage for all the knowledge our culture has amassed is already very much in doubt.

One of my readers thus responded to last week's post by asking me how her field, mathematics, might preserve some of its knowledge base for the future. That's a daunting question, for which I know no easy answers. Right now mathematicians in the more abstract and less practical branches of their field can draw a salary to pursue their researches only because a longstanding social habit encourages governments and donors to cover the costs. The same thing is true of many other branches of scholarship, and of those fine arts that haven't quite finished the process of devolving into the manufacture of high-end collectibles for the rich. Outside of university mathematics departments, it's hard to find anyone who has even heard of most of today's hot topics in math, much less anyone who would be willing to study and teach them in their off hours, for no pay, out of the sheer love of the subject.

That sort of constituency will be hard for any part of today's elite culture to find, and without it, there's a minimal chance that anything more than fragments of that culture will reach the future. Still, there is a wild card in the deck, and its name is religion. Nearly all the classic examples of cultural conservation have drawn their motivating force from religious beliefs. Is it possible that some of today's scientific and cultural heritage will find a welcome within the ambit of a present or future religious movement? Next week's post will explore these options.

89: RELIGION AND THE SURVIVAL OF CULTURE

(Originally published 4 June 2008)

Among the more interesting things I've had occasion to notice, during the time The Archdruid Report has been online, is a common assumption shared by the two popular viewpoints about the future of industrial society — the belief in a future of perpetual progress and the belief in a future of sudden collapse. Despite their disagreements, both viewpoints embrace the claim that there is nothing to be learned from the past; our present situation, both insist, is unlike anything else in history, and therefore history cannot be used as a yardstick to measure the possible shapes of the future ahead of us.

It will not come as an unbearable surprise to readers of this blog that I find this claim unconvincing. It's true, of course, that the current predicament of industrial civilization differs in some ways from the equivalent challenges that faced, and overwhelmed, civilizations of the past. It's equally true that historical patterns never repeat themselves precisely. Still, it's worth suggesting that despite the differences, our predicament is analogous to those earlier examples, and the experiences of the past thus may turn out to be useful as we face our own future.

One pattern found very commonly in the decline and fall of civilizations, as I pointed out in last week's post, is the transmission of cultural heritage from one civilization to its successors through the medium of a newly established religious movement. The classic example, which has seen a certain amount of discussion in futurist circles since Roberto Vacca's The Coming Dark Age (1973) introduced it to contemporary culture, is the role played by monasteries in Europe in preserving Greek and Roman literature, philosophy, and scientific knowledge through the worst years of the Dark Ages.

The same thing has happened often enough elsewhere that Arnold Toynbee made the concept a key theme in the later volumes of his massive A Study of History. In Toynbee's view, the fading years of every civilization form a seedbed for new religious movements; one or more of these movements break free of the others as decline continues, to become a major cultural force; as the civilization that nurtured it collapses completely, the new religious movement fills the vacuum, salvaging what remains of the old civilization's heritage, and the concepts central to that religion become the framework on which a new civilization begins to take shape.

Toynbee's account of this process, like so much of his historical vision, derives primarily from Roman history, and some of his details do not wear well when applied to other historical examples. In his view, for example, the religions that rise from one civilization to pass on cultural heritage to another are newly minted or recently imported missionary religions with a sense of universal mission, and this is by no means always true.

The Jewish and Zoroastrian religions provide persuasive counterexamples. Both were old religions that underwent major retooling after the collapse of their national communities, the Roman depopulation of Israel after 70 CE and the Muslim conquest of Persia in the seventh century respectively. Both abandoned universalizing ambitions to become ethnic religions, holding outsiders at arm's length through a formidable body of custom and taboo. Both nonetheless played a significant role in passing on the cultural heritage of the classical Middle East to rising cultures in Europe and the Arabic world, in the case of the Jews, and India, in the case of the Parsis.

Broaden Toynbee's insight to embrace a wider range of religious phenomena, though, and his basic claim — that religion very often serves as the conduit by which the cultural treasures of one civilization reach the waiting hands of the next — is true much more often than not. It's easy enough to see why this should be so.

In a time of social disintegration, when institutions collapse and long-accepted values lose their meaning, only the most powerful human motives can ensure that the economically unproductive activities needed to maintain cultural heritage will be carried out in the teeth of the difficulties. Religion is the only cultural force that consistently provides motivation strong enough for the job; the same sense of transcendent value that leads martyrs to sing hymns as they are burnt alive can just as easily inspire scholars and scribes to preserve and transmit knowledge to a future they will never see.

Nor was Toynbee wrong to point out that the religions that accomplish this function are rarely identical to the established faiths of the old civilizations. Both Rabbinic Judaism and the Zoroastrian faith of the medieval and modern Parsis differ in significant ways from the forms the same faiths took in the ancient world; the forms of Buddhism that enabled classical Japanese culture to survive the breakup of the Heian period were not the forms that thrived under the patronage of the Nara and Heian courts; even in imperial China, where a cult of cultural continuity persisted for some five thousand years, the end of a dynasty generally meant the rise of a new form of Buddhist or Taoist spirituality.

Here again, the reasons behind this changing of the guard are straightforward enough, though certain features of a civilization in decline have to be taken into account. In Toynbee's view, as a civilization moves into its imperial phase, it suffers a schism between the dominant minority, which benefits from the imperial project, and the bulk of the population of the imperial state, which does not. As this schism in the body politic widens, the bulk of the population — the internal proletariat, in Toynbee's terms — becomes alienated from the values of their own culture, which becomes identified with the interests of the dominant elite.

Religion is among the things most affected by this sense of alienation, and so one of the classic signs of a society on its way to collapse is a widening religious schism along class lines. America offers an interesting example of this process in motion. As it entered its imperial phase around 1900, a significant minority of Americans began breaking away from the religious consensus of their culture—a consensus that used the forms of mainstream Protestantism but, in the name of the "social gospel," transformed that faith into an anthropolatrous worship of progress.

The vehicle for the countering schism was Christian fundamentalism. Twice, however—in the 1920s and then again in the 1980s and 1990s—fundamentalist leaders proved all too eager to cash in their ideals in exchange for crumbs of political power from the tables of the dominant minority; the result in the first case was a near-total implosion of the fundamentalist movement, and a repeat of that process seems increasingly likely today as fundamentalist churches move further away from their once-challenging role as social critics to embrace unthinking partisan loyalties nicely calibrated to support the status quo.

The failure of fundamentalism to establish itself as an alternative to the values of the dominant minority left the field open to other new religious movements. Some of those have proven just as willing to sell out as their fundamentalist equivalents; others never did veer far enough from the values of the mainstream to attract a following outside the privileged classes.

At the same time, the mainstream Protestant-progressive religiosity of the elite has widened into a consensus shared by most varieties of American Judaism, much of the English-speaking wing of the American Catholic church, and several forms of Americanized Buddhism, not to mention a very large number of people who would insist they follow no religion at all. What is often portrayed as a rising tide of tolerance among these traditions actually marks the widespread embrace of a common ideology of social progress unrelated to the central historic commitments of the faiths in question, but easy to insert into the shell of any religious (or irreligious) tradition once awkward questions about transcendent values are quietly put on the shelf.

Thus it's hard to name a religious movement in contemporary America, or for that matter most other parts of the industrial world, that is well placed just now to rise to the occasion as industrial civilization begins the long slow process of its decline and fall. At the same time, it's crucial to remember that we are still in a very early stage of that process. A Roman scholar of 150 CE, say, who tried to guess at the religious forms that would rise to prominence during the empire's decline, would have faced a ferocious challenge in sorting through the contenders; his world was awash in new religious movements, some homegrown and many others from elsewhere in the Mediterranean world; nothing special marked out the destinies of Christianity and Judaism from those of their many competitors, and the religion that arguably played the largest role in passing classical culture to the medieval world, Islam, didn't even exist yet.

Thus one of the religious movements that will pick up the remnants of modern culture and pass them on to the future might well, at the present time, consist of a few dozen people gathered around a charismatic teacher in a commune in Kentucky. Another might have been founded fifty years ago in Brazil or Bangladesh, and still awaits the brilliant missionary who will bring it to Europe or America and transform it into a mass movement. A third might still be an inchoate current of ideas that will not find its prophet for another two hundred years. The one thing that can be predicted in advance is that those movements will draw on the religious heritage of contemporary culture, but reshape it in unexpected ways that will inevitably be at odds with the conventional wisdom of our age.

Yet new religious movements there will be, and it's far more likely than not that they will attract a growing number of followers as the industrial age stumbles toward its end. It's often said that there are no atheists in foxholes, and there tend to be very few in times of social decay and collapse. In every age in which people believe that their own efforts can bring them the material goals their culture sets before them, it's common for them to stop worrying about the transcendent dimension of life; it's only when those goals become too obviously unreachable that the majority will raise their eyes to other possibilities and, as Augustine of Hippo phrased it, perceive a difference between the City of Man and the City of God.

Efforts to turn this religious impulse to foster the survival of today's cultural heritage will succeed or fail, I think, on their willingness to let go of the assumptions of contemporary culture, and to make peace with religious forms that offend modern sensibilities. Thus, for example, there seems to be little hope in the suggestion made now and then that today's scientific thought ought to redefine itself as a religion for this purpose. The raw material of religion certainly exists in modern science, or rather scientism, the belief system that has grown up around the simple but powerful logic of the scientific method; Carl Sagan, who did more than any other recent thinker to cast that belief system in religious terms, is arguably one of the significant theologians of the 20th century.

Yet scientism as it exists today, certainly, embodies the attitudes and values of the dominant minority at least as well as any of the more obviously religious forms mentioned above. From its long struggle to seize intellectual authority from religious institutions, too, the culture of contemporary scientism embraces a bitter hostility to more explicitly religious belief systems. This no man's land of the Western mind forms perhaps the single most troublesome barrier to the survival of science in the deindustrial world of the future. The prospects of crossing it, and transmitting the modern world's greatest intellectual adventure to the future, will be the focus of next week's post.

90: SAVING SCIENCE

(Originally published 11 June 2008)

Last week may just find its place in the history books as the point in time when peak oil became a social fact. Combine a drastic spike in oil prices — up US$16 in two days for one widely watched benchmark grade of crude oil — with an announcement by General Motors that the Hummer, that overblown icon of an era of excess, will no longer be manufactured, and you've got a snapshot of the transformation now hitting an unprepared and unwilling world.

As this particular milestone takes its place in the rear view mirror of contemporary history, it's important that we try to glimpse the upcoming milestones on the road ahead. The one I'd like to address here, as I suggested at the end of last week's post, is the need to preserve the heritage of modern science through the challenges of the coming deindustrial age.

From today's perspective, mind you, it may seem silly to suggest that science may need saving at all. Not only does scientific research play a huge economic role in modern society, science has become an ideology that fills most of the roles occupied by religion in older civilizations than ours. Scientific institutions have profited accordingly, expanding into an immense network of universities, research institutes, foundations, and publishers, subsidized by many billions a year in government largesse.

Yet the same thing could have been said about the priesthoods of Jupiter Optimus Maximus and his fellow gods in the glory days of the Roman Empire, or the aristocratic priest-scribes of the Lowland Maya city-states in the days before Tikal and Copán were swallowed by the jungle. Civilizations direct huge resources to their intellectual elites, because they can, and because the payoff in terms of each civilization's values are well worth the expenditure. The downside is that the intellectual heritage of each civilization becomes dependent both on the subsidies that support them and on the ideological consensus that makes those subsidies make sense. In the decline and fall of a civilization, both the subsidies and the consensus are early casualties; thereafter, the temples of Jupiter get torn apart to provide stones for churches, and the intricate planetary almanacs compiled by Mayan astrologers rot in the ruins of the temples where their authors once contemplated the heavens.

Project the same process onto our own future and the vulnerabilities of science are hard to miss. Imagine, for example, a world forty years from now in which rates of annual production of oil, coal, and natural gas have dropped so low that only countries that produce them can afford to use them at all, and then only to meet critical needs. Half the surviving population in the nations with remaining fossil fuels, and 90% in the others, labors at subsistence agriculture, and most of the remainder work in factories converting salvaged materials into needed goods with hand tools. Worldwide, dozens of nations have collapsed into violent anarchy, and whole populations are on the move as sea level rises and rain belts shift. In America, the old canal network is being reopened by men with shovels, as fuel shortages hit a rail network that never recovered from its 20th-century dilapidation. Meanwhile army units face guerrilla forces in the mountain West, while refugees from starving Japan, packed into the hulks of abandoned container ships, ride the currents en masse toward the west coast.

In such a world, what role will modern science have? Certain branches of applied science, especially those applicable to energy and the military, will get funding as long as anything still exists to fund them. Most other applied fields will have to scrabble for scraps, though, while pure research will go begging, because the resources to support them in their current style won't exist. The facilities that make advanced research possible will be boarded up when they haven't been looted for raw materials.

Significant science could still be done in such a future. It bears remembering, after all, that such epochal scientific discoveries as the theory of natural selection and Mendelian genetics were made with equipment would be considered hopelessly inadequate for a high school science class today. The problem is that the entire mindset of today's science militates against research on this scale. The transformation of science from a pursuit of gifted amateurs to a profession supported by government and corporate funds was complete most of a century ago; today it would be hard to find many scientists who would be able to pursue their research unassisted in a basement lab with homemade equipment, and I'm by no means sure how many of them would be willing to do it without pay, on their own time, after their day jobs.

Thus science faces the same predicament as other elements of today's cultural heritage: it needs a constituency to carry it through the process of decline and fall, or it risks vanishing entirely. James Lovelock, one of the few scientists to glimpse this problem, has suggested creating a single large book containing scientific discoveries — "the scientific equivalent of the Bible," in his phrase — that can be printed on durable materials and distributed widely in advance of the crash. This begs a crucial question, though: when we talk about preserving science, exactly what are we trying to save?

That word "science," after all, includes a great many things under its umbrella. It's common to divide them by subject into disciplines such as biology, physics, chemistry, and so on. In the present context, though, another division has more value. We need to look separately at science as product, science as profession, and science as process to make sense of our predicament and craft a strategy for its survival.

Science as product is the sort of thing Lovelock is discussing: those facts and theoretical models about the universe currently accepted as true by the majority of scientists in the relevant fields. This is in some ways the easiest part of science to save, since a single book preserved in some dusty library could preserve a huge amount, the way that Ptolemy's Almagest preserved nearly the whole body of Greek mathematical astronomy intact. Just as the Almagest became a millstone around the neck of later astronomers, though, science as product easily fossilizes into dogma. By treating science wholly as product, Lovelock's proposal risks reducing science to the rote repetition of doctrines accepted on the basis of blind faith.

Science as profession is the system of trained personnel and infrastructure that keeps today's science going. This dimension of today's science is fatally vulnerable to the impacts of decline, for reasons already discussed; the economic troubles, political chaos, and desperate exigencies of an age of decline will shred the support system for today's science in fairly short order. In a time when the destructive legacies of technology may loom larger than its fading benefits, too, the possibility of a violent popular backlash against science cannot be dismissed out of hand

That leaves science as process: the scientific method, that elegantly simple fusion of practical logic and applied mathematics that was birthed in the 17th century and gave birth in turn to the modern world. This is the dimension that arguably deserves saving ahead of anything else, since it allows science to be done at all; ironically, it is also the most vulnerable of the three, since few people except professional scientists have any exposure to it. Lovelock's appalling dream of scientific Holy Writ, to some extent, simply reflects current reality; science as product has eclipsed science as process, so that people outside the scientific profession are taught to accept scientific doctrines on faith, rather than being encouraged to practice science themselves. If today's professionalized science faces extinction over the next century or so, there's a real possibility that it could take the scientific method with it to the grave.

A number of eloquent voices have argued that this might not be a bad thing. Such writers as Theodore Roszak and Lewis Mumford have pointed out that the practical benefits of science must be weighed in the balance against the dehumanizing effects of scientific reductionism and the horrific results of technology run amok in the service of greed and the lust for power. Others have argued that scientific thinking, with its cult of objectivity and its rejection of human values, is fundamentally antihuman and antilife, and the gifts it has given us are analogous to the gewgaws Mephistopheles brought to Faust at the price of the latter's soul.

These arguments make a strong case against the intellectual idolatry that treats science as a surrogate religion or a key to ultimate truth. I'm not convinced, though, that they make a case against the practice of science on the much more modest basis to which it is better suited, and on which it was carried on until quite recently: that of a set of very effective mental tools for making sense of material reality. As the age of cheap abundant energy comes to an end, and the reach of our sciences and technologies scales back to fit the realities of life in a world of strict ecological limits, the overblown fantasies that encouraged people to make science carry the burden of their cravings for transcendence are, I think, likely to give way sooner rather than later.

At the same time, the survival of the scientific method will be crucial to the task of creating sustainable societies in the future ahead of us. That process will be very hard to pursue without the touchstone of quantitative measurement and experimental verification. Thus I suggest that preserving the scientific method as a living tradition belongs tolerably high on the priority list as the Long Descent begins around us.

How could this be done? With today's institutionalized science unlikely to survive, at least two options present themselves. The first is that other social forms better suited to withstand the rigors of an age of decline might choose adopt the practice of scientific research. One example is emerging just now in the movement I know best, the modern Druid community. I don't think it's a secret to many people that Druids care passionately about the environment, and are interested in learning about nature; the Druid order I head, for example, requires participants in its study program to learn about the natural history of the area in which they live.

With that as foundation, we are building a framework for Druids to take part in environmental sciences as active participants. It takes very little in the way of hardware to identify pollinators visiting a backyard garden, or to track turbidity and erosion along the banks of a local stream; it takes very little more to turn the knowledge gained in these ways to the work of ecological healing — providing nesting boxes for orchard mason bees, seeding erosion-controlling plants, and many other small steps with potentially huge consequences. A grasp of scientific method will be crucial in this work, and if it proves valuable to the survival of human communities and the ecosystems in which they live—as I am convinced it will—the method will be handed down to the future.

Now it's only fair to say that Druidry, as one small religious movement among many, has no special privilege in this regard. Any other religious tradition, or for that matter any nonreligious one with enough passion and commitment to survive the coming troubles, could make a similar choice, adopting some branch of science useful to its work. It's a tried and true method—trace the survival of Greek logic by way of Christian and Muslim religious traditions, or the parallel survival of Indian logic in Hinduism and Buddhism, and you'll find a similar process at work. I hope other groups rise to the challenge; in the meantime, we Druids are doing what we can.

Yet scientists themselves might explore the possibility of creating new social forms to keep science going as a living tradition once today's lavishly funded institutions become tomorrow's boarded-up buildings and another century's crumbling ruins. How those new forms might take shape, and how they might best cope with the crises ahead of us, is anybody's guess just now; my own background leads me to imagine something along the lines of Freemasonry, say, or the occult lodges that kept Renaissance esoteric traditions alive during the age of science, using the keys of narrative, symbolism and ritual to turn dry philosophies into unforgettable experiences; still, this is only one option among many.

The crucial point, it seems to me, is to recognize that no special providence guards science, or for that matter any of the opulent cultural heritage we enjoy nowadays. It has been said, and rightly, that nothing seems so permanent as an empire on the verge of collapse, or so invulnerable as an army on the eve of total defeat. Like the broken statue of Ozymandias in Shelley's poem, a few fragments of today's science might someday stand in an metaphorical wasteland once filled with the cyclotrons and observatories of a vanished age. Our job, as I see it, is to salvage what seems most likely to be of value to the future while we still have the chance.

91: THE TRIUMPH OF HISTORY
(Originally published 18 June 2008)

Nearly two decades have passed now since Francis Fukuyama announced the end of history. The chorus of catcalls that greeted this claim was by no means undeserved. Still, his theory deserves a second look today, not least because the logic that underpinned it also guides a great many claims about the shape of the future in the age of peak oil.

Fukuyama's proclamation appeared in a 1989 article titled "The End of History?" and was further expanded a book released later that same year, The End of History and the Last Man. His arguments were misunderstood generally enough that a brief summary of them is probably worth offering here. From the 19th century German philosopher G.W.F. Hegel, Fukuyama took the concept of history as a process of repeated conflicts and syntheses between contending forces, leading to a final state of perfection in which the ideal becomes manifest in historical time.

In Fukuyama's reading, the contending forces are different systems of political economy, and history is the competition among them that ends with the victory of the best. The collapse of the Soviet Union and the intellectual bankruptcy of Marxism, he argued, marked the completion of that process, because liberal democracy — his term for the hybrid corporate-socialist bureaucratic states currently governing most of the world's industrial societies — has proven to be the best of all possible systems. Thus the historical process is at an end; in the years to come, those states that have not yet adopted liberal democracy will do so, and the world thereafter will bask in an endless afternoon, the closest approximation to Utopia that human nature allows.

A profound irony surrounds this argument, for at every point, it duplicated the Marxist theory Fukuyama dismissed so caustically—a point Fukuyama himself admitted in a later book. Not all that many years before "The End of History?" saw print, quoting Hegel and portraying history as a grand process leading to the best possible society were the distinctive badges of the Marxist intellectual. There was never much that was new, and even less that was genuinely conservative, in the thinking of the neoconservatives who embraced Fukuyama's claims so enthusiastically, but his proclamation in many ways marked the nadir of the process by which the American right turned into a mirror image of the Marxism it thought it was opposing.

Fukuyama's claims, though, deserve attention on their own right. In doing this it's crucial to note the special sense he gave to the word "history." He was not claiming, as many of his critics suggested, that what might more broadly be called historical events will stop happening; while he claimed that liberal democracy is the best possible system, he admitted its imperfections, and allowed that those imperfections may still lead to wars, political and economic crises, and a great deal of human misery. The end of history, rather, means that no one can ever propose a better system to deal with these difficulties than the one already in place; the challenges faced by the posthistoric world will be matters of management, not of fundamental change or reconsideration.

It's at this point that Fukuyama's argument finds common ground with a great many other claims about the future that circulate these days. Most proponents of today's science, for example, argue that the scientific progress of the last century or so does not simply reflect the maturation of one culture's way of thinking about nature but, rather, traces the discovery of objective truths that can be refined but not refuted; the more enthusiastic of today's science writers, in fact, look forward to a time not too far in the future when all nature's fundamental laws will be known, and researchers will have to content themselves with filling in minor details.

More generally, the collective imagination of the industrial world these days seems increasingly unable to imagine a future that isn't either a rehash of the present or a sudden, cataclysmically driven lurch backward into the past. Today's peak oil debates are a case in point. The mainstream consensus these days treats peak oil as a challenge to be solved by finding some other convenient fuel to power the existing machinery of industrial society; move toward the fringes and you'll find most discussions center on a return to the past, ranging from the moderate — back to the 18th century — through the extreme — back to the hunter-gatherer lifestyle — to the limiting case — back to a world without human beings, or even without life. All these claims, just as much as Fukuyama's, treat the modern industrial world as the culmination of a historical process that runs in one direction to one foreordained conclusion.

What makes these proclamations of the end of history so fascinating is that they are themselves a historical phenomenon. The assurance of today's scientists that the universe's last mysteries will be solved in due time has its precise equivalent in the confidence of medieval scholastics that the nature of the world would be known for good once the last few problems with Ptolemy's astronomy were worked out. Equally, Fukuyama's confidence that liberal democracy was the final shape of human society has its mirror in the panegyrists of the Roman Empire, who saw the arrangements of their own time as the last word in human social structures.

As these examples suggest, claims that history has reached its final and unchanging state appear at a distinct stage in the development of cultures, and also in such cultural phenomena as science. Claims that Rome's empire would last forever surfaced just as that empire's expansion neared its limit, and took on a more insistent tone with each stage in the following decline. In the same way, Ptolemy's earth-centered cosmology became steadily more entrenched in medieval culture as the problems fitting it with the observed facts became harder to ignore. Proclamations of an end to history, in fact, are one of the standard phenomena of periods in which the prospect of historical change has transformed itself from a promise to a threat.

It's worth noting that the same stage of history also gives new impetus to the seemingly opposed belief that total cataclysmic change is imminent, and the existing order of things is about to pass away "in the twinkling of an eye." The opposition here is more apparent than real, however; the new world waiting on the far side of apocalypse, whether it's defined as the Kingdom of God, the dictatorship of the proletariat, the neoprimitivist hunter-gatherer utopia, or what have you is just as immune from history, at least in theory, as Fukuyama's liberal democratic consensus. The only point under dispute is whether the ahistorical world of the future is the fulfillment of the present, or its total repudiation.

The rhetorical force and theoretical conviction of these expectations of an end to history cannot be doubted. Equally, though, it's clear that every such claim that has been tested by events has been flattened by the steamroller force of historical change. The learned doctors who pronounce history dead, and the poets, prophets, and philosophers who write her epitaph, keep on being inconvenienced by the patient's awkward refusal to lie down and stop breathing. Today's prophets of history's end commonly insist that it's different this time, but then so did their predecessors, right back to the beginning of recorded history.

A meaningful philosophy of history, by contrast, needs to take history itself as its guide — not the few decades of history in which the Marxist-capitalist quarrel played out, as Fukuyama did, nor the few centuries from the end of the Middle Ages to the flowering of today's technology, as the contemporary myth of progress does, but as broad a view as possible, embracing every human culture and every age of which sufficient details survive to make the exercise worthwhile. One lesson taught by any such broad view of history is that proclamations of the end of history are always premature. Another is that such proclamations are always popular at a time when attentive minds come to suspect that if history continues, the attainments of the present may not turn out to be as lasting as their propagandists claim.

To me, at least, it seems symptomatic that so many historians who attempt such a grasp of history as a whole come to see it in cyclical terms. From ibn Khaldun and Giambattista Vico to Oswald Spengler and Arnold Toynbee, the theorists of historical cycles have argued that the historical process has no endpoint. Their logic cuts to the core of the argument Fukuyama borrowed from Hegel, and it also challenges some of the most common assumptions of today's debates concerning peak oil, anthropogenic climate change, and the other manifestations of the crisis of contemporary industrial civilization.

The central problem with Fukuyama's argument, from the point of view of a cyclical conception of history, is that it treats the idea of "the best possible society" as an abstraction, divorced from any sense of context and any awareness of the inevitable dependence of human societies on the nonhuman world. What is possible at one time is not possible for all times, and what is good at one point in history may turn out to be far from good at another. Whether what Fukuyama calls "liberal democracy" is the most satisfactory form of human society, then—a point I don't propose to address here—it depends utterly on radically unsustainable relationships with the planetary biosphere, with the societies it exploits, and with the majority of its own population.

While it's popular just now to argue that these problems can be fixed without undercutting the system itself, the evidence increasingly points the other way. The American way of life, for example, depends on arrangements that allow 5% of the world's population to exploit some 33% of its natural resources. The convulsions set off in recent years by modest improvements in China's and India's standards of living demonstrate that on a finite planet with rapidly depleting resources, Fukuyama's vision of a world made over in the image of America is a pipe dream.

Thus, as the theorists of historical cycles have been pointing out all along, history has no end; the consequences of each stage in the historical process set in motion the forces that lead to the next. The question we need to be asking as peak oil makes the transition from a theory to a hard reality, in turn, is not how we can impose an ahistorical permanence on a historical situation that, by its very nature, is unsustainable; nor how we can get ready for an apocalyptic transformation to some other, equally ahistorical future; but instead, how we can cope with the triumph of history over our fantasies of immutability with some measure of grace.

92: THE SILENT RUNNING FALLACY
(Originally published 25 June 2008)

One of the privileges a wry providence has granted to the arts is that even their missteps have more to teach than the best productions of more sensible men. I was reminded of that a few days ago when a discussion among Druid friends turned to the 1972 SF movie classic Silent Running.

I have no idea how many of my readers remember that film, so I'll summarize it here. Bruce Dern plays Freeman Lowell, a geeky ecologist on Valley Forge, one of a fleet of orbiting space freighters with domes containing the last wild plants and animals from a future Earth where only human beings and their technologies remain. His fellow crew members simply want to get through their one-year tours and get back to a world where there is no more poverty or disease and it is always 70° F. everywhere, but the forest is Lowell's obsession and his life.

Then the order comes to jettison the domes, destroy them with nuclear charges, and return the freighters to commercial service. Lowell rebels, kills the other three crew members on his ship, and flees into the outer solar system with only the ship's robot drones for company. When Valley Forge's sister ship Berkshire locates him again months later, Lowell rigs lights in the last remaining dome to keep the forest viable, jettisons it on a course into interstellar space, and uses the last of the nuclear charges to blow up himself and his ship.

It's a powerful and profoundly moving film, and a favorite of mine for many years. Still, even the first time I watched it—I was ten years old at the time, dropping most of a week's allowance on a tall root beer and tickets to the Saturday matinee at the local movie house in suburban Federal Way, WA—I had trouble believing two of the movie's core plot elements. The first was a vague sense of doubt about the premise that there could be a world full of healthy, happy humans with no biosphere to support them. The second was more specific: when Lowell sent the dome into deep space, I wondered, where did the electricity for its lights come from?

It took me more than a decade to realize that these two points both pointed to the same common but disastrous misunderstanding which—with apologies to an excellent movie—I've named the Silent Running fallacy. Like most of the garbled thinking that has doomed our civilization and threatens the survival of our species just now, it's a simple error with profound consequences, and it's thus best approached indirectly.

Start with some details of the movie's premise, then. How much energy would it take to maintain the Earth's entire surface at a steady temperature of 70° Fahrenheit? The Earth's atmosphere does a relatively efficient job of distributing heat from the sun around the planet via the intricate heat engine we call weather, but even so, the temperature on a hot day in the Sahara can differ from the temperature on the same day at the South Pole by more than 200°F. Balancing that out would be ferociously expensive in energy terms.

How much energy would it take to keep a planet full of people free from poverty? Our current industrial civilization hasn't even come close; average out today's income per capita over the population of the Earth and you get a Third World existence—and of course there's the hard question of just how long we can maintain today's profligate energy expenditure of 450 exajoules (that's 450,000,000,000,000,000,000 joules, for the prefix-challenged) per year.

The short answer to both of those questions, in other words, is "more than we've got." That's generally the answer when the question comes up about the costs of replacing any significant process in the biosphere by human means. When a working group headed by Robert Costanza tried a few years ago tried to work out the economic value of the free services provided to humanity by the Earth's biosphere, for example, the mid-range estimate they came up with was around three times the total value of all human economic activity. For every dollar of economic value you get, in other words, 25 cents was produced by human beings and the other 75 cents was produced by nature.

The reality of our dependence on living nature goes well beyond this, however. Consider the oxygen in the air we breathe. It doesn't just happen; it's put there, moment by moment, by complex ecological cycles centering on photosynthesis in green plants. If those cycles go away, so does the oxygen, and so do we. The Earth's supply of fresh water, similarly, is renewed by intricate biogeochemical cycles in which a wide range of living things play a part. The experiment of producing food by treating soil as an abiotic sponge into which petrochemicals are dumped is proving to be a long-term failure; here again, only natural cycles in which countless living things participate put food on our table and keep us all from starvation.

It's in this context that we can define the Silent Running fallacy; it's the mistaken belief that human industrial civilization can survive apart from nature. It's this fallacy that leads countless well-intentioned people to argue that nature is an amenity, and should be preserved because, basically, it's cute. That sort of argument invites the response, just as stereotyped and more appealing to our culture's governing narratives, that hard-headed practicality takes precedence over emotional appeals and nature can therefore be ravaged with impunity.

Yet nature is not an amenity, and the "practicality" that leads current political and business leaders to ignore the disastrous consequences of their own actions doesn't deserve the name. If anything, industrial civilization is the amenity, and it's not particularly cute, either. Nature can survive without industrial humanity, but industrial humanity cannot survive without nature—no matter how hard we pretend otherwise, or how enthusiastically we stuff our brains with science fiction fantasies of electronic reincarnation and the good life in deep space.

What makes this irony mordant is that nature is also a great deal more resilient than industrial humanity. A recent book on global warming, Six Degrees by Mark Lynas, argues that a global temperature rise of 11°F or so would cause global catastrophe. It's a common claim these days, but Lynas apparently failed—as so many prophets of apocalyptic change have failed—to check his claims against the evidence of history.

A little more than 14,000 years ago, according to recent research on Greenland ice core samples, global average temperature jolted up 22°F in some fifty years. A couple of thousand years later, it lurched back down a similar amount, only to pop back up again 1200 years later. Climate shifts like these are apparently fairly common in Earth's long history.

Does this mean that we have nothing to fear from global warming? Quite the contrary. We—meaning here human beings living in industrial societies—face dire consequences even from so modest a temperature shift as Lynas' six-degrees-Celsius rise. In such a future, widespread crop failures caused by unpredictable shifts in rain belts, and the drowning of half the world's largest cities due to the breakup of the Greenland and West Antarctic ice caps, are likely events. Even without the other causes driving modern industrial society down the long ragged slope of catabolic collapse, a century or more of regular famines and rising sea levels would likely do the trick; added to the rest of the predicament of industrial society, they promise a harsh future with far less room for our species than we have come to expect.

In such a future, on the other hand, the living Earth will be fine. Temperature changes as large or larger than the one we are facing have happened countless times in the last 500 million years or so, and the planet we live on has flourished at much higher temperatures than our mismanagement can produce even in the most extreme scenario. From the perspective of deep time, it has to be remembered, the crises of the present are barely a blip on the planet's radar. They will pass, and so, in due time, will we.

We have all grown up, in other words, thinking of nature as an adorable, helpless bunny that some of us want to protect and others, motivated by the will to power that is the unmentionable driving force behind so much of contemporary culture, want to stomp into a bloody pulp just to show that they can. Both sides are mistaken, for what they have misidentified as a bunny is one paw of a sleeping grizzly bear who, if roused, is quite capable of tearing both sides limb from limb and feasting on their carcasses. The bear, it must be remembered, is bigger than we are, and stronger; it is also better adapted to survival in the world outside the fragile shell of our industrial society. We forget this at our desperate peril.

The stunningly beautiful final image of Silent Running shows the last of Earth's wild plants and animals, cradled in a dome of glass and steel, lit by artificial lights and tended by a robot drone, as it moves through deep space toward the stars. Brilliant cinematography though it is, it also makes a perfect image of the fallacy I've been outlining here. Long before the industrial civilization needed to build the dome, power the lights, and manufacture the robot can get around to stripping the Earth of its green fabric of life, that civilization will have been overwhelmed by the consequences of its own ecological mismanagement: as predicted in the Seventies, and as beginning to manifest around us right now.

Swap out nature for technology and vice versa in that final scene, in fact, and it becomes a good image of the best hope for what will be left of our industrial civilization in the future we're making for ourselves right now. In that image, a frail and vulnerable scrap of modern society, surrounded and supported by the strong arms of nature, moves forward through the starry void along with the rest of the living Earth. How that process might be set in motion will be central to the next few posts on this blog.

93: LESSONS FROM AMATEUR RADIO

(Originally published 2 July 2008)

Of the many recent signals that peak oil has come of age as a social reality, the one I find most interesting is the efforts being made, on nearly all sides of the cultural spectrum, to find reasons not to talk about it. The ongoing superspike in the price of oil, for example, has been blamed on almost everything under the sun except the simple, easily verifiable fact that worldwide petroleum production has been stuck on a plateau since late in 2004, and shows no sign of going anywhere but down in the foreseeable future.

Now of course it's true that speculation has played a role in driving up the price of oil, though as many speculators have bet on a decline in oil prices as on a continued rise — check the short interest on oil futures on any of the exchanges in recent months if you doubt that. It's also true that Russia, for example, has been using its newfound energy wealth as a political weapon, though there's rich irony to be savored in watching pundits in the United States, which built an empire on its own now-depleted petroleum reserves, criticizing Russia for doing the same thing. If oil production was still increasing at 2% per year, none of that would matter.

Look at the situation in the light of the relationship between supply and demand and the nature of the current crisis is hard to miss. Over the last year, the price of oil has approximately doubled. According to conventional economics, a price increase on this scale ought to stimulate new production, since oil reserves that were economically marginal when oil was $70 a barrel are much less so when oil is $140 a barrel. During the same period, despite frantic drilling on the part of oil companies, production has remained stuck in a narrow band. This only makes sense if production is constrained by non-economic factors. That, in a nut-shell, is the peak oil concept: at a certain point, geology trumps economics, because you can't pump oil that's not there any more.

This may seem obvious enough. To most of the people in the world's industrial nations right now, though, this sort of logic is unthinkable, for intensely personal reasons. Accept the reality of peak oil, and the future most people have planned for themselves and their children stands revealed as one of history's all-time bad jokes. Worse still, the reality of peak oil means that all those who turned their backs on the lessons of the 1970s energy crises, and wallowed in the quarter century of excess that followed, have personally contributed to making the world their children will inhabit a poorer place. That's a hard pill to swallow at the best of times, and this goes a long way to explain the passion for finding someone else — anyone else — to blame for the unfolding crisis.

They'll get over it eventually, when it becomes clear that what I have called the age of scarcity industrialism is the new reality, and no amount of scapegoat-hunting is going to change that fact. In the meantime, it seems to me, it's crucial that the peak oil movement keep going forward. Ten years ago, when the idea of oil priced above $100 a barrel was considered laughable by serious people, we correctly predicted the shape of the future. Now it's time to move on, and propose constructive responses to that future as it takes shape around us.

And that, dear readers, is what landed me in a converted World War Two barracks building the Saturday before last, with a multiple choice test on the table in front of me and a group of elderly men from the American Radio Relay League waiting to grade it.

A few words of explanation are probably in order at this point. One of the major achievements of the last two hundred years, it seems to me, is the emergence of communications networks that allow news and information to move from one side of the planet to another at a faster pace than messengers on horseback or sailing ships can travel. Though there had been plenty of earlier attempts, using semaphore and other visual systems, the telegraph revolutionized communication across the industrial world, and launched a series of more complex media — telephone, radio, television, and finally the internet. Not all these were an unmixed blessing, it has to be said; every technology has its downsides, but on the whole, widespread access to long-distance communication has been much more a blessing than the opposite.

There are also few dimensions of modern industrial society more vulnerable to breakdown in the age of scarcity now beginning. The internet, the crown jewel of modern communications, depends on a huge and energy-intensive infrastructure that may well prove unsustainable in the future. A single server farm can use as much electricity as a small city, and the technology that makes the internet possible in the first place requires plenty of energy, exotic raw materials, and a very high level of technology — none of which can necessarily be guaranteed in the decades to come. On a broader level, most of today's telecommunications, including the internet, support themselves through advertising sales, and the economic model that makes this work will have a hard time surviving the collapse of the consumer economy.

At the same time, electronic communications media need not be as dependent on today's industrial systems as they are. It's quite possible to build a vacuum tube — the backbone of radio communications in the days before transistors — from commonly available materials using hand tools; Peter Friedrichs' excellent book Instruments of Amplification, which details how to do this, has become popular reading on the more outré end of the do-it-yourself crowd. Fifty years ago, widely available books for the teen market such as Alfred P. Morgan's The Boy's First (and so on up through Sixth) Book of Radio and Electronics taught aspiring young electricians how to build remarkably sophisticated gear out of oatmeal boxes, spare parts and salvaged scrap. The possibility of viable electronics in a post-peak oil era deserves exploration.

What would a viable long-distance communications network in the age of peak oil look like? To begin with, it would use the airwaves rather than land lines, to minimize infrastructure, and its energy needs would be modest enough to be met by local renewable sources. It would take the form of a decentralized network of self-supporting and self-managing stations sharing common standards and operating procedures. It would use a diverse mix of communications modalities, so that operators could climb down the technological ladder as needed, from computerized data transfer all the way to equipment that could be built locally with hand tools. It would have its own subculture, of course, in which technical knowledge and practical expertise would be rewarded, encouraged, and fostered in newcomers. Finally, it would take a particular interest in emergency communications, so that operators could respond to disruptions and disasters with effective workarounds at times when having even the most basic communications net in place could save many lives.

The interesting thing, of course, is that a network that fills exactly these specifications already exists, in the form of amateur radio. During a long and complex history, the original loose network of radio experimenters who pioneered the airwaves in the first three decades of the 20th century morphed into a worldwide community of radio hobbyists, who are assigned their own segments of the radio spectrum. Licensed and occasionally encouraged by governments, "ham radio" — the origins of the nickname are a subject of some debate — flies almost completely under the radar of the wider culture these days, surfacing only when someone in the media notices that in the wake of some natural disaster, a group of local radio amateurs stepped up and kept emergency communications going when all other channels shut down.

All this was in my mind when I sat down two Saturdays ago and prepared to take the first of a series of FCC exams that would qualify me for an amateur radio license. Like a fair number of my generation, I'd been involved in amateur radio in my teen years — my Boy Scout troop had a ham radio club — but it got lost somewhere in the tangles of a difficult adolescence. Six months of study had, I hoped, prepared me for the most challenging test of all, the Element Four exam required to get an Amateur Extra class license, which authorizes operations on all amateur bands and all modes. Longtime readers of this blog will have already guessed that I had my Pickett slide rule with me, to crunch numbers as needed.

As it happened, that six months of study paid off, and the Pickett performed splendidly. I passed all three required exams, and a week later got an envelope from the FCC containing my Amateur Extra "ticket," call sign AD7VI. The next task is to assemble a station; given the limits on my budget, that will involve a good deal of scrounging and probably some homebuilt gear as well, but that's hardly a disadvantage; a Druid interested in appropriate technology has much to gain by practicing technological salvage and getting some facility with a soldering iron.

All this has several lessons that may be worth considering as we move deeper into the age of peak oil. First, of course, members of the peak oil community interested in practical responses to the future ahead of us could do worse than look into amateur radio. The internet has been the crucial framework for peak oil organization and information sharing since the dawn of the peak oil scene in the late 1990s. If the net becomes unstable, or outlying areas begin to lose access—both real possibilities as energy prices rise and infrastructure falters—having something else in place as a backup has much to recommend it. The Druid order I head has similar concerns, and similar plans in process.

Second, many other technologies vulnerable to the impacts of peak oil, climate change, and the other impacts of the predicament of industrial society have potential backups and replacements in the large and little-known world of hobby subcultures. An astonishing number of what we might as well call "trailing edge technologies," from black powder firearms through handloom weaving to long-distance sailing on windpowered boats, have survived intact to the present in the form of hobbies pursued by their own community of aficionados. Those communities, and the knowledge they preserve, are potentially an immense resource as we look for more sustainable ways to do things in the aftermath of the age of oil.

A third lesson, though, may be the most relevant of all. I've suggested elsewhere that our civilization is the first, and thus the most clumsy and tentative, of a new class of human societies—technic societies—as distinct from earlier forms as the first urban agricultural societies were from the tribal cultures that preceded them. One of the inevitable blind spots our historical position imposes on us is a tendency to confuse the particular cultural forms evolved by our technic society with the requirements of technic societies in general. Amateur radio is a reminder that there are ways to handle long-distance electronic communications that do not involve, say, mass broadcasting supported by huge energy inputs and the financial payback of a consumer economy. This is worth keeping in mind as we begin the long transition toward the ecotechnic societies of a sustainable future.

94: TRAILING EDGE TECHNOLOGIES

(Originally published 9 July 2008)

One of the worst of the booby traps built into the contemporary mythology of progress, it seems to me, is the notion that the way out of any difficulty is to keep moving the way we are already going, and do it faster. It may seem obvious that if you've gone down a blind alley, the only way out begins by shifting into reverse, but it takes very little attention to the current political scene to notice that this bit of common sense is far from common just now.

For a case in point, listen to the pundits — a sizeable chorus of them just now — who insist that the only way to bring soaring prices of oil, food, and other commodities back to earth is to push forward with the project of economic globalization. The problem here is that globalization was never more than an artifact of the final blowoff of the age of cheap oil, and as that age ends, so do the economic factors that made globalization work.

During the quarter century from 1980 to 2005, the cost of transport was so close to negligible that it seemed to make sense — and certainly made profits — to arbitrage labor costs by building sweatshop factories in Third World countries and shipping their products around the globe to markets in the industrial world. Far from being the wave of the future, as so many of its promoters claimed, or a malign conspiracy, as so many of its enemies insisted, it was simply the most profitable solution of an equation in which fuel costs, prevailing wages, and the relative strengths of various currencies were the most significant factors.

That equation is changing now. A recent news article noted that the cost of shipping a container of freight from China to Europe is now three times what it was before the current oil price spike began, and US companies that had offshored their production lines to distant continents were beginning to reopen long-shuttered domestic factories to cut transport costs. As the age of cheap oil dwindles in the rearview mirror, companies that choose the same strategy will prosper at the expense of those who cling to the mirage of the global economy.

The same sort of reversal, I'm coming to think, may affect many more aspects of life in the near future, as a great many apparent waves of the future turn out to be temporary adjustments to the short-term aberration that sent energy prices plunging down to levels that, in constant dollars, they never reached before — and almost certainly will never reach again. Any number of examples come to mind, but the one I'd like to discuss here is technology.

Few aspects of contemporary life are as heavily freighted with mythic significance as the way that technologies change over time. It's from this, more than anything else, that the modern myth of progress draws its force — and yet there are at least two very different processes lumped under the label of "technological progress."

The first, progress within a particular technology, follows a predictable course driven by the evolution of the technology itself. The first clumsy, tentative, and unreliable prototypes are replaced by ever more efficient and reliable models, until something like a standard model emerges; thereafter, changes in fashion and a slow improvement in efficiency supply what variations there are. Compare a sewing machine, a clothes dryer, or a turboprop engine from the 1960s with one fresh off the assembly line today, and in the underlying technology, the differences are fairly slight.

The difference lies in the control systems. The sewing machines, clothes dryers, and turboprops of the 1960s used relatively simple mechanical means of control, guided by the skill of human operators. Their equivalents today use complex digital electronics, courtesy of the computer revolution, and require much less human skill to run effectively. On a 1960s sewing machine, for example, buttonholes are sewn using a simple mechanical part and a great deal of knowledge and coordination on the part of the seamstress; on a modern machine, as often as not, the same process is done by tapping a few virtual buttons on a screen and letting the machine do it.

Changes of this sort are generally considered signs of progress. This easy assumption, though, may require a second look. It's true that the primitive computers available in the 1960s would have had a very hard time sewing a buttonhole, and the idea of fitting one of the warehouse-sized mainframes of the time into a home sewing machine would have seemed preposterous; computer technology has certainly progressed over that time. Yet the change from mechanical controls and operator skills with digital electronics is not a matter of progress in a single technology. It marks the replacement of one technology by another.

It's at this point that we enter into the second dimension of technological change. Mechanical controls and home economics classes did not gradually evolve into digital sewing machine controls; instead, one technology ousted another. Furthermore, both technologies do an equally good job of making a buttonhole. The factors driving the replacement of one by the other are external to the technologies themselves.

In the case of the sewing machines, as in so many similar technological transformations of the last sixty years or so, the replacement of one technology by another furthered a single process — the replacement of human skill by mechanical complexity. What drove this, in turn, was an economic equation closely parallelling the one that guided the rise of the global economy: the fact that for a certain historical period, all through the industrial world, energy was cheaper than human labor. Anything that could be done with a machine was therefore more profitable to do with a machine, and the only limitation to the replacement of human labor by fossil fuel-derived energy was the sophistication of the control systems needed to replace the knowledge base and nervous system of a skilled laborer.

For most people today, that equation still defines progress. A more advanced technology, by this definition, is one that requires less human skill and effort to operate. The curve of progress thus seems to point to the sort of fully automated fantasy future that used to fill so many comic books and Saturday morning cartoons.

One of the major mental challenges of the near future, in turn, will consist of letting go of this image of the future and retooling our expectations to fit a very different reality. Behind the clever robots who populated the collective imagination, and the less clever but more tangible bits of household automation marketed so obsessively to the middle classes in recent decades, lies the replacement of human energy by mechanical energy derived mostly from fossil fuels. During the age of cheap abundant energy, this made economic sense, because the energy — and the machines needed to use it — were so much cheaper than the skilled labor they replaced. In the decades to come, as energy stops being cheap and abundant, that rule will no longer hold. What looked like the wave of the future, here as elsewhere, might well turn out to be a temporary adjustment to a short-term phenomenon.

It's hard to think of an aspect of modern life that will not face drastic reshaping as a result. The collapse of American education, for example, was a consequence of the same economic forces that put computers into sewing machines; for the last few decades, it was more cost-effective to hand over bookkeeping chores to computers and equip word processors with spell checkers than it was to teach American children how to do arithmetic and spell correctly. In the future, this will very likely no longer be true, but the sprawling bureaucracies that run today's education industry are poorly equipped, and even more poorly motivated, to deal with the need to teach the skills that will be needed for humans to replace the machines.

Now of course not all the machines will need to be replaced at once. Many modern technologies, however, demand very large energy inputs that will not be reliably available in the future. Many more cannot be repaired when they break down — during the age of cheap energy, it was more cost-effective to throw a machine away when it broke, and buy a new model, than it was to pay a repairman's wages. Furthermore, the extraordinary levels of interconnection that pervade today's technology mean that the failure of a single component that cannot be replaced or repaired can render an entire system useless.

It's probably too late to avoid the future of systems failure the choices of the recent past have prepared for us, but quite a bit can be done to mitigate it. The first priority, it seems to me, is precisely to break free of the dubious assumption that the kind of technology that was more cost-effective in an age of cheap abundant energy will be well suited to the age of scarce and limited energy now dawning around us. The second is to redirect our attention and efforts to those technologies better suited to the new realities of our future.

Among the most useful resources in this context, in turn, are precisely the technologies that fell out of fashion in the last extravagant decades of the age of abundance, and the skills necessary to use them. As a culture, we've pursued cutting edge technologies for so long that shifting attention to trailing edge technologies may seem almost willfully perverse. Nonetheless, those older technologies that work effectively with relatively modest energy inputs, and rely on human hands and minds in place of energy- and resource-intensive electronics, may turn out to be much more viable in the long run.

That 1960s sewing machine—designed to allow for maintenance and repair, built of easily replaceable parts, and relatively easy to convert to foot pedal power if electricity becomes scarce— is likely to have a much longer working life in an age of decline than the computerized models filling showrooms today. In the same way, a great many trailing edge technologies—and the skills needed to use them, many of which can still be learned from living practitioners today—are worth preserving. The question, of course, is how many people will do that while the opportunity still exists.

95: DREAMS OF A BETTER WORLD

(Originally published 16 July 2008)

As it launched the modern worldview on its trajectory, the intellectual revolution of the 18th century — the Enlightenment, as it's usually called — passed on a legacy with profoundly mixed consequences for the future. Central to the Enlightenment ethos was the claim that myths were simply inaccurate claims about fact, and should be replaced by more accurate claims founded on reason and experiment. This seems like common sense to most people nowadays, but like most things labeled "common sense," it begs more questions and conceals richer ironies than a casual glance is likely to reveal.

One of those ironies became central to a discussion sparked by last week's Archdruid Report post, when a reader took issue with my characterization of progress as a myth. Like most people nowadays, he assumed that "myth" meant a story that isn't true, and drew the usual distinction between myth and science — that is, between the cosmological narratives of other cultures, which don't usually make experimentally testable claims about the natural world, and the cosmological narratives of ours, which does. It took, as it usually does, several exchanges before he realized that the popular definition of myth he was using is not the only game in town.

What makes this ironic is that the definition of myth he was using is itself part of a myth: the very one I mentioned in the earlier post. Only from within the myth of progress — the belief that all human existence follows a single line of advance leading straight from the caves to today's industrial societies, and beyond them to the stars — does it make sense to treat the belief systems of the past as inadequate attempts to do what we do better. The notion that other mythologies might have other purposes, and accomplish them better than ours does, is practically unthinkable these days. Yet many traditional belief systems have done a fine job of enabling the people who hold them to live their lives in harmony with their environment for millennia, while modern industrial cultures have proven hopelessly inept at this basic and necessary task.

Now of course there are plenty of people nowadays who use arguments such as this last to stand the myth of progress on its head, and insist that these traditional cultures are more advanced than ours. As I see it, though, the predicament we are facing demands something subtler. Rather than swapping one narrative for its mirror image, it may be time to step back and look at our mythic narratives as narratives, rather than imposing them by force on the world around us.

This backward step has a useful if uncomfortable effect: it reveals the awkward fact that the cultural narratives we use to make sense of the world today, however new they look, are generally rehashes of myths that have been around for a very long time. The anthropologist Misia Landau pointed out some years ago, for example, that contemporary scientific accounts of the rise of Homo sapiens from its prehuman ancestors are simply rehashed hero myths that follow Joseph Campbell's famous typology of the hero's journey, point for point. In the same way, those like Ray Kurzweil who argue that the perfect human society is to be found in a hypertechnological future, just as much as those who argue that the perfect human society is to be found in a return to the hunter-gatherer past, are simply projecting the myth of paradise onto one or another of the very few locations a secular worldview offers for it.

All this has to be kept in mind when considering an odd phenomenon that has become steadily more prominent in recent months, and seems likely to become even more so in the near future.

Well over a dozen times in the last six months, I've found myself in conversations with people who believe that the imminent crash of industrial society will inevitably lead to the birth of the sort of society they themselves most want to live in. What I find most interesting is that no two of them agree on exactly what sort of society that will be. Some of them come to the discussion with detailed plans for their perfect future, backed up figuratively—and now and again literally—with a backpack stuffed with supporting documentation laboriously cherrypicked from their favorite authors and the media; on the other end of the spectrum are those who have no idea what the world of the future will look like, but cling to an unshakable faith that it must be better than the world of today.

This astigmatism of the imagination is remarkably common. A good friend of mine once recounted a conversation he'd had in the last days of 1999 with someone who confessed she was deeply worried about the imminent Y2K problem. He assumed that she meant she was worried about the struggle for survival in the aftermath of the massive systems collapse some people were still predicting at that point, but she quickly set him right. Her job was unsatisfying, her marriage was on the rocks, and her life was at a standstill; what worried her was the possibility that she might wake up on January 1, 2000 to find that nothing had changed.

For my part, I knew quite a few people who became profoundly depressed when the world still worked after Y2K came and went, and there are many more people placing similar hopes on the potential catastrophes of the present and near future. It might seem that coping with a boring job, a troubled marriage, and a midlife crisis would still be preferable to starving to death in a burned-out basement in the aftermath of a cataclysmic social unraveling. The fact that many people in America today see things differently is one of the least noted and most troubling indicators of the temper of our times.

History has a good deal to do with the popularity of the belief in utopia through apocalypse these days. Over the course of the 20th century, the dizzying range of political-economic ideologies that once jostled for position in the western world narrowed gradually down to two—free market capitalism and Marxism—and then to one, which combines most of the objectionable features of both. The collapse of the New Left in the aftermath of the Sixties, and the abandonment of traditional conservatism by the pragmatist Right of the Reagan era, left a political vacuum that has yet to be filled. For some years now, as a result, most radicals of left and right alike have pictured their task in the purely reactive language of resistance and opposition, while the mainstream parties abandoned their old commitments in favor of the pursuit of business as usual for its own sake.

This has spared all sides the daunting challenge of coming up with constructive proposals for the future, but the downside is that those who sense the necessity for change are left with nothing but fantasies of a perfect world after an apocalyptic collapse to feed their hopes. In the process, it has been all too easy for many people to forget that in every other example in history, the decline and fall of a civilization leads not to utopia, but to a long and difficult age of warfare, mass migration, population decline, impoverishment, and the loss of priceless cultural treasures. Just as revolutionaries who insist that nothing can be worse than the status quo are often unpleasantly surprised to find just how much worse things can get, those who insist that today's industrial societies comprise the worst of all possible worlds may find themselves pining for the good old days of suburbs and freeways if they get the collapse they think they want.

Furthermore, especially but not only in America, the last few decades has seen the emergence of a culture of political demonology in which the slight differences between competing political parties get redefined in terms of absolute good and evil. Vigorous debate over the relative merits of candidates for office is the lifeblood of a republic, but when opponents of a public official don't seem to be able to walk past his picture without screaming obscenities at it — and I have seen this on both sides of the widening political chasm in America today — something has gone seriously wrong. Carl Jung's useful concept of "projecting the shadow" is more than a little relevant here; too many Americans nowadays have fallen into the seductive but disastrous habit of blaming their political adversaries for their own feelings of shame and resentment. Even the briefest glance at history shows where that sort of scapegoat logic leads, and it's no place any sane human being would want to go.

Still, sanity may be in short supply as the crisis of industrial society deepens around us. Lacking a clear sense of the logic of myth — and the legacy of the Enlightenment has made such a sense uncommonly hard to gain these days — it's far too easy for people in crisis to get so deeply entangled in mythic narratives that they lose track of the direction those narratives are leading them. A good deal of what happened during Germany's "few years in the absolute elsewhere" between 1933 and 1945, as Jung pointed out in a prescient essay, can best be understood as this type of entrapment in a myth, with a grand Wagnerian Götterdammerung as finale. It's entirely possible that some similar madness could grip America in the years to come.

Whether or not anything so ghastly happens, the unfolding crisis of industrial society is likely to bring in a bumper crop of misplaced myths and self-defeating ideologies unless we can manage to gain a wider recognition of the role of myth in public life, even — or, rather, especially — in those modern societies that pride themselves on their hard-headed rationality. When claims that an imminent catastrophe will inevitably result in the coming of a desired new world are seen for what they are — religious myths of apocalypse decked out awkwardly in secular drag — it's easier to see through them, and also to notice that the same claims have failed catastrophically every time in recorded history that they have been projected onto the inkblot patterns of current events.

If we can regain a certain degree of mythic literacy, and apply it to the myths that shape our public life, we might even be able to stop thinking of modern industrial society as either the best or the worst of human cultures, and recognize it as the ramshackle product of a long process of evolution, containing much that is worth saving alongside much that belongs in history's compost bin. We might also find ourselves realizing in time that catastrophe is no guarantee of Utopia, and a better society will emerge out of the wreckage of this one only if a very sizeable number of us are willing to muster the courage, forbearance, and capacity for hard work needed to make that happen.

96: POST-PEAK POLITICS

(Originally published 23 July 2008)

The recent downward lurch in the price of oil, among its other effects, has provided a good look at the downward arc of a cycle of public discourse about energy that will likely become all too familiar during the months and years ahead of us. As oil prices rose to new records a few weeks back, the media bristled with pundits warning about an imminent energy crisis in language ranging from sober to apocalyptic. Now that prices are cycling down again, another round of pundits has surfaced in the media, insisting that the first lot were wrong and we really can burn as much energy as we want.

These same frenetic swings in popular media and public opinion showed up in the 1970s, of course, and this is not the first such cycle we've seen since energy prices began climbing out of the basement in 2003 or so. I suspect a comparison of the rate of pro- and anti-peak oil pieces in the media with upward and downward movements in the price of oil would find a solid positive correlation, though my college statistics classes are far enough in my past that I'll let someone else apply for the grant.

Such short-term gyrations deserve attention. As I've suggested in several posts here, much of the impact of peak oil — and indeed of the wider crisis of industrial society, of which peak oil forms only one aspect — takes the form of increased volatility rather than linear change. This in itself is a source of serious economic and social disruption; if governments, businesses, and families have no way of knowing whether gasoline, or diesel fuel, or home heating oil will be $3 a gallon or $6 a gallon six months from now, planning for the future becomes an exercise in high-stakes gambling, especially as the same uncertainty percolates through the rest of the economy in the form of unstable energy and raw material costs.

Still, these short-term effects are only half the story. Behind them, and more than half hidden by them, is the long-term trend that has lifted energy prices from the all-time lows of the 1980s and 1990s to today's troubling levels. If that trend continues into the future, as seems most likely, not many of the economic arrangements of the last thirty years are well equipped to survive the experience. The resulting transformations will play out on many levels, but one of the most important—and the one I want to talk about today—is the political sphere.

The politics of peak oil form one of the most explosive and least often understood dimensions of the emerging crisis of industrial civilization. Too often, when questions of politics enter the peak oil discourse, they focus on the belief that the problem of peak oil can be solved by throwing one set of scoundrels out of power so that another set of scoundrels can take their place. This seems hopelessly misguided to me.

To start with, peak oil is not a problem that can be solved. It's a predicament—a phenomenon hardwired into our species' most fundamental relationships with physical and ecological reality—and like any other predicament, it cannot be solved; it can only be accepted. It differs in detail, but not in kind, from the collisions with ecological limits that punctuate the historical record as far back as you care to look.

Like every other species, humanity now and then overshoots the limits of its ecological support system. It's our misfortune to live at a time when this has happened on a much larger scale than usual, due to our species' recent discovery and reckless exploitation of the Earth's once-abundant fossil fuel reserves. Expecting a change of leaders, or even of systems, to make that reality go away is a little like trying to pass a bill in Congress to repeal the law of supply and demand.

Still, leaders and governmental systems make great scapegoats, and just now scapegoats are very much in fashion. Consider the rogue's gallery of villains blamed in the media for recent surges in the price of oil: speculators, oil companies, environmentalists, Arab sheiks, Nigerian rebels, and the US government, which — succumbing to a rare fit of common sense — refused to drain the nation's strategic oil reserve so that vacationers could have cheap gas for their holiday driving. Veer away from the mainstream media, in turn, and you'll find that the list of culprits for soaring oil prices has expanded far beyond an archdruid's capacity to catalogue.

Missing from nearly all these lists, however, is the simple geological reality that there's only so much oil in the Earth's rocks, we've pumped out most of the really large and easily accessible deposits, and it's becoming increasingly difficult to maintain current production levels — much less increase them — by drawing down the smaller and less accessible deposits that remain. It's not hard to show that this is a major factor in the current energy crisis; when a commodity's price doubles in a year, but the production of the same commodity fails to budge outside of a narrow range, it's a reliable bet that physical limits on the supply of the commodity are to blame.

The difficulties with this otherwise sensible observation, of course, are twofold. It offers no easy answers; if we've reached the physical limits of petroleum production, that's a fact we have to learn to live with, no matter how inconvenient or uncomfortable it may be. At the same time, it offends against a common assumption of modern thought, the belief that human beings — and only human beings — play an active role in history. Older civilizations understood that nonhuman forces shared in the making of history, and there's a fine irony in the way that our civilization, having rejected the nonhuman world as a historical agent, now finds its own history being shaped by a nonhuman reality with which it steadfastly refuses to come to terms.

Bring historical irony into the political sphere, though, and as often as not it turns explosive. The example of Germany in the aftermath of the First World War is instructive. Faced with the collision between an imperial ideology of world domination and the hard fact of military defeat, a great many Germans after 1918 searched feverishly for an explanation for that defeat that did not require them to recognize the geopolitical limits to German power in the dawning age of oil.

As the economic troubles of the postwar period mounted, so did the quest for scapegoats, until finally a fringe politician named Adolf Hitler came up with an answer that most Germans found acceptable. Germany's second attempt at world conquest proved, even more conclusively than the first, that in an age of oil, a small country with no oil reserves and no defensible borders has no business dreaming of global empire. Still, it took the most destructive war in human history and the horrors of the Holocaust to bring that simple fact to the attention of the German people.

One factor that made the political situation in Weimar Germany so vulnerable to this sort of self-destructive evasion of crucial realities was the intellectual bankruptcy of the mainstream political parties at the time. The late 19th century saw the emergence of a political consensus across the then-industrial world that united all mainstream parties behind the principles of free trade, governmental noninterference in economic affairs, and imperial expansion into the Third World. Finding substantive differences between Liberals and Conservatives in Britain, Democrats and Republicans in America, and equivalent parties in other countries around the turn of the last century was a task best pursued with a magnifying glass. It took decades of crisis, culminating in the economic debacle of the Great Depression, to break the grip of that consensus on the political imagination of the industrial world.

We are in a similar situation in America today. If anything, contemporary political thought is far more impoverished than it was in 1908, when the radical fringes of society swarmed with alternative theories of political economy. Since the collapse of classical conservatism in the 1960s, and the implosion of the New Left in the 1970s, political debate in the American mainstream has focused on finding the best means to achieve a set of ends that few voices question at all, while a great deal of debate outside the mainstream has abandoned political theory for a secular demonology in which everything wrong with the world—including the effects of the Earth's ecological limits, of course—is the fault of some malevolent elite or other.

The current presidential race in America is a case in point. Neither candidate has addressed what, to my mind at least, are the crucial issues of our time: for example, whether America's interests are best served by maintaining a sprawling military-economic empire with military bases in more than a hundred nations around the world; what is to be done about the collapse of America's economic infrastructure and the hollowing out of its once-prosperous heartland; and, of course, how America's economy and society can best deal with the end of the age of cheap abundant energy and the transition to an age of scarcity for which we are woefully unprepared.

Instead, the candidates argue about whether American troops should be fighting in Iraq or in Afghanistan, and whether or not we ought to produce more energy by drilling for oil in the nation's wildlife refuges. Meanwhile, the partisans of each of these career politicians strive to portray the other as Satan's own body double, while a growing number of those who are disillusioned with the entire political process hold that both men are pawns of whatever reptilian conspiracy happens to be fashionable on the fringes these days.

Maybe it's just me, but this sort of evasion of the obvious seems utterly counterproductive. If Weimar America is to have a less disastrous future than its 20th century counterpart, we need to move toward serious debate over the shape that future is going to have, and our economically ruinous empire, our disintegrating national economy, and our extravagant lifestyles need to be among the things up for discussion. The radical right have already begun to scent a major opportunity; Nick Griffin, head of the neofascist British National Party, has already commented that his party is precisely one major crisis away from power, and he may well be right.

More generally, the first political movement to come up with a plausible response to peak oil will likely define the political discourse around energy and society for decades to come. Griffin and his peers are eager to take on that role; their response may not look plausible to most people now, but then neither did Hitler's, before the Great Depression lowered the bar on plausibility to the point that he could goose-step over it. Unless some other movement comes up with a meaningful politics for the post-peak world, Griffin's ideas may yet win out by default.

That would be a tragedy, and for more than the obvious reasons. One advantage of crisis is that it becomes possible to make constructive changes that are much harder in less troubled times. While I am no fan of utopian fantasies, and the possibility always exists that well-intentioned changes could make things worse, it's hard to argue against the idea that the dysfunctional mess that is modern American politics could stand some improvement. That might involve learning a few things from other democracies; it might also involve returning to something a little more like the constitutional system on which this country was founded, which after all worked well in a pre-fossil fuel age. One way or another, though, it's time to take a hard look at some of our most basic assumptions, and replace scapegoat logic with a reasoned discussion about where we are headed and what other options our society might want to consider.

97: REVIVING THE HOUSEHOLD ECONOMY
PART ONE: THE WORLD OUTSIDE THE MARKET
(Originally published 30 July 2008)

As the current pullback in oil prices continues—one of the bench-mark grades dropped to a little over $120 a barrel yesterday, though it jumped back up $4 in early trading today—peak oil skeptics have seized the opportunity to insist that there's nothing wrong with the petroleum market that a few more trillion-dollar giveaways to the oil industry wouldn't fix. One interesting lesson worth drawing from the current barrage of punditry is that most of people who reject the concept of peak oil don't actually seem to know what the phrase means.

A case in point is a recent opinion piece that denounced peak oil as "nonsense," on the grounds that the world still has some forty years of oil left at today's rate of production. The author of this piece somehow managed not to notice that the peak oil theory focuses on precisely the point he took for granted, the sustainability of today's rate of production. The world may well have the equivalent of forty years' worth of current annual petroleum production left in its reserves, but if the amount it can produce each year plateaus and then begins to shrink due to geological limits, a global economy founded on ever-expanding energy supplies is in trouble. That's the essence of the peak oil position, and waving around claims about the absolute size of global reserves doesn't address it at all.

Still, it's not surprising that so many people are finding such ingenious ways just now to avoid understanding the implications of peak oil. As worldwide oil production remains stuck in its current plateau—a plateau that increasingly has had to be propped up by massive production of high-cost biofuels and tar-sand products—some of the most basic presuppositions of the modern world are turning out to be well past their pull dates. Once production begins to slip down the far side of the world's Hubbert curve, that process is likely to accelerate, and much of what counts as conventional wisdom today will end up sitting in history's dumpster next to phlogiston and the divine right of kings.

One example with sweeping implications unfolds from a particular mismatch between current economic theories and the practical realities of the age of peak oil. Perhaps the best way to introduce this example is to invite my readers to put on their walking shoes, pick up their canvas shopping bags, and join me in one of yesterday's errands.

In the southern Oregon town where I live, Tuesday is the day of the weekly grower's market, and so yesterday, as we do nearly every Tuesday between March and November, my wife Sara and I walked the 3/4 of a mile or so to the National Guard armory parking lot where local growers and ranchers sell their produce. Among our purchases was a flat of fresh raspberries, and this afternoon we'll be turning those into home-canned raspberry jam for the year to come.

Now it's unquestionably true that we could just buy an equivalent volume of commercially manufactured raspberry jam and eat that instead. Still, these two ways of putting by a supply of raspberry jam are by no means equal. Set aside for a moment the higher quality of homemade jam, which (in this case, at least) is made of fresher ingredients and prepared in small batches; one of the most important differences between the two processes is that the homemade jam represents a much more efficient use of fossil fuels.

The grower who produced the raspberries used organic methods, which saved the petroleum and natural gas that would otherwise have had to go into pesticides and fertilizers. While she used a pickup to bring her crop to the market, the ten miles or so she drove compares favorably to the thousands of miles agricultural products are routinely shipped in their journey from farm to factory, warehouse, and supermarket, and even if we owned a car and drove to and from the market, the extra mile and a half of gas wouldn't shift the balance much.

Turning berries into jam and canning the result probably takes about an equal amount of energy per pint of jam whether it's done in a home kitchen or a huge factory, though it's a lot easier to provide the energy via a solar cooker or other renewable source on a small scale. Even without that, though, the homemade jam takes a small fraction of the energy to go from raspberry canes to our pantry than commercial jam requires. One measure of these energy economies is that, including all expenses, our homemade jam costs us only about two-thirds as much as the same volume of commercial jam.

Compare the homemade jam with its commercial equivalent from the viewpoint of conventional economic measures, though, and the balance swings the other way. In terms of its impact on the gross domestic product — generally considered the broadest measure of national prosperity — our homemade jam is practically an economic disaster. The very modest price of raspberries, sugar, pectin, and new lids for our much-recycled canning jars is the only contribution it makes to the economy. By contrast, making, shipping, storing, and selling the commercial jam requires, directly and indirectly, the expenditure of a very large amount of money, all of which counts mightily toward a higher gross domestic product.

Consider the economics from the perspective of the participants in the creation of the homemade jam, though, and things take on a very different shape. Even aside from the other reasons Sara and I might want homemade jam, we have a potent economic motive; by making the jam ourselves we get a superior product at a lower price. The raspberry grower, in turn, benefits handsomely from the same decision; the price she gets for her berries when sold directly to the consumer is several times the price she can get from wholesalers. According to conventional economics, the end result of individuals freely pursuing their own interest in a market should be the maximization of prosperity — and yet if prosperity is measured by the gross domestic product, our free pursuit of our own interest decreases our contribution to national prosperity.

What is happening here, of course, reflects one of the largest of the blind spots of contemporary economics: the assumption that market transactions mediated by money are the only significant form of economic activity. Our household jam-making activities drop off the economic radar screen the moment we finish paying for the raw materials. Value is being produced — the same jam offered for sale at next week's market would bring substantially more than the cost of the raw materials — but it's being produced outside the market economy, and therefore has no official existence in an economy measured entirely by market metrics.

What makes this particularly relevant in the twilight of the age of cheap oil is that the world's industrial nations, and above all the United States, have spent most of the last century transferring as much as possible of the household economy into the market sphere. In making our own jam, among other things, Sara and I belong to a minority of American households. Glance back a hundred years, by contrast, and nearly every family in the country outside the very rich and the very poor had an active household economy that produced a large fraction of the total goods and services they consumed. Many factors contributed to this dramatic shift, but one of the most significant is the availability of cheap abundant energy.

Most of the economies of scale that make mass production of processed foods economically viable, after all, are economies only because the cost of transportation is low enough to permit them. As recently as the first half of the 20th century, most consumer products in the US were produced locally for regional markets, in large part because transportation costs were still high enough to make national distribution a costly proposition. (Those brands that did find a nationwide niche, such as Coca-Cola™, did it by franchising out manufacturing and bottling to local firms.) It took the birth of a new transportation network of diesel-powered trucks using a massive new interstate highway network to create today's national distribution chains, and cheap petroleum provided the foundation on which the whole system arose.

The twilight of cheap oil, in turn, bids fair to throw this process of economic centralization into reverse. As transportation costs rise to become a major part of the cost of consumer products, the economies to be gained by local production will sooner or later outweigh the economies of scale that shape the current system, opening economic niches for small and midsized firms nimble enough to move with the currents of economic change. Equally, though, the financial advantages of the household economy will become overwhelming. In a world of scarce oil, anything that can decrease the amount of fossil fuel energy that has to go into an product will pay off handsomely, and if the transition to scarcity involves widespread impoverishment—as seems most likely just now—the choice faced by many households throughout the industrial world may well come down to doing things themselves or doing without.

At the same time, it's crucial to recognize that the forces holding the current economic order in place reach beyond the realm of simple economic calculations into murkier areas of culture and collective psychology. For those who have access to fruit growers—and with the growth of farmers markets across the US and elsewhere, this has become a tolerably large fraction of the population—making one's own jam, and a great many other food products, is already a paying proposition; so are many other activities that once formed part of the household economy, and very likely will do so again; yet these activities remain the hobbies of a minority of today's Americans, and most of their neighbors turn to the market economy to get inferior products at higher prices instead. The forces motivating this sort of economic irrationality will be the focus of next week's post.

PART TWO: THE DECLINE AND FALL OF HOME ECONOMICS
(Originally published 6 August 2008)

Raspberry jam, the ostensible subject of last week's Archdruid Report post, is only one of hundreds of goods and services that until recently were produced almost entirely in the household econo-

my, outside the reach of the market. Nowadays, by contrast, nearly all those goods and services are either produced commercially
or are not available at all. This represents an economic transformation on a massive scale, and yet it's one that has seen remarkably little discussion by economists.

It also represents a social transformation of equally massive
scope. Visit the library of an American public university that has
not yet taken up the currently fashionable habit of purging its collection of "outdated" materials, wander through the stacks until
you find the dingiest and most neglected shelves in the building,
and odds are that you'll be looking at the mummified remains of
a field of study, a profession, and a university department as dead
as the dinosaurs, and a good deal less popular nowadays: home
economics.

Not all that many decades ago, an impressive network of
home economists working for universities, county extension services, and private industry provided an extensive support system
for the household economy. Backing that network, and the by no
means negligible expenditures that supported it, was an almost
universal consensus that recognized the social and economic importance of the household economy. The experience of two world
wars, in which government-promoted home economics measures
had played a major role in softening the impact of food rationing
and enabling the United States to feed armies and allies alike,
gave support to that consensus.

At the same time, the household economy had long faced
steady pressure from the expansionistic habits of the market economy. Beginning around the end of the 19th century, and acceler-
ating over the decades that followed, the market seeped into the
domestic sphere with a steady stream of "convenience" products
and "labor-saving" devices. Many of these were neither convenient nor labor-saving, but the massive marketing programs that
backed them up made them highly fashionable, especially in the
newly prosperous middle classes that emerged as the 20th century wore on and America entered on its age of empire.

These two major social forces — the broad consensus surrounding the domestic economy and the expanding pressure of a met-

astatic market economy—finally collided head on in the decades following the Second World War. A third force, however, played what may well have been the decisive role in the collision. Bringing up that third force at all may be problematic, for it's remained a hot-button issue in American culture right down to the present, and very few people seem to be able to discuss it dispassionately just now. Still, what happened to the household economy is impossible to understand without taking it into account. That force, of course, is the role played by the economics of gender in launching and shaping the second wave of American feminism in the 1960s and 1970s.

Many currents of social change flowed together to launch the women's movement of the 1960s, but one factor that has not always been given its due is the impact of the abrupt changeover from the war economy of the 1940s to the consumer economy that followed it. As the troops came home, government and industry alike did everything in their very considerable power to get Rosie the Riveter off the factory floor and turn her into Suzy Homemaker as fast as possible, in order to free up jobs for millions of demobilized soldiers. At the same time, the quest for markets to fuel the consumer economy's expansion and employ those same millions threw the market assault on the household economy into overdrive.

Postwar propaganda—"advertising" is too mild a word for the saturation campaigns that flooded the popular media in the late 1940s and early 1950s—presented middle class families with a glittering image of affluence in which convenient, up-to-date consumer products provided by the market would replace the dowdy routine of the domestic economy with a life of elegance and leisure. The reality behind the facade turned out to be much less palatable. Denied both the place in the market economy they had occupied during the war years, and the role in the household economy their mothers had held before that, millions of middle class women across America found themselves expected to lead a purely decorative and essentially purposeless existence.

As a motor for rebellion, deprivation of meaning is even more potent than deprivation of food, and so an explosion was inevitable. Many of the forms that explosion took were altogether admirable. A great many injustices were set to rights, or at least challenged, and social roles that had become hopelessly restrictive for women and men alike came in for a much needed reassessment. Still, as the feminism of the Sixties and Seventies percolated outward into popular culture, it suffered in some measure the common fate of progressive social movements in the modern West: instead of challenging the system of male privilege, and the presuppositions that underlay it, a great many women who considered themselves feminists simply set out to seize their share of the positions of privilege within the existing system.

In the process, no small number of them embraced the manners, mores, and attitudes of those they hoped to supplant. Compare an issue of Playboy from the 1960s with an issue of Cosmopolitan from the 1980s, for example, and it's impossible to miss the parallels, all the way from the shared obsession with sexual conquest, conspicuous consumption, and personal appearance, to the mutually interchangeable cover girls meant to allure potential readers. The astonishing thing is that the "Playboy man" and the "Cosmo girl," those airbrushed icons of consumer culture, were both considered to be liberated, and liberating, in their day.

The household economy, or what was left of it, was one of the casualties of the process that made these dubious figures popular. The feminist movement might have posed hard questions about the relative social value assigned to the household and market economies, and indeed some of the subtler minds within the movement made forays in this direction, but their ideas found few listeners. Instead, many feminists—and ultimately a great many American women—simply accepted the relative values their culture assigned to the two economies, and aspired to the one that they were taught to consider more valuable. The ensuing shift in attitudes cut the ground out from under the consensus that once made home economics relevant; by the 1980s most universities had closed their home economics departments, and county extension agencies and private firms followed suit.

Still, the old social roles assigned to women carried so much emotional force in the collective imagination for so long that they had to go somewhere. To a remarkable extent, they came to be applied to the institution that supplanted the economic roles once held by women: the market itself. Look at the rhetoric applied to the market over the last few decades and you'll find every cliché applied to women in 1950s men's magazines present and accounted for.

The market, in effect, has become American society's coquettish and curvaceous sex kitten, its June Cleaver mom complete with patriotic flags and apple pie, its nubile innocent waiting to be rescued from the lustful grasp of government regulations and tax collectors. Placed on a rhetorical pedestal as absurdly florid as anything Coventry Patmore ever said about Victorian womanhood, and abused and exploited as ruthlessly as Victorian women so often were, the market is America's pinup girl, the focus of overheated notions every bit as detached from real life as the fantasies that filled the pages of Playboy or Cosmo in their prime.

Any attempt to rebuild the household economy in the wake of peak oil will inevitably have to contend with these issues. It's not at all uncommon today, for example, to find couples for whom the cost of professional childcare, an extra car and commuting expenses, and the other costs of a two-salary lifestyle add up to more money than the second salary brings in. In many cases these families would come out substantially ahead if one of the adults were to stay home and provide the same services within the household economy, but in the present social climate, this option is very nearly unthinkable for many people.

As a longtime househusband, I can speak to this from a certain degree of experience. During slightly more than half of 24 years of married life, it made a great deal more economic sense for my spouse, a bookkeeper, to work in the market economy, while I tended the garden, cooked the meals, did most of the cleaning, and worked my way through the long learning curve of a career as a writer in my off hours. I came in for a fair amount of criticism for making this choice, though I have to say it was a great deal less savage than the treatment meted out, mostly by other women, to women I knew who made the same choice. Despite the pressure, though, it was unquestionably the right choice for us; it enabled us to maintain a very comfortable lifestyle on a modest income.

That choice is likely to be at least as valuable an option for a great many more people as the market economy contracts in the wake of peak oil. The abandonment of the household economy, after all, was only viable in the first place because of the temporary conjunction of American imperial expansion with the rapidly expanding fossil fuel production of the postwar years. As America's empire frays and global energy production falters, the costs of the energy-intensive economic structure we have built over the last sixty years will fairly rapidly begin to outweigh its benefits. In that context a renewal of the household economy offers one valuable set of tools for taking up the slack and providing needed goods and services, and those dusty books in the home economics section of your local college library may turn out to be valuable once again.

Such a renewal, though, will require a reassessment of social roles and values as ambitious as anything the pioneering feminists of the 1960s envisaged. Measures of value evolved within the market, and shaped to a large degree by market-centered ideologies, fall flat when applied to nonmarket economies in which custom, reciprocity, and collective benefit govern exchanges, rather than the quest for individual profit. Money itself, that abstract fiction that has very nearly smothered the real economy of goods and services it originally evolved to support, may be a good deal less relevant as alternative forms of value become ascendant. The form that will be taken by those alternatives in the ecotechnic world of the future is probably impossible to guess at this point, but an openness to options and a willingness to look beyond the market are likely to be valuable steps just now — and a renewed household economy may just turn out to be the seed from which the economics of the future can take root and grow.

98: IDOLS OF THE MARKETPLACE
(Originally published 13 August 2008)

As last week's post suggested, the forces that keep American families stuck on an economic treadmill, trying to meet new and challenging conditions with old and increasingly dysfunctional responses, are by no means entirely economic in nature. Despite the polite fiction that all players in the economic game are rational actors pursuing their own interests in free exchanges, most of the decisions individuals make in the course of that game involve precious little of the sort of rational deliberation the fiction suggests.

To begin with, of course, a great many of the choices are enforced. I think it was Anatole France who pointed out that equality under the law, as often as not, amounts to forbidding the rich as well as the poor to sleep under bridges, steal bread, or beg for coins in the street. For many Americans, and most people elsewhere in the world, the freedom to exchange their labor for money amounts to a Hobson's choice between sweatshop labor at poverty wages, on the one hand, and starving in the streets on the other. America's caste system is somewhat more flexible than average, and its privileged classes long ago figured out the advantages of opening their doors to a trickle of aspirants from below, but access to economic opportunity in America still depends to a very large extent on how much money your parents made.

Yet the power of cultural narratives and myths, a frequent theme in these essays, also plays a massive role in leading supposedly rational actors into the irrational decisions that shape so much of our collective lives these days. The twilight of the household economy, the theme of last week's post, is a good example.

A number of my readers responded to the post with emails describing couples they knew who maintained two salaries, even though the costs incurred by doing so—professional childcare, commuting, office clothing, and more—far exceeded the income of the less lucrative of the two jobs. This is quite common nowadays, because the cultural narratives surrounding employment make it impossible for most American families to notice that their economic status might be improved noticeably by giving up one salary in exchange for full-time involvement by one family member in the household economy.

Behind the narratives that prop up this curious blindness, though, lies a broader pattern, and it's this that I want to discuss this week. For reasons rooted in history, it's difficult to talk about the theme I have in mind without stirring up passions of the most irrational and intemperate kind. Still, the attempt has to be made, because the narrative in question is turning out to be a massive barrier to constructive change as we approach the twilight of the industrial age. The cultural story I have in mind is the myth of the market.

The measure of a narrative's power is the extent to which its believers miss the fact that it's a culturally conditioned narrative, and treat it as an objective reality obvious to any unbiased observer. This condition is widespread enough in the case of today's market mythology that it's probably necessary to sketch out the narrative in some detail. In simplest terms, the myth of the market starts from the belief that all human economic activity naturally involves free exchanges of value in a free market, mediated by an accepted measure of value—that is, by money. The myth goes on to claim that any economic activity outside the world of market exchanges either doesn't count, doesn't contribute to prosperity, or is a bad thing that can only be redeemed by bringing it within the sacred precincts of the market. Finally, the myth insists, anything that restricts or regulates the choices made by participants in market exchanges is a bad thing, guaranteed to hinder prosperity, because the market itself—guided by Adam Smith's famous "invisible hand"—inevitably maximizes the benefits received by all its participants, so long as it's given the freedom to do so.

I have used the word "myth" here deliberately, with an eye both of its current meanings. Its older meaning—the sense possessed by its source, the Classical Greek word muthos—defines a myth as an important cultural narrative, a story that every full participant in the culture can be expected to know, that serves as a paradigm for some aspect of humanity's experience of itself and the world. Its more recent, derivative, and polemical sense defines a myth as an important cultural narrative that happens to be false. In this second sense, proving that something is a myth doesn't mean showing that it plays a crucial role in some society's view of the world; it means showing that whatever it says about the world is untrue.

Now it so happens that some cultural narratives are myths in both senses of the word: they are crucial elements of a society's view of the world, and they also make statements about the world that can be shown to be untrue. The myth of the market falls into this interesting category. Just now, in America and some other industrial nations, it plays a central role in defining how people think about the economic dimension of their lives. At the same time, some of its core assumptions, and many of the statements about the world that derive from it, are hard to support on any basis but blind faith.

This is where the intemperate passions I mentioned earlier enter the picture, of course, because the myth of the market is not simply a cultural narrative; it's also an ideology supported by a great many people just now. There's a complicated history behind its current ideological role. The grand geopolitical struggle between the American and Russian empires that occupied most of the twentieth century, and still makes headlines today, followed the usual custom and borrowed ideological garments to provide a scrap of decency to the clash of naked ambitions.

The American empire's first choice of ideologies to counter Russia's Marxist polemics was Christianity—this is why, for example, the words "under God" were tacked onto the Pledge of Allegiance during the Eisenhower administration, and why the word "Russia" rarely appeared in American political speech for more than two decades without the adjective "godless" in front of it. This turned out to be a bad choice, though, not least because it had little appeal outside America's borders. A secular ideology had to be coined, and free market capitalism filled that need. It's not accidental that many of its active proponents in recent years were Marxists during their years of adolescent rebellion in the 1960s; much of what now passes for economic thought in America simply takes Marxist assumptions and stands them on their head, in the same way that Satanists borrow most of Christian theology but root for the other side.

The Siamese-twin relationship between Marxism and today's free market ideology can be seen most clearly, perhaps, in the insistence on both sides that the only valid position on the spectrum of possible relations between government and the economic sphere lies at the two extremes: either all economic activity should be controlled by the government, or the government should have nothing to do with the economic sphere at all. I doubt anyone just now needs to be shown that the Utopian promises of Marxism don't work in practice, but the current ideology of the free market is another matter. Still, the evidence of history simply doesn't support the claims made by free market advocates.

Track the economic history of the United States in the 20th century, for example, and an interesting pattern emerges. Until the 1920s, a free market ideology far more principled than its current equivalent dominated American politics; government kept its hands off business until the crash of 1929 and the Great Depression made that politically impossible. During the Depression years, politicians imposed an alphabet soup of regulations on the American economy, and those remained in place until the early 1980s, when most of them were removed. If the myth of the market is to be believed, the American economy should have been more prosperous before the mid-1930s and after the mid-1980s than in the intervening period.

The problem, of course, is that this isn't what happened. Until the 1930s, the American economy was racked at regular intervals by a disastrous cycle of booms and busts that drastically limited American prosperity and made severe economic depressions a frequent experience. As the New Deal took hold, the economic cycle damped down to livable levels, and the United States entered the longest period of general prosperity in its history. That prosperity waned in the 1970s as US oil production peaked and began to decline, but the deregulation of the 1980s did not bring it back. For most Americans, per capita income in constant dollars has declined since the early 1970s, and many other measures of effective wealth have slumped accordingly; the rate of infant mortality in America today, for example, is roughly on a par with that of Indonesia.

What has returned, and in spades, is the old cycle of boom and bust. Since the beginning of the Reagan years, speculative booms and their inevitable implosions have once again become a dominant feature of the economic landscape. So far, the US government has responded to each popping bubble by ignoring its own free market rhetoric and flooding the economy with borrowed money. There seems to be some doubt about whether that strategy will work in the aftermath of the most recent incarnation of the process, the real estate frenzy of 2002-2006; one way or another, though, US government, corporate, and individual debt has soared to unsustainable levels after these binges of borrowing, and a reckoning cannot be avoided forever.

Of course it's possible to argue that the regulations established in the 1930s and eliminated in the 1980s had nothing to do with the period of relative economic stability and rising national prosperity that arrived in the 1930s and ended in the 1980s. Look beyond US borders, though, and the same patterns show up. The nations with the highest standards of living today, for example, are not those that have embraced an unrestricted free market, or for that matter those that have subordinated all economic activity to the political sphere. Rather, they're nations that have found a middle ground, leaving economic activity in private hands but regulating it where necessary for the public good, and in particular, preventing it from indulging in the self-destructive excesses it pursues when left to itself.

That middle ground, granted, lacks the simplistic good-and-evil categorization that makes for a popular ideology these days. It's pragmatic, it's sloppy, and it requires constant tinkering and a willingness to deal with the reality of conflicting interests. All that can be said for it is that, by and large, it does seem to work better than the alternatives.

Well, that may not be quite all that can be said for it. One of the fundamental axioms of ecology is that an ecosystem becomes more stable and productive as it becomes more balanced. Cycles of boom and bust are common in marginal ecosystems, where nothing controls populations except the crude forces of food supply and starvation; as ecosystems develop complexity and richness, subtler factors come into play, and conflict and chaos give way to equilibrium. Economic systems may well be subject to the same rule.

Political systems certainly are; the success of democratic systems of governance, after all, depends precisely on the extent to which they establish and maintain a balance of powers in which no one has unchecked authority. Today's market economies may be badly in need of a dose of the same medicine. Part of the countervailing force that's needed to pull them out of the vicious cycle of speculative boom and bust will likely come from government regulation, but the same principle may need to be applied in other ways, not least to keep government power from ballooning further out of control than it already is.

Just as it's clearly not true that the unregulated market automatically brings prosperity — the invisible hand, it turns out, is quite capable of giving us the finger — the issues raised in the last two posts suggest that it's also not true that all economic activity ought to be subject to the market's vagaries. Economies outside the market system could play a large role in helping to balance out the market's wobbles. The household economy is one potential balancing force; another could come from local economies driven by the very different forces of reciprocity and custom, in which surplus products are exchanged as gifts between neighboring families. Other economies beyond the market also deserve exploration.

The crucial thing to keep in mind, it seems to me, is that subservience to the intellectual idols of the contemporary marketplace may well turn out to be profoundly counterproductive in the years ahead of us. The market economy is already having to deal with rising transportation costs and the twilight of the short-lived global marketplace, and will shortly have to face the desperate need to retool our lives and productive capacities to meet the requirements of the dawning age of scarcity industrialism. In such a context, remaining stuck in a rigid, ideologically based stance about the proper relationship between the market economy and other sectors of society may be a luxury we can no longer afford.

99: THE TEMPO OF CHANGE
(Originally publsihed 20 August 2008)

One of the lessons of history is that change, no matter how drastic it appears on the pages of history books, is rarely anything like so sudden for those who live through it. Read an account of the French Revolution, for example, and events seem to follow one another like bangs from a string of firecrackers from the final crisis of the Ancien Régime straight through to the fall of Napoleon. For the man or woman in the French street, though, these happenings were scattered threads in a fabric of months and years woven from the plainer cordage of ordinary life.

Partly this is a function of the way historical narrative compresses time. It bears remembering that a teenage Parisienne who sat daydreaming of her upcoming wedding on the day that Louis XVI summoned the États-General in 1788 would most likely have been a grandmother on the day the Allied armies marched into Paris after the battle of Waterloo in 1815. Equally, though, it's rare for historical events to have the same apparent importance at the time that they are assigned in the historian's hindsight, not least because the everyday process of making a living and moving through the stages of human existence plays a larger role in most lives than the occasional tumults that make the history books.

This lesson needs to be kept in mind as we try to make sense of the implications of the crisis of industrial society, not least because it offers some protection against the common bad habit of projecting daydreams onto the inkblot patterns of the future. That habit of thinking is more than usually at issue in exploring the theme of this week's post, the nature of daily life in the decades ahead of us.

The role of wishful thinking in driving the apocalyptic expectations so common in contemporary culture rarely shows itself so clearly as here. In the weeks leading up to the Y2K noncrisis, I knew quite a respectable number of people whose conviction that industrial civilization was about to undergo total collapse was all too clearly motivated by the belief that this meant that come January 1, 2000, they would no longer have to continue living the lives they had made for themselves. You'd think that the prospect of mass death would be a good deal more daunting than even the most humdrum modern existence, but it's always part of the narrative of imminent apocalypse that dieoff only happens to other people; no matter how poorly suited the people in question were to the strenuous task of surviving the overnight collapse of a civilization, each one of them believed that they'd be among the lucky few.

The same sort of logic pervades certain corners of the peak oil scene. I've met far too many people who don't know enough about plant care to keep a potted petunia healthy, and have very likely never put in an eight-hour day of hard physical labor in their lives—most middle class Americans haven't, after all—and yet who nonetheless talk enthusiastically about the life they expect to lead in a self-sufficient rural lifeboat ecovillage as industrial civilization crashes into ruin a comfortable distance away. It's all very reminiscent of the aftermath of the Sixties, when a great many people headed back to the land with equally high hopes; the vast majority of them straggled back to the cities a few months or years later with their hopes in shreds, having discovered that fantasies of the good life in nature's lap make poor preparation for the hard work, unremitting discipline, and relative poverty of life as a subsistence farmer.

The would-be communards of the Sixties had an advantage not shared by their counterparts in the peak oil movement. Rural land was relatively cheap, and money was fairly easy to come by, not least because the counterculture scene always had a sprinkling of members with large trust funds who functioned as the sugar daddies of the movement. As the Summer of Love gave way to the summer of Altamont and the urban neighborhoods

that nurtured hippie culture went to seed, communes in the countryside were a significant option, and a great many of them—I
don't know that a census was ever done, but there were certainly
thousands—sprouted as a result.

That has not happened in the wake of peak oil. Partly, of course,
it's one thing to leave the city behind for a rural commune when
you're nineteen years old and can put all your worldly goods into
a knapsack, with plenty of room left over for dreams; it's quite
another thing to do that when you're forty and comfortably middle-class, with a family to support, a career to think of, and the
prospect of retirement sufficiently visible on the horizon of your
future that the impact of your choices on your pension is always
somewhere in your thoughts. Today's peak oil activists very often
resemble the second of these categories a good deal more than
the first, which goes a long way to explain the gaping difference
between the number of lifeboat ecovillages that have gotten onto
the drawing boards and the number of them that have actually
been built.

Still, this is only one reflection of a much broader problem,
which is that lifeboat ecovillages do not make economic sense in
today's world. However self-sufficient they may turn out to be in
the deindustrial future their planners envision, they are anything
but self-sufficient here and now, when they have to be built and
paid for. Nor is it at all clear how soon they will become self-sufficient if the future turns out to be a gradual descent into the deindustrial age, rather than the sudden plunge so often imagined
these days.

This is where the perspective I brought up at the beginning of
this essay—the difference between history as read in retrospect,
and history as lived at the time—becomes crucial. Seen in retrospect, the changes that will follow the decline of world petroleum
production are likely to be sweeping and global. From the perspective of those who live through them, however, those changes
are much more likely to take gradual and local forms. This will
make them harder to notice, but paradoxically easier to meet.

Imagine, for example, a scenario in which worldwide production of conventional crude oil drops by an average of 5% a year,

and other fossil fuels follow gradual depletion curves of their own. Especially at first, the gap can be offset with biofuels, tar sands, and other unconventional sources; yearly production totals for liquid fueld may even increase, though this won't include an accounting of the fuel burnt to extract oil from tar sands or the petroleum products used to grow biofuel crops, and thus will hide the fact that there's less energy available for other uses. The need to funnel an ever-increasing fraction of fuel into producing more fuel, coupled with expanding global population and the ongoing transfer of economic and political power from an aging American empire to its successors, will tend to drive fuel prices up; economic contraction driven by the twilight of cheap energy will tend to decrease demand, and drive them back down; factor in speculation, and you get wild gyrations in energy costs, coupled to cycles of economic boom and bust of an intensity not seen in the Western world since the nineteenth century.

All of this spells trouble, without a doubt. To rising energy prices and contracting economies, add the public health consequences of increasing poverty and the likelihood that the end of the American empire will result in wars as bloody and protracted as those that followed the decline of every other major commercial empire in recent history, and you get a recipe for massive change. I've argued in previous posts that these changes mark the first stage of the decline and fall of Western industrial civilization — the change from affluence industrialism to scarcity industrialism — and that it will be followed by further stages of contraction and social transformation, leading into a dark age several centuries long from which our successor societies will eventually emerge.

From the perspective of some future Edward Gibbon of the year 3650 or so, outlining The Decline and Fall of the American Empire as he strolls past sheep grazing on the mossy ruins of ancient Washington DC, all this will doubtless seem traumatic enough. For those who experience that transformation first hand, though, it will likely have a much different appearance. The young Parisienne whose image I invoked at the beginning of this essay, after all, did not go to sleep one night in the agrarian, half-feudal France of the Ancien Régime and wake up the next morning as a grandmother in the nascent industrial nation that France became in Napoleon's wake. Even those changes in the interval that brought her grief — any sons she had, for example, would have faced high odds of dying a soldier's death — would have been spread out over the years, part of a fabric of many other experiences.

Similarly, the unraveling of today's industrial society can be expected to follow a similar tempo of change. If the scenario I've outlined above is anything close to the shape the future holds for us, we can expect to witness economic, social, and political turmoil beyond anything the industrial world has experienced in living memory. We will all be attending more funerals than we do nowadays, and our appearance as the guest of honor at one of them will likely come noticeably sooner than it otherwise would. Most of us will learn what it means to go hungry, to work at many different jobs, to have paper wealth become meaningless, and to watch established institutions go to pieces around us. A quarter century or so from now, the world may be a very different place, but on the way there each of us will have had to deal with the same unoriginal challenges of everyday life we face today.

The continuity of history as a lived experience imposes requirements on planning for the post-peak future that haven't always been noticed. Like the imaginary lifeboat ecovillages that would make perfect economic sense in an imagined world, but can't even scrape together the funding to get built in this one, a good many of the plans and projects that have been discussed as a response to peak oil make no provision for the fact that people will still have to live their lives and make a living while they wait for those projects to justify themselves. Those projects that make good practical sense here and now, or at least place no great burden on the people who choose to pursue them, will be a good deal more viable than those that can only support themselves in a radically different world than the one we inhabit. In the weeks to come I plan on sketching out some outlines of how such an approach to the future might be crafted.

100: NO DIFFERENT THIS TIME

(Originally published 27 August 2008)

The chorus of "Georgia On My Mind" that has flooded the Western media with broken-record persistence for the last few weeks, though it's accomplished little else, has at least provided a few delicious snippets for connoisseurs of historical irony. We've seen the same politicians who backed the invasion of Iraq and the partition of Serbia insist that nations should not invade other nations, and that the territorial integrity of even the most jerry-rigged of today's nation-states must be considered sacrosanct. Even by contemporary standards of moral posturing, this is breathtakingly disingenuous.

The Russians, for their part, are having none of it. The insistence of Western powers on treating Russia as a conquered province, rather than a proud nation with valid security concerns along its own borders, made an explosion inevitable; goad a bear often enough, and sooner or later it will turn on its tormentors. The war in Georgia, furthermore, is much more likely to be the beginning of a Russian response than the end. When the United States raised the stakes by signing an agreement to base missiles in Poland, the Russian government promptly replied by promising a military response. It seems unduly optimistic to hope that this response will consist of harmless gestures.

Amid the gunfire and oratory, though, a point with much broader application seems mostly to have been missed. Fifteen years ago, by most definitions of the term, Russia was a failed state, with a government coming apart at the seams, a military on the verge of mutiny, an economy being systematically looted by Western business interests and homegrown plutocrats alike, and an impoverished population struggling to survive in the face of food shortages, collapsing public health, and spreading pockets of local anarchy. All this followed one of the most dramatic discontinuities in modern history, the collapse of the Soviet Union.

That collapse has been used as a central piece of evidence for the claim that other industrial nations, especially the United States, could face similar discontinuities in the near future. Uncomfortable though this suggestion might be, it has quite a bit of merit, and several recent books—Dmitry Orlov's mordant Reinventing Collapse in particular—have made a solid case for the possibility. Still, that case needs to be put in a wider context. Two decades on, Russia is no longer the failed state it briefly became at the bottom of the arc of collapse. Resurgent, resentful, and by no means unwilling to use its substantial natural resource base as a geopolitical weapon, Russia is back, and its return to the international scene as a major player is just as relevant as its earlier collapse.

The Russian trajectory from superpower status through collapse, contraction, stabilization, and recovery makes an interesting contrast, in particular, with the more common imagery of collapse that circulates in the peak oil community and elsewhere these days. While the events of the Soviet collapse were dramatic enough, the things that did not happen during that collapse are in many ways as important as the things that did. Despite economic collapse, for example, urban populations did not turn into starving mobs roving the landscape. Instead, as existing supply chains broke down, local entrepreneurs jerry-rigged new ones, and the backyard gardens of the Soviet era went into overdrive to keep most Russians fed even in the darkest days of the collapse.

In the same way, while Russia's social order frayed to the breaking point and entire regions became battlegrounds for warring criminal gangs, this glimpse into the abyss of a Hobbesian war of all against all was not followed by the vertiginous plunge into anarchy that plays so large a part in today's imagery of collapse. Instead, the great majority of Russians responded by moving in the other direction, backing the reestablishment of state power in the late 1990s even at the cost of individual liberty. Given the way that the rhetoric of democracy had been used to justify the looting of Russia's economy and natural resources in the decade before then, after all, it's hardly surprising that a common bit of Russian humor these days twists demokratiya — the Russian word for "democracy" — into dermokratiya, which works out to "rule by excrement."

More generally, one of the crucial lessons of the Soviet Union's collapse is that it was a self-limiting process. As bad as it was — and as Orlov and others have documented, it was much worse than anything Americans have experienced in living memory — it did not keep on getting worse; it bottomed out, stabilized, and then gave way to recovery. While Orlov's own take on the prospects of American collapse is much more nuanced — and, at least to my mind, much more realistic — it's very common to see this side of collapse roundly ignored in discussions of the fate of industrial society in America and elsewhere.

In these essays, and in much more detail in my book The Long Descent, I've suggested that this gap between the realities of collapse in history and the imagination of collapse in contemporary culture unfolds from the presence of cultural narratives that were originally borrowed from religious sources and repeatedly mapped onto secular history despite their consistent failure to anticipate the shape of any actual future. Recently, that claim has come in for some sustained criticism, ranging from suggestions that it misses the real points at issue to claims that it's simply a rhetorical straw man used to brush aside competing viewpoints.

It's not surprising that an attempt to contextualize today's peak oil debates in this way would come in for criticism. Still, it can be shown that talking about the wider context of those debates is neither an irrelevancy nor a rhetorical gimmick. Perhaps the clearest way to do this is to point to another example of the same phenomenon — one that, just now, shows the relationship of narrative to reality with unusual clarity.

Two or three years ago, it was quite common to hear people insist that investing in real estate was the opportunity of a lifetime, a can't-lose deal guaranteed to make the fortune of anyone canny enough to get on board. An impressive array of pundits, many of them equipped with Ivy League degrees, backed up these claims with books, articles, and seminars arguing that a new economic era had dawned and prosperity was within reach of all. The few critics who challenged these claims were denounced, often in heated terms, for failing to notice the huge and important differences that distinguished the real estate boom from failed speculative bubbles of the past.

Today, with housing prices in freefall and most of the industrial world's largest banks scrambling to stay solvent under a cascade of failed mortgage loans, it's clear that the pundits were wrong—totally, wildly, disastrously wrong—and their critics were right. What makes this relevant in the present context is that most of those critics did not make their case by examining the real estate bubble in fine detail. Instead, they recognized the real estate bubble shared a common cultural narrative with every other speculative bubble in modern history, from the Dutch tulip mania of the 17th century to the tech-stock bubble of the 1990s. They understood, as a result, that whenever anybody claims that a new economic era has arrived and some asset or other will increase steeply in value forever—no matter what the asset is, or what the circumstances happen to be—the proper response is to head for the exits as fast as possible.

This insight proved accurate because the arguments for a permanent real estate boom weren't simply the straightforward response to circumstances that most real estate speculators believed they were. The speculators, and the pundits who encouraged them, were projecting a cultural narrative onto the inkblot pattern of a temporary and, to start with, relatively modest rise in real estate values. That narrative isn't simply the generic conviction that real estate, or tech stocks, or tulips are destined to rise in price forever; it includes nearly all the rhetoric deployed in defense of that indefensible claim. (Read John Kenneth Galbraith's trenchant The Great Crash 1929 and then look through the overenthusiastic articles on real estate that peppered the popular press in 2004 and 2005, and you'll find any number of stock-jobbers' claims from the flapper era recycled, sometimes word for word, for the twenty-first century's first boom and bust.)

One of the essential claims made by the speculative bubble narrative, in turn, is precisely that "it's different this time," and the hard lessons of the past not only can but must be disregarded. Since any speculative bubble you care to name has some unique features — there had never before been a global real estate bubble, for example, and the ramshackle financial architecture tacked together to keep the bubble going was mostly brand new — it's always possible to defend, at least to the satisfaction of speculators, the claim that the bubble in question isn't a bubble and won't pop. Events refute that claim over and over again, but it remains unassailable in each instance until and unless the underlying narrative is seen for what it is.

My argument, basically, is that the narrative of total collapse is another example of the same kind. Since the late 19th century, when religious apocalyptic began to lose its grip on the Western imagination, a narrative as stereotyped and dysfunctional as the narrative that drives speculative bubbles has circulated in the industrial world. That narrative claims that the world faces collapse of a historically unprecedented kind: sudden, complete, and final. Like the bubble narrative, the collapse narrative brings its own rhetoric with it, and applies that rhetoric to currently favored catastrophes — peak oil, global warming, the Y2K crisis, nuclear war, race conflict, every major comet of the last century and a half, you name it — in the same way that the bubble narrative applies its rhetoric to the asset class du jour. Like the bubble narrative, in turn, the collapse narrative always insists that the failures of the past don't matter, because it's different this time.

The narrative of collapse shares another feature with the bubble narrative: it produces consistently inaccurate predictions about the future. Again, people have been predicting collapse in the terms of the narrative for around a century and a half, using arguments identical in form to the ones now being used to justify the same predictions today, and the results have not been good. This isn't simply a function of the future's obscurity, for other approaches — based on other, more nuanced narratives — have yielded better results. Arnold Toynbee and Oswald Spengler both made predictions about the cultural evolution of the modern West, for example, that have proved quite prescient. For that matter, the central argument of The Limits to Growth — that unlimited economic expansion would bring industrial civilization up against hard planetary limits in the first half of the 21st century, leading to an age of crisis and contraction — seems far more plausible now than it did when first published.

This reasoning undergirds my suggestion that it's crucial to recognize the collapse narrative for what it is, and set it aside as a guide to the future, just as anyone hoping to make sense of economics in the real world would be well advised to start by setting aside the bubble narrative. Insisting that it's different this time, and a way of thinking about collapse that has consistently produced false predictions for a century and a half is going to turn out accurate this once, just doesn't seem plausible to me.

I suspect Dmitry Orlov is right that America is facing a collapse along the same lines as the Russian experience. If that happens, though, it's just as likely that twenty years on, something like the rest of the Russian experience will have replicated itself as well, and an approximation of today's United States will have undergone some degree of recovery from collapse. Equally, other regions of the world will likely be experiencing their own trajectories through the twilight of the petroleum age, and some of those trajectories will include sudden downward jolts of varying severity. Over the long term, as I've suggested, all those trajectories will trace out a broad pattern of decline, but history shows that the decline of a civilization is a complex thing, and there's no reason to think that it will be different this time.

101: THE POST-PETROLEUM WANT ADS
(Originally published 3 September 2008)

The mismatch between the narratives of sudden apocalypse that shape so much of today's debate about the future, on the one hand, and the sluggish pace at which the predicament of industrial society unfolds in the real world, on the other, found a poster child of sorts last weekend. During the days of uncertainty before Hurricane Gustav's arrival on the Louisiana coast, some enthusiastic soul posted claims to the peak oil newsblog The Oil Drum that the hurricane would bring industrial civilization itself crashing down in ruins.

I was pleased to note that this announcement seems to have fallen on unsympathetic ears. The Oil Drum's forte is shrewd technical analysis, and its staff—if I may so describe the loose association of regular posters and commenters who give that excellent site its tone and direction—set aside such speculations and did their usual exemplary job, mapping out the oil platforms and refineries likely to be affected by Gustav and posting damage estimates that turned out to be fairly close to the picture now emerging on the ground. Gustav was a moderately strong storm; it forced the evacuation of nearly every offshore and coastal petroleum facility in the Gulf of Mexico, causing substantial short-term production losses; the long-term effects of the storm will not be clear for weeks, but all by itself, $30 billion or so in estimated damage piled atop an already faltering economy will certainly have an impact.

The difference between the fantasy of sudden collapse and the reality of one more localized jolt piling additional burdens on a stumbling society is well worth keeping in mind. Like the proverbial frog in the saucepan, those who think of apocalyptic collapse as the only way industrial civilization can break down are far less likely to notice the gradual changes in their environment that are leading in the same direction, just more slowly. It's as though, to shift stories, the boy who cried wolf was convinced that immense armies of wolves would suddenly swoop down and eat up all the sheep in the world at once, and mistook every whistle of wind in the trees for the distant howling of the wolf pack to end all wolf packs; meanwhile, practically under his nose, real wolves — scruffy, undersized, and quite depressingly few in number compared to the massed uber-wolves of the fantasy — were picking off a sheep or two each day from the fringes of the flock.

As both these metaphors suggest, the fixation on sudden collapse has practical disadvantages. If you're a frog in a saucepan, and the only idea of heat you're willing to consider involves all the water in the saucepan suddenly flashing into steam, you probably won't jump while your legs are still uncooked enough to do so; if you're guarding sheep from wolves, and groups of wolves numbering fewer than fifty are beneath your notice, your sheep are going to be eaten. In the same way, there are plenty of practical steps that can be taken here and now by individuals, that will likely make the slow unraveling of industrial society much less horrific than it might otherwise be. Most of those steps would be, or at least appear to be, irrelevant in the face of sudden global catastrophe, and in fact it's not uncommon to find believers in some such catastrophe dismissing these practical steps in exactly those terms.

Mind you, there are other reasons why those steps are easy to dismiss. Every one of them has a price tag of some sort, denominated in money, labor, comfort, convenience, or unimpeded access to the smorgasbord of distractions today's industrial civilization offers its inmates. By contrast, our culture's two dominant narratives about the future — the narrative of apocalypse and its twin and shadow, the narrative of inevitable progress — are popular at least in part because they push the necessity and the costs of change onto somebody else: the "they" who are expected to think of something just in time to keep progress on track, for example, or the supposedly faceless billions who are expected to hurry up and die en masse so that the flag of some future utopia can be pitched atop their graves.

I've talked about some of the steps in question already on this blog, but today I'd like to turn to something a bit different from those previous discussions: the question of how people will make a living during the long unraveling of the industrial age.

That's a question that has received surprisingly little attention in recent years, and a good deal of that neglect, I think, can be laid at the door of the apocalyptic narrative. According to that narrative, after all, nothing much changes until everything does; you keep on punching the timeclock at your present job until the day that civilization falls apart, and then, if you happen to be among the survivors, you step into whatever new role the apocalypse has ordained for you — subsistence farmer, tribal hunter-gatherer, protein source for the local cannibal population, or what have you. At the same time, the absence of a 9-to-5 routine on the far side of apocalypse is likely to be an important source of the narrative's popularity; I'm far from the only person who noticed, during the runup to the Y2K noncrisis, how many people predicting imminent doom seemed exhilarated by the notion that they would not have to go to work on January 2, 2000.

If I'm right and the descent into the deindustrial future unfolds over generations, though, that enticing prospect is not in the cards. Rather, the vast majority of us will need to earn our livings in a world that, while it will be changing around us, is extremely unlikely to change in ways that will make that process any easier than it is now. During the period I've described in other posts as the age of scarcity industrialism, something like today's money economy will likely remain firmly in place, though the household economy and other forms of production and exchange outside the money economy will likely play a steadily growing role. During the age of salvage economies that I expect to follow the twilight of the industrial system, money of some sort will likely remain in use on a small scale, as it does in most dark ages, but most day-to-day transactions will take place via barter or other systems of exchange outside the money economy; again, that's standard practice in dark ages. In both periods, though, people will work for their livings—and will likely work a good deal harder than many Americans do today.

Nor will their jobs be the same as the ones that employ most Americans nowadays. The flood of cheap abundant energy that surged through the industrial world during the twentieth century reshaped every dimension of the economy in its image, and nearly all the things we have grown up considering normal and natural are artifacts of that highly abnormal and unnatural state of affairs. Very few people in the industrial world today spend their workdays producing goods or providing necessary services; instead, pushing paper has become the standard employment, and preparation for a paper-pushing career the standard form of education. The once-mighty archipelago of trade schools that undergirded the rise of America as an industrial power sank with barely a trace in the second half of the twentieth century. I once lived three blocks away from the shell of one such school; it had been engulfed by a community college, and classrooms that once hummed with the busy noises of machine-shop equipment and the hiss of hot solder were being used to train a new generation of receptionists, brokers, and medical billing clerks

The postindustrial economy proclaimed by Daniel Bell many years ago, and accepted as an accurate description of economic reality since then, was never much more than a shell game. The societies of the industrial world were every bit as dependent on industry as they had ever been; they simply exported the industries to Third World countries where labor was cheap and environmental regulation nonexistent, and continued to reap the benefits back home. Those arrangements only worked, however, because cheap abundant energy made transport costs negligible, and systematic distortions in patterns of exchange pumped wealth from the Third World to a handful of industrial nations, providing the latter with the wherewithal to pay a very large fraction of their populations to do jobs that don't actually need to be done. As energy becomes scarce and expensive again, and the imperial systems that concentrated the world's wealth in a minority of nations are shredded by the rise of new centers of power, those arrangements will break down. As that happens, a great many goods and necessary services now done offshore will need to be done at home once again, and a great many professions that produce no goods and provide no necessary services will likely drop off the economic map.

Prophecy is a risky business at the best of times, but it's worth hazarding some guesses about the jobs that will fill the post-petroleum want ads here in America over the next generation or so, through the years of the Great Recession and the disintegration of America's overseas empire. Farmers are among the most likely candidates for the top of the list. By this I don't mean subsistence farmers in rural ecovillages — their time is much further in the future, if it ever comes at all. Rather, market farmers tilling what is now suburban acreage to feed the dwindling cities, and rural farmers producing grains and other bulk crops for foreign exchange, will likely be in high demand, along with support professions such as agronomists.

Engineers form another set of trades likely to do well in the generation to come, especially those who know their way around energy production and distribution and the design, building, and maintenance of low-tech transportation networks. In the not too distant future, rail and canal transport will have to take over much of the work now done by trucks, and energy networks will have to cope with a fractious mix of alternative resources, dwindling fossil fuels, and massive conservation programs. The people who actually put the plans of engineers into effect, from skilled machinists all the way down to the gandy dancers who lay the rails, will also be able to count on steady paychecks.

Another suite of professions likely to do well barely exists today, though demolitions experts, junkyard workers, and people who run recycling and composting operations represent tentative forays into the territory. A huge fraction of America's potential wealth in the postpeak years consists of manufactured objects that can either be refurbished and put back into circulation, or stripped of raw materials for reuse. When the electricity needed to power elevators and run heating and cooling systems is dizzyingly expensive when it can be had at all, for example, skyscrapers will be worth more as sources of refined metal than as buildings, and most of them will come down. On the other end of the spectrum, a great many consumer products that are now consigned to landfills when they break will be worth salvaging, repairing, and reselling once the cost of the necessary labor is cheaper than the cost of the energy and raw materials for a new model—a state of affairs that existed in America until the 1960s and will likely exist again within a decade or two. The salvage industries, as we may as well call them, may well turn out to be one of the major growth industries of the twenty-first century.

Other professions have their own possibilities. It's a useful exercise to locate a city directory from the first half of the twentieth century and flip through the pages, noting the businesses that existed then but are nowhere to be found today. Those that meet actual needs, however unpopular they are as career tracks today, are likely to be more viable and more lucrative in a deindustrializing future than many professions fashionable today. The pundits and publicists of our economic system never seem to tire of explaining that tomorrow's jobs will not be the same as today's, and I suspect they may just be right; what they don't expect, and I do, is that many of tomorrow's hottest jobs will have more than a little resemblance to the careers of yesterday.

Those people who make preparations now to move into such jobs as they come open will be doing themselves and their communities alike a favor of no small worth. These preparations need to begin soon—while the time, resources, and knowledge base for many necessary skills are still readily accessible—and this requires, once again, some sense of the way civilizations actually fall, and a willingness to apply that slow, stumbling, unromantic but realistic model to the events going on around us right now.

102: THE RETROFIT ECONOMY

(Originally published 10 September 2008)

I've suggested several times in these essays that the broad shape of the most likely future facing industrial society, at the end of the age of cheap abundant energy, can be sorted out very roughly into three phases: the age of scarcity industrialism, the age of salvage societies, and — if we are lucky — the ecotechnic age, when new societies based on sustainable high technology will rise on the ruins of our own unsustainable time. For a variety of reasons, any typology of this sort is easy to misunderstand, and it seems worthwhile just now to clarify what I intend to say, and what I don't, in proposing this model of the future.

The most important point that needs making, it seems to me, is that these three phases are to some extent ideal types, and the forms they take on the ground of actual history will be far more complex, messy, and idiosyncratic than the simple outline suggests. This isn't simply a result of the fact that none of these phases have arrived yet. The same thing can be said, after all, of the use of economic phases to talk about history that's already happened.

When a historian suggests that England embraced a mercantilist economic system in the sixteenth century, for instance, she does not mean that the English economy shifted gears all at once on January 1, 1501. Nor does she mean that the English economy in that century lacked important features of the older feudal-agrarian economy or foreshadowings of the capitalist economy that replaced mercantilism later on, nor that the English mercantilist economy was identical to all others. Rather, she means that the traits implied by the term "mercantilism" — an export-based economy geared toward generating a favorable balance of trade with competing nations, foreign policy initiatives pursuing overseas colonies and the expansion of naval power and a merchant marine, and the like — provide a workable sketch of the shape toward which the English economy moved over the course of the century in question.

The same rule applies to the phases I've outlined here. The transition from today's industrialism of abundance to the scarcity industrialism of the near future, for example, will likely be just as slow and ragged a process as the rise of mercantilism. Some nations — Russia, for example — have already implemented the political control of resource markets that I've suggested as a core feature of the phase; other nations have barely begun to move in that direction, and other features of the phase are just as unevenly distributed. For that matter, the 1950s-era American autos cruising down the streets of Havana today, repeatedly rebuilt with scavenged and jerry-built parts, show certain core features of the salvage economy already in existence in some parts of the world right now.

Thus the world of a hundred years from now, say, will include nations at many different points along the scale. It will very likely be dominated by nations that have embraced scarcity industrialism, while the powers of today's age of abundance will be the fallen empires and failed states of that day. Meanwhile, those nations that draw the short straws in the geopolitical lottery may already be well into the salvage society phase, mining the refuse of the industrial age to meet local needs and to pay for whatever foreign trade can still be had. Nations that lack both fossil fuels and valuable salvage, in turn, will either have fallen back to agrarian or nomadic economies or, given plenty of luck and the necessary knowledge base, may be pioneering the first rough sketch of an ecotechnic society. All of this will take place amid the turmoil of ordinary history: that unending and uneven rhythm of crises, struggles, and the rise and fall of governments and peoples whose embarrassingly premature obituary Francis Fukuyama wrote a few years back, and which tends to hide the slower and broader shifts in economy and subsistence from contemporary eyes.

Fast forward another century, when Hubbert's curve will

have finished its trajectory and fossil fuels will be rare geological specimens, and the powers of the age of scarcity industrialism will most likely have collapsed in their turn. Those areas with a wealth of salvageable scrap and the political and military savvy to hold onto them will be the regional powers of a world in which global reach no longer exists, while other areas — the modern conception of the nation-state will probably have fallen into history's recycling bin by then, to be replaced by some other form of geopolitical arrangement — will have only sustainable resources to rely on; some of those will likely have settled into some nonindustrial mode for the long term, while others may be building on the first tentative foundations of an ecotechnic system. All these changes, once again, will take their shape amid the rough and tumble of historical events, and may be difficult to track against that wildly variable background.

One implication of this vision is that appropriate steps for the present and the near future are not limited to those that have some obvious relationship to the scarcity industrialism of the near future. If, unlikely as it seems, any of my readers belong to the political, economic, or military leadership of one of the world's leading or rising powers, their attention will be, and indeed should be, riveted to the coming of scarcity industrialism; the nations they lead, not to mention their own positions of influence and privilege, depend utterly on how well they are able to manage that difficult transition. For the rest of us, though, a broader focus and a less limited toolkit has many advantages. The end of the age of abundance industrialism means the end of the trickle-down economy that provided so many economic benefits to the middle classes and raised the industrial world's working classes out of abject poverty. To some extent, while the political classes will be entering a new industrial order, those outside that circle may just find themselves passing directly into the world of Dark Age salvage societies. What this implies, in turn, is that the skills and habits of the age of salvage may be well worth cultivating right now.

One obvious example unfolds from the implications of the sprawling speculative subdivisions that surround so many American cities just now, in the aftermath of the late housing bubble.

For decades now, people interested in sustainable housing have focused their attention on innovative methods of new house construction: cobb and adobe, straw bale, and many more. These are useful and in some cases brilliantly successful technologies, but their application to our present predicament is limited by one overarching factor: here in America, at least, we already have many more houses than we need or can afford, and the economic system we use to pay for new houses is so badly broken just now that it may take a generation or more to get a new one up and running.

That being the case, the dream of sustainable Levittowns of cob-built, earth-sheltered, solar-heated houses will remain out of reach for a good long time. The possibilities before us are more limited. We can either struggle on with the hopelessly inefficient housing stock we have now in its current state, or we can learn how to rework our existing homes to improve their energy efficiency: that is, we can learn to retrofit.

The word "retrofit" was coined in the 1950s, but its common use is one of the legacies of the energy crises of the 1970s. During those years, a great many homeowners discovered that houses built to take advantage of cheap energy lost most of their advantages when energy stopped being cheap. At the same time, the soaring interest rates and stagflation of that decade made buying a new home a good deal less economically viable than it had been during the preceding years. Many people responded by figuring out cheap, effective ways to improve the energy efficiency of their existing homes. Insulating blankets found their way around hot water heaters, caulk guns traced lines around leaky foundation plates, insulated Roman blinds replaced fashionable curtains, and a surprising number of people discovered that it really is just as comfortable to put on a cardigan as it is to turn up the thermostat on a cold evening.

One of the less noticed phenomena of these same years, in turn, was the emergence of home energy retrofitting as a viable economic sector. In every American city and a great many smaller towns, contractors no longer able to find work building houses found a new niche installing insulation, storm windows, and solar water heaters, while hardware stores found room for a new section of home energy efficiency supplies. It was never a large sector, and its growth came to a sudden stop in the early 1980s in the flurry of political machinations that crashed the price of oil and threw away our best chance for a transition to sustainability, but it was one of the few success stories at a time when most American industries were contracting and most families' standard of living was slipping year after year.

Many of those same conditions are repeating themselves on a much larger scale as the world stumbles across the uneven plateau on top of Hubbert's peak. Despite the recent volatility in the futures markets, oil remains far more expensive than it was a year ago; one step down for every two steps upward still amounts to steady upward movement. The approaching Great Recession promises to make the stagflation of the Seventies look mild, but to American families it still poses the same challenge of having to get by with less. Thus it's tolerably likely that the same sort of retrofit economy will emerge in the next few years, as those homeowners who stayed clear of the blandishments of fast-talking mortgage salesmen, and keep their homes, find that they have no choice but to make the best of the homes they have.

The same considerations apply to other sectors of the economy. The auto industry is facing a similar transition, for example, as mechanics and hobbyists across the country turn used cooking oil into biodiesel, convert hybrid cars into plug-in vehicles, and equip bicycles and scooters with electric motors and batteries. Detroit's much-ballyhooed electric cars, when they finally get around to appearing on the market, are likely to find themselves eating the dust of thousands of ingenious retrofitters who, unburdened with the institutional inertia of Fortune 500 corporations, are getting products to local markets right now. These retrofits won't allow what James Howard Kunstler has usefully labeled "the paradise of happy motoring" to continue; on the other hand, they may well enable a great many Americans to deal with the downside of a social geography designed for cars rather than people, during the inevitable lag time while that social geography becomes a bad memory.

A great many more dimensions of American life are likely to need retrofitting in the years to come; nearly every aspect of our economy, culture, and politics depends on cheap abundant energy and will have to be rebuilt to deal with the new reality of energy scarcity. That will apply to little things—for example, plenty of home appliances now controlled by computer chips can be made to work with thermostats, spring-driven timers, and the like, given a little ingenuity and a willingness to tinker—and to much bigger ones as well. In a very real sense, given the sharp limits we face in the near future, our entire lives will need to be retrofitted to deal with the realities so many of us have been trying to avoid for so long. The first job of this foreshadowing of the salvage economy, in other words, will be to haul a viable future out of the scrap heap of the present, and get it back into some semblance of working order while there's still time to do so.

103: THE EFFLUENT SOCIETY

(Originally published 16 September 2008)

The latest round of convulsions in the world's financial markets has caused a great deal of panic among pundits and ordinary citizens alike. I have to admit, though, that I don't share their consternation. One benefit of living on a writer's limited means is that I don't have the funds to spare for investment — like most of my generation, I'll never be able to afford the luxury of retirement; unlike most of my generation, I'm well aware of this fact — and the lack of any personal stake in the fate of Wall Street makes it possible to sit back and watch the carnage with a certain degree of detachment.

Of course it doesn't hurt that most of the money lost in the recent troubles never existed in the first place. The wealth allegedly created by rising house prices, for example, consists of nothing more than the belief that a great many houses could be sold by their owners for more than their previous purchase price. Only a small fraction of said owners can actually sell their homes at any one time without crashing the price — this is, after all, how housing bubbles inevitably end — but while the bubble lasts, even the most theoretical increase in value is treated as cash on the barrel. The popping of the bubble, in turn, simply dispels the delusion that these evanescent gains are actually worth anything.

Still, my habit of reaching for the popcorn instead of the panic button when the stock market swoons has another source. It's sitting on a bookshelf a few steps from the desk where I'm writing this: a much-read copy of The Great Crash 1929 by the late John Kenneth Galbraith. The Great Crash is considered the definitive history of the speculative bubble and bust that ushered in the

Great Depression; it is also the funniest work of serious economic history ever written. Galbraith's wry humor and his superb grasp of economic process make it arguably the best introduction to the way that markets run amok and bring about their own worst nightmares.

As this suggests, bubbles rise and burst with tolerable regularity. The crucial lesson of Galbraith's book is that what's happening now has happened before. Dozens of times in the past, people convinced themselves that the world had entered a new economic era in which getting something for nothing was the way things worked. Dozens of times in the past, markets driven by this giddy conviction soared to absurd heights, then plunged back to earth with a resounding thud. Even the rhetoric repeats itself so precisely that you can time the market by it; when leading political figures respond to a market slump, for example, by insisting that the economic fundamentals are in good shape – an utterance that has already passed the lips of several American politicians, including John McCain – it's always time to head for the exits.

What this implies, of course, is that the end of a bubble is not the end of the world. This is not to say it will have no impact. A great many people who thought they had huge amounts of money, and who made dismally bad decisions on that basis, will have to deal with the consequences. A great many companies made the same mistakes on an even larger scale, and face bankruptcy in many cases and massive layoffs in others; the impact on employment levels, tax revenues, and many other aspects of our collective life will not be small. If the consequences are handled clumsily enough by government and the upper levels of business, the end result could be – well, since the word "depression" has been gently shepherded out of the realm of public discourse, let's call it the Great Recession, a period of economic contraction and retrenchment that could easily run on for a decade and leave America's economic and political life in shreds.

All this has happened before. Only the comfortable delusion of American exceptionalism – a belief that manages to ignore all of American history before 1950, and assumes that the second half of the 20th century will repeat itself in a tape loop until the end of time—makes many Americans think that it can't happen now, or that it won't happen again. Yet that same delusion makes it hard to remember that our society survived this same process many times before, and will doubtless survive it once again. Nations have perished for many reasons, but curiously enough, financial collapse is not one of them—a reminder, if one is needed, that money is not wealth, but simply a tool for facilitating the exchange of that real wealth that consists of goods and services provided by people for people.

Over the last two decades or so, I've had quite a few occasions to reflect along these lines. Beginning with 1987's Black Friday, which ushered in the current era of financial instability, economic crashes and convulsions of one sort or another have come at fairly regular intervals, and each time Galbraith's book has offered a useful counterpoint to the pronouncements of the moment. This time, though, has been spiced with an additional dose of irony, for a few weeks ago one of the used book stores here in Ashland provided me with a dog-eared old copy of what was once Galbraith's most famous book, The Affluent Society.

Some economists spend their lives writing in obscurity, and some become famous without seeing their ideas put into practice. Galbraith was not so lucky. Published in 1958, The Affluent Society argued that the United States had achieved a self-sustaining level of opulence to which the old laws of economic scarcity no longer applied, and that this abundance could support sweeping public programs to eliminate poverty and provide amenities for all. These claims became holy writ in mid-20th-century liberal circles, and drove most of a generation of American public investment, from Johnson's Great Society on down. In the process, it committed America to unsustainable public expenditures that set the stage for the economic troubles of the Seventies, and helped drive the backlash of the Eighties that replaced tax-and-spend Democrats with borrow-and-spend Republicans. By the time Galbraith died in 1997, he was treated by most economists with that dismissive fondness reserved for proponents of failed ideologies.

The Affluent Society has been much critiqued by those economic thinkers whose faith in the omniscience of the free market rivals a medieval peasant's trust in the miracle-working powers of the bones of the local saint, but it seems to me that the book's major flaw has been missed by these writers. Ironically, Galbraith in The Affluent Society fell into the same trap he critiqued in The Great Crash: the belief that economic reality had changed and the old rules no longer applied. He was quite correct to note that America in the 1950s had become stunningly wealthy, but he was quite wrong to think that this wealth was more than a temporary phenomenon.

Two factors gave postwar America the longest period of sustained economic expansion in its history. First, the accident of geography that put nearly all the battles and air raids of the Second World War on other nations' territory left the United States in a unique position at the war's end. Every other industrial power on the planet had had its factories and cities pulverized by enemy action; America, and only America, was left with its industrial plant intact. For more than a decade after 1945, as a result, America dominated the world's markets for most industrial goods, and profited mightily as a result. By the time The Affluent Society saw print, though, this dominance was already fading, and within another decade it would be a thing of the past.

Just as important as America's industrial predominance was its role as the world's largest producer of crude oil. In 1950, for example, the United States produced as much petroleum as the rest of the world put together. Its huge market share allowed it to prosper in the same way that oil sheikdoms are prospering today. By the end of the 1950s, however, the vast American thirst for cheap energy had turned the United States into a net importer of oil; by 1970, US petroleum production peaked and began its irreversible decline as America's oil reserves began skidding down the far side of Hubbert's peak. All this made the opulence of the Fifties a passing phase, and turned Galbraith's prescription for a better society into an expensive flop.

Behind both these failures, it seems to me, is the besetting sin of modern economics, the failure to ground economic factors in their historical and ecological contexts. The index of The Affluent Society contains no entries for "energy," "coal," or "petroleum;" while Galbraith briefly raises the issue of resource depletion at the end of his book, he presents it purely as a challenge that could be solved with an adequate supply of scientific talent. The role of contingent historical events in launching American society on its trajectory through affluence and out the other side gets equally short shrift in Galbraith's book. Neither of these faults is unique to Galbraith; they pervade the entire discipline of economics, which has consistently tried to impose timeless laws on the grubby historical realities of economic life, and has just as consistently ignored the role of natural systems as a primary source of economic value.

It's for these reasons, I've come to think, that a society guided by economic ideas treats pollution as an amenity problem, rather than a factor that can reduce the Earth's ability to support human societies, and treats resource scarcity as something that can be solved by investing more money, rather than a hard limit to growth. On a larger scale, it's for these reasons that the three-hundred-year boomtime of industrialism looks normal to so many people today. Looked at with an eye tempered by the cycles of history and the principles of ecology, it takes on a very different shape; its similarity to a speculative bubble is hard to miss; its dependence on reckless, unsustainable exploitation of half a billion years of stored photosynthetic energy, in the form of the Earth's fossil fuel reserves, becomes just as visible as the dependence of the late housing bubble on wild overestimates of how much future buyers would pay for homes.

Thus the last three centuries of industrialism have given us, not an affluent society, but an effluent one: effluent in the literal sense — one that pours out its waste on the living Earth that supports it — and also in the deeper sense of its Latin roots, ex-fluere, to flow out or away. By ignoring its own dependence on functioning natural systems and the nonrenewability of the resource base that allows it to function, it is causing the historic and ecological conditions that allowed it to emerge and flourish to trickle away out of reach. The history of industrial humanity may therefore turn out to be a repetition, on a much larger scale, of the same sequence of bubble and bust that is heading to its normal conclusion in the world's financial markets right now; it's pleasant to think that a future equivalent of John Kenneth Galbraith might someday write the history of that larger boom and bust for the edification of our descendants.

104: RX: DEPRESSION
(Originally published 24 September 2008)

By the time you read these words they will have been sitting on my computer for most of a week; the chance to attend the annual ASPO peak oil conference in Sacramento was too good to pass up, and I'll be on the road during the window of time I normally use to compose these essays. It's an interesting time to be second guessing the future, too, for as I type these words, the world's financial markets are in chaos. The collapse of Lehman Brothers, one of the longest established brokerage houses in the New York market, followed by the forced sale of Merrill Lynch and the near-collapse of insurance giant AIG, seem finally to have made it clear to the world's investors that the mountain of unpayable debt weighing on the global economy is a problem that can no longer be ignored.

Just how bad that problem will become is anybody's guess. Stock markets worldwide are down steeply but, at least as of this writing, not yet in freefall, and massive government intervention in the credit markets has staved off a liquidity crunch. Over the longer term, though, investments supposedly worth trillions of dollars are going to have to be written off, and companies that padded their balance sheets with those investments are now facing a scramble for survival that many will fail. An entire economy built around the exchange of exotic IOUs is coming apart at the seams, and the economic structures that will replace it are not yet in sight.

A growing number of voices are proclaiming that the current crisis marks the beginning of a major economic downturn; the word "depression," until recently taboo in polite financial company, is even being heard. Now it's worth pointing out that we have as yet no way of knowing whether or not things will get that bad. The 1987 "Black Friday" crash, which saw the Dow Jones Industrials lose 22% of their value in a single day of trading, was followed by the same sort of proclamations; so was the unraveling of the tech boom in 2000. Both slumps, severe as they were, led to relatively modest recessions. It's possible — though admittedly not very likely — that the same thing could happen this time.

Yet it also has to be remembered that not too long ago, economic depressions were simply a fact of life. In the 19th century, before government regulation restrained the excesses of the business cycle, major economic depressions happened every twenty or thirty years on average; most people could expect to live through two or three of them. The New Deal reforms of the 1930s, which restricted the vagaries of the business cycle, made depressions a thing of the past; still, those reforms were tossed aside in the deregulatory frenzy of the 1980s and 1990s, and unless they get put back in place, we will all likely have to get used to depressions again.

Counterintuitive though it may seem, furthermore, a serious depression right now may just be the best thing that could happen to the United States. I don't say this by way of passing judgment, or in the spirit of schadenfreude that seems to surround so many predictions of social catastrophe. Rather, a good many of the dysfunctions that are dragging America to ruin will be immediately unsustainable in a time of depression, and a certain amount of economic suffering now could spare the American people a far worse experience later on. Here are some examples.

1. The End of American Empire

Right now America is as addicted to empire as any inner-city crackhead to cocaine. We support the world's most bloated military, with troops and bases in more than a hundred countries, in order to enforce a global economic order that allows the 5% of the world's people who live in the United States to use roughly a third of the world's resources. At the same time, empires are costly pets, and ours — like every other empire in history — is becoming an economic burden our nation can no longer support; at the same time, the drastic decrease in US living standards that would follow the end of American empire is a political time bomb nobody wants to touch. Caught in that dilemma, the United States seems determined to follow the usual course of past empires, allowing its imperial commitments to drag it down.

A depression, however, would force the issue. In the midst of economic collapse, the United States would be no more able to maintain a global military presence than Russia was after its own collapse. The troops would have to come home — not just from Iraq and Afghanistan, but from the whole far-flung web of US military bases — and resources now being drained by the incubus of empire would be available for more constructive tasks, such as preparing for the onset of peak oil.

2. Energy Availability

A serious depression would also have predictable effects on energy use. The economic troubles of the 1970s and early 1980s, mild as they were by depression standards, played a noticeable role in causing energy use to drop sharply during those same years; when people don't have money, they don't spend it on unnecessary energy, and they are also likely to take conservation measures that cut into energy use even further.

By many estimates, we are only a few years from serious decreases in world petroleum production. Any significant response to this crisis will, ironically enough, require more fossil fuel energy — it takes energy, after all, to manufacture insulation, rebuild railways, and make wind turbines, and most of that energy will have to come from existing sources. If energy prices spiral out of sight, many such projects will be out of reach. A depression, on the other hand, will force down demand, keeping prices from rising and making it possible to build for the post-fossil fuel era. Public works projects such as the Depression-era Civilian Conservation Corps could also be directed toward energy conservation and renewable resources.

3. From Offshoring to Onshoring

Another likely result of a serious depression would be the re-birth of a domestic manufacturing economy in America. Right now the US economy produces very little but debt; that's the way the tribute economy of America's global empire works. The results have been profitable not only for the political classes but also for the middle class, which gets to buy all the consumer goods it wants without having to pay what it would cost to hire Americans to make them; the poorer two-thirds of the population, by contrast, has been hammered by predatory economic policies that replace well-paid factory jobs with minimum wage positions flipping hamburgers.

The global economy that made offshoring possible, though, will be an early casualty of a serious depression, and when the US either defaults on its national debt or hyperinflates its currency — and it will have to do one or the other of these, sooner or later, to get out from under the burden of unpayable debt — the unraveling of the global marketplace will be complete. Once that happens, goods and services for the American market will have to be produced here, and the rebuilding of domestic manufactur-ing capacity will follow. This will make it much easier for Amer-ica to survive the transition to the age of scarcity industrialism now dawning around us.

4. Decreasing Income Disparities

Meanwhile, the huge disparities in income that separate the upper third of Americans from the rest of the population will unravel. Economic boomtimes are always periods of increasing social inequality, because investment income is concentrated in the upper income levels; depressions are income levelers for the same reason. In the 1920s, income disparity soared to levels that were not reached again until the Reagan years; in the 1930s, as investments of all kinds plunged in value, the gap between the rich and the rest dropped to historic lows. The same thing is true today; essentially all the exotic investments that drove the recent boom were available only to the rich, who thus have earned the privilege of losing their shirts as those investments unwind.

The narrowing of income disparities isn't simply an issue of class jealousy; it powerfully affects the functioning of the economy. When the working classes have money, they spend it on goods and services, helping to maintain economic well-being. When the rich have money, they are more likely to invest it in speculative instruments that contribute much less. Speculation is a parasite on the economy, and it is quite capable of killing its host; that's essentially what's going on right now. An economy with lower income disparities is more stable and productive than one with the drastic disparities we have now, and we need a more stable and productive economy in order to deal with the instabilities that will follow the end of the age of cheap fossil fuels.

5. We're Headed There Anyway

The most important impact depression could have is also the one that most people will enjoy the least: most of us will have to learn to make do with fewer of the comforts, conveniences, and opportunities that we have all learned to expect. For the last sixty years most Americans have enjoyed lives of relative opulence, even as the resource base and manufacturing economy that made that opulence possible has trickled away. The last few decades have seen desperate attempts to replace these losses with exotic financial instruments and an increasingly strident imperial policy overseas. These measures worked for a while, but now the bill is coming due.

At the same time, the end of America's age of opulence comes as the world's ability to supply itself with cheap abundant fossil fuels is becoming steadily more problematic. In a world of scarce energy, the opulence of the recent past will no longer be in reach for anybody. The sooner we begin retooling our lives to deal with that reality, the better off we will all be in the future. A depression would thus bring about changes that are going to happen anyway, and would do it at a time when the world could still devote significant amounts of energy to the transition.

No matter what we do, the way there won't be easy. Hard times are hard times, and it's a waste of time trying to sugarcoat that fact. Still, an economic contraction beginning now — before peak oil has a chance to force the issue — could give us a crucial margin of lead time.

105: CASSANDRA'S VIEW

(Originally published 1 October 2008)

As I mentioned in last week's post, I took the opportunity this year to travel to Sacramento to attend the annual conference hosted by ASPO-USA — the acronym-impaired may want to know that this is the US branch of the Association for the Study of Peak Oil and Gas, the largest and most respected organization in the peak oil field. It was, as the Grateful Dead might have put it, a long strange trip, and ever since my return I have been wondering just how to talk about the experience on The Archdruid Report.

That the conference needed to be discussed here I had no doubt. Some of the presentations at the conference were profoundly insightful. Others were profoundly obtuse — and this very fact is worth noting, as a marker of the extent to which intelligent people with the best intentions in the world can still miss the most crucial implications of the systemic crisis facing the industrial world just now. Still, inspiration chooses its own path; it wasn't until I unpacked a book I'd found in a very different place the day before the conference, and flipped idly through its pages, that I knew how to say what needed to be said.

Perhaps the most surprising personal discovery I made at the conference was that while many people there had encountered these essays, most of them apparently thought that the word "archdruid" in the title was a cute internet handle rather than a job description. I am in fact the elected head of a Druid order, and in that capacity I travel now and then to events hosted by other Druid organizations around the country. It so happened that the ASPO conference took place just after one such event, a harvest festival for Sacramento's Pagan community, celebrating the autumn equinox.

That's where I was on the two days prior to the conference, celebrating the coming of autumn with Sacramento's Druids and Pagans in a sunny, pleasant park east of town. That's where I wandered into a bookstall in the row of vendors, and bought a copy of an old favorite, Bulfinch's Mythology; and it was as I paged through the volume, thinking mostly of the challenges involved in finding a place for it on my already overcrowded bookshelves, that I found a reference to the old story of Cassandra.

Most people nowadays have heard the name, but those of my readers who had what passes for an education in the American public schools may not be familiar with the story. Cassandra was a daughter of Priam, the last king of Troy; Apollo gave her the gift of prophecy in an attempt to seduce her but, when she refused him, put a curse on her so that nobody would believe her predictions. She thus had to watch helplessly as all her warnings were ignored and her father's city plunged headlong into the catastrophe of the Trojan War.

When Troy fell to the Greeks, the Greek commander Agamemnon took her home with him as a captive. In a scene portrayed with stunning force in Aeschylus' play Agamemnon, she foresaw his murder—and her own—at the hands of Agamemnon's estranged wife; no one believed her then, either, and captor and captive died together. The crowning irony is that Apollo's curse has lost none of its power today; more often than not, when someone is described as "a Cassandra" these days, the phrase implies that the dire events that person predicts will not happen.

In terms of the original tale, though, the whole cast of Cassandra's story was present and accounted for at the ASPO conference last week. The event took place in an expensive hotel across the street from the California state capitol, with skyscrapers filling in for the fabled towers of Troy, and King Priam played by Arnold Schwarzenegger, who did not attend the conference but prefers a penthouse suite in the same hotel to the less private comforts of the governor's mansion up the street. Lunches, finger food for breaks, and hors d'oeuvres for the evening receptions all tended toward the overly precious, and the uniformed hotel staff bustled about like servants at a Bronze Age royal court.

In this setting, the presentations and talk at the conference took on a surreal quality, as though the global civilization we were discussing—the one running out of cheap and easily available fossil fuels—was on some other planet. I'm not at all sure how many of the attendees took the time to connect the energy that provided climate-controlled air, fluorescent lighting, PowerPoint slideshows and overabundant snacks for the conference with the sinking lines on graphs that tracked our world's rapidly depleting oil, coal, and natural gas reserves. I'm even less sure how many of them traced out those graphs to their logical conclusions and thought through the likely impacts on their own lives; even in peak oil circles, this is surprisingly uncommon

Some of the presentations, certainly, showed no trace of such reflections. To my mind, at least, the most pathetic of them—and I use this word with its full meaning of "evoking pathos," not in its current sense as a general-purpose insult—was offered by Christer Lindstrom, a pleasant Swedish businessman who wants to solve peak oil by building countless millions of little four-seat computer-guided monorail cars to replace today's urban automobiles. No hint of the fantastic capital expenditures needed to build a new transportation grid in cities sprawled across three continents, no reference to the immense burden on the electric grid such a project would impose, darkened his presentation.

Instead, we watched pretty computer graphics and video footage of prototypes circling a little test track in Uppsala. In a world blessed with cheap abundant energy, some such thing might be worth considering. Still, one of the core implications of peak oil is precisely that the huge projects of the recent past—the interstate highways and the Apollo programs—are slipping out of reach as the surplus energy that made them possible depletes out from under us. Ignore this essential point, and it's easy to come up with technological fixes that will solve the peak oil problem; applying them to the real world is another matter.

None of the other presentations were quite so detached from the realities of our predicament, but some came close, clinging to a model of business as usual that has already been outstripped by events. Other presenters showed a clearer grasp of the situation Among them were geologist Ken Verosub, who provided a crisp summary of the fundamentals of petroleum science and the steep and ongoing decline in American oil reserves; David Hughes, another geologist, who put coal into the energy picture and showed the dubious figures behind claims that coal—currently being used at the same rate per capita as in 1910, and itself subject to drastic depletion—can replace our declining oil supplies; and engineer Robert Rapier, familiar to readers of The Oil Drum, who sorted out sales hype from reality in the biofuels industry.

What set these presentations and others apart from the more facile ones, at least from my viewpoint, is that the former recognized that we are long past the point of ready answers. The cry for solutions is a common one, and understandably popular. Still, thinking of peak oil as a problem we can solve by some grand project, or combination of projects, misses some of the most crucial features that define the crisis of the contemporary industrial world.

The essence of that crisis is that we no longer have the resources or the time to bring about changes in our infrastructure or technology large enough to make a significant difference on a national or international scale. We threw away that opportunity when the industrial world abandoned the steps toward sustainability taken in the 1970s. The quarter century from 1980 to 2005, when energy was cheaper and more abundant than ever before in human history, could have been used to launch the transition to sustainability, but that opportunity was wasted—along with all those billions of barrels of oil—and all the wishful thinking in the world will not bring either one of them back.

The Limits to Growth, the most insightful (and thus the most vilified) of the warnings issued during the Seventies, outlines the resulting predicament in detail. One of the central themes of that study was that constructive change had to happen while there was still a surplus of energy and other resources to fuel it. By the time significant shortfalls begin, all available resources are already committed to current needs, and any attempt to free up resources for some new project comes into conflict with the demands of existing economic sectors. The US government may be in a position to loan Wall Street $700 billion it doesn't have — in today's economic world, money is so close to a mass hallucination that it's not surprising to see it wished into being so casually — but actual resources such as fossil fuels, trained labor forces, and time are not so flexible.

The recent troubles set in motion by attempts to promote ethanol production show how the resulting limits work. Diverting corn to ethanol production boosted US gasoline supplies over the short term, but sent food prices soaring, sparking inflation across a wide range of products and causing a cascade of problems elsewhere in the economy. This was a relatively modest example, because ethanol production for motor fuel used existing pipelines, gas stations, and other infrastructure; something on the scale of an attempt to replace gasoline with hydrogen — which would require a completely new infrastructure from top to bottom — could draw down remaining resource stocks so drastically that, pursued with enough misplaced enthusiasm, it could drive an economic collapse all by itself.

Thus a focus on grand solutions is self-defeating, even when those solutions are not as obviously beside the point as Lindstrom's dream of a mini-monorail in every garage. We need to start with a close look at the resources that are actually available for change in the real world, with all its political, economic, and cultural complexities. We need to recognize that the apportioning of resources to any economic sector, however absurd it seems, has a constituency that backs it and can be counted on to fight against attempts to divert it. We need to accept that no one is likely to agree cheerfully to cuts in their standard of living unless they themselves see a very good reason for the change — and after so many decades of predictions of imminent doom by purveyors of apocalyptic fantasies, another round of warnings just isn't cutting it.

These hard limits sketch out the range of action available to today's industrial societies in the first years of the age of peak oil. They do not make a cheerful picture; Cassandra's view never does, and this is why clear assessments of unpleasant realities so often get pushed aside in favor of grand, elegant, and optimistic visions flawed only by the minor fact that they are unworkable in the real world. I don't claim to know whether this habit will one day bring down Sacramento's towers in flames, as it did the towers of Troy; still, as those towers shrank in the rear window a week ago, the possibility was hard to dismiss out of hand.

106: THE POWER OF THE NONRATIONAL

(Originally published 8 October 2008)

For the release of a book on the end of industrial civilization, it was certainly good timing. Over the last week or so, as my book The Long Descent: A User's Guide to the End of the Industrial Age hit the bookstores, the wheels came off the global economy. As stock markets crashed worldwide and governments panicked, I found myself wondering if the marketing people at my publisher, New Society, had managed to pull off the great-grandmother of all publicity stunts.

Now of course the crisis now under way has been building since the early 1980s, when politicians who had forgotten the lessons of the Great Depression threw out the prudent regulatory firewalls that kept banks from speculating with other people's money. Deregulation was the word du jour, driven by a blind faith in markets that did its level best to ignore the lessons of history, and each of the crises that followed — the 1987 stock market crash, the currency implosions of the 1990s, the dotcom bubble and bust at the turn of the millennium, and the orgy of delusional finance that drove the global real estate bubble thereafter — simply brought cries for more of the same deregulation that caused the trouble in the first place.

For a quarter century, those who recalled Charles Mackay's Extraordinary Popular Delusions and the Madness of Crowds and its many successors, and pointed out that uncontrolled speculation always ends the same dismal way, were told that they ought to shut up until they learned something about economics. Sober warnings from distinguished scholars were drowned out by a chorus of cheerleading, while less prestigious voices were pushed out to the fringes of the blogosphere. What is now painfully clear is that those marginalized voices were right all along, and their warnings could have spared us a massive economic disaster if the pundits and politicians who dismissed them had listened instead.

All this raises a question that deserves more attention than it usually receives: what makes a society accept or reject any given set of warnings about the future? At the ASPO-USA peak oil conference last month, a slightly more focused version of this question was much in the air. Several of the speakers expressed their frustration at the way warnings of global climate change have been picked up by the media and turned into an international cause célèbre, while warnings of the imminence of peak oil are still being dismissed as a nonissue by most people straight across the political and cultural spectrum.

It's a fascinating question, not least because there are at least two serious problems with the case for global extinction via climate change currently being splashed across the media. The first of these was pointed up by several of the presenters at the ASPO conference: the scenarios of drastic climate change being offered by the IPCC, the government-supported panel of scientists responsible for the most widely accepted predictions, assume that the world's production of petroleum, coal, and natural gas can increase steadily through the year 2100.

That's a problematic assumption, to say the least. The world's peak production of conventional petroleum happened in 2005; massive infusions of tar sand products and biofuels have kept the numbers from falling significantly since then, but with production at most of the world's oil fields dropping steadily, the IPCC's assumptions of steady increase are hard to support. Natural gas worldwide is expected to hit peak production around 2030. Coal is more complex, because all coal is not created equal; the most energy-intensive coal, anthracite, is all but exhausted already, and most of what remains is low-quality "brown coal," much of which will cost more energy to extract than it yields; by 2040 at the latest, the energy yield from coal production will have reached its limit and begun an irrevocable decline. By 2100, our total consumption of all fossil fuels put together will have fallen to a very modest fraction of today's levels, simply because there won't be enough left to produce.

Yet there's another difficulty with the scenarios of global eco-logical collapse being offered by activists and the media just now: even if the IPCC figures for production made sense, a 6°C increase in the Earth's temperature over a century is well within the normal range of variation for our planet. The latest Greenland ice cores show, for example, that at the end of the last ice age, the Earth's av-erage temperature spiked up 12°C in fifty years or less; similar jolts up and down, some of them even more extreme, have happened many other times in Earth's long history, and for most of the last billion years, this planet has been much, much warmer than it is now. Not that many millions of years ago, it bears remembering, alligators lived on the shores of the Arctic Ocean, and tropical and subtropical forests covered most of the planet.

This doesn't mean, mind you, that we can simply dump CO_2 into the atmospere and ignore the consequences. What counts as normal variation for the Earth is far more than a fragile industrial civilization can cope with, and the prospect of drastic food short-ages driven by wild climatic swings, plus a 50-foot rise in sea levels drowning every coastal city on Earth, should be reason enough for second thoughts. The point I hope to make, rather, is that extreme scenarios of planetary extinction have been widely accepted in popular culture, despite some very significant weaknesses, while the predictions of the peak oil community — which have a much more solid basis in fact — have been dismissed out of hand. Why?

That question cannot be answered without straying out of sim-ple matters of fact into the murky territory of beliefs and cultural narratives. Many of the critics of these essays, and indeed some of the people who have praised them, have dismissed this side of the conversation I've tried to start as irrelevant to our predicament. The problem with this sort of thinking is that it's only in the de-lusions of raving economists that human beings make decisions on the basis of a purely rational assessment of objectively known facts. In the real world, facts are never objectively known, and rea-soning is the willing slave of its preconceptions; we project our be-liefs onto the inkblot patterns of experience, and so understanding those beliefs is essential if we're to understand the forces driving today's choices—and thus making tomorrow's hard facts.

Look at the beliefs underlying the idea of catastrophic global climate change and you'll find, at their core, a story about human power. We have become so powerful through our technological progress, according to the narrative, that we are able to threaten our own survival and that of the Earth itself. The only limits most climate change advocates seem to be able to imagine are those they think we must place on ourselves; even if climate change leads to our extinction, we will at least have the glory of doing the deed ourselves. It's almost a parody of the old atheist gibe: to prove our own omnipotence, we made a crisis so big not even we can lift it out of our way.

Underlying the idea of peak oil, though, lies a different and far more sobering view of things, because peak oil is not a story about human power; it's a story about human limits. If the peak oil narrative is correct, the power we claimed as our own was never really ours; we got it by breaking into the earth's treasure of stored carbon and burning them up in a few short centuries. Despite the clichés, we never conquered nature; instead, we borrowed her assets and blew them in a three-hundred-year orgy of lavish consumption. Now the bills are coming due, the balance left in the account won't meet them, and the remaining question is how much of what we bought with all that carbon will still be ours when nature's foreclosure proceedings finish with us.

These differences matter, because the basic assumption of the climate change narrative—the belief in human omnipotence—is a core article of faith in contemporary industrial societies. It's so pervasive that its effects are rarely noticed, but it undergirds an astonishing range of popular attitudes and ideas. It's axiomatic in the industrial world that anything unsatisfactory is a problem in need of a solution, and equally axiomatic that a solution can be found for it. The suggestion that some deeply unsatisfactory conditions may not be problems that can be solved but, rather, are predicaments that must be lived with, is at once unthinkable and offensive to a great many people these days.

Yet this is exactly what the peak oil narrative suggests. If the world's conventional petroleum production peaked in 2005 and faces imminent declines, as all the evidence suggests; if none of the proposed replacements for petroleum can take up the slack, and many of them, especially the other fossil fuels, are themselves closing in on their own peaks and declines; if the technological revolutions and economic boom of the last three centuries were a product of extravagant use of these nonrenewable resources, not of such impressive intangibles as "the human spirit," and will not outlast their material basis; if, in other words, human life is subject to hard ecological limits—if these things are true, the narrative of human omnipotence falls, and a popular and passionately held conception of humanity's nature and destiny falls with it.

Now I have to confess that I find the narrative of human omnipotence, and the secular mythology that has grown up around it, utterly unconvincing. From the perspective of my own Druid faith, all that rhetoric about humanity's conquest of nature is absurd; it's as though a leaf were to daydream about conquering the tree that brought it into being, presently sustains it, and will let it fall in due time; the attitudes that lead us to picture ourselves as creation's overlords strike me as nothing more than an extraordinary case of egomania. Still, the fact remains that, in an age that has abandoned the traditional forms of religion without uprooting the emotional needs that religions meet, many people rely on these beliefs as a source of meaning and hope.

In turn, the peak oil movement's problems finding a hearing in the wider discourse of our time has nothing to do with a shortage of solid facts or compelling reasoning; it has both of these in abundance. Rather, I have come to think, those difficulties are rooted in the movement's failure, at least so far, to address these deeper, nonrational issues. If the peak oil message is correct, then the Great God Progress is dead; however misguided the faith of his votaries may turn out to be in hindsight, it's a deeply held faith, and those who rely on it to give their lives meaning and hope can be counted on to cling to it until and unless some convincing alternative comes their way. That their clinging may keep our civilization from finding useful responses to a crisis even more challenging than today's financial debacle is simply one of the ironies of our present situation.

107: THE FLIGHT INTO ABSTRACTION

(originally published 15 October 2008)

My decision some two and a half years ago to launch a weekly blog on the future of industrial society has had its share, or more than its share, of unexpected results. The original plan was to start a conversation about the future within the contemporary Druid community, which is not precisely one of the largest religious movements in America these days, and I would have considered the project a success if the blog's total readership topped fifty. That The Archdruid Report somehow failed to stop there still astonishes me.

Just as unexpected has been the impact on my own writing process. Some writers, like the hero of Edward Gorey's wry tale The Unstrung Harp, have orderly habits: on November 18th of alternate years, with the creaking predictability of an old orrery, you can be sure that Gorey's protagonist Mr. Earbrass will start a new novel. By inclination, at least, I fall on the other end of the spectrum, and it happens as often as not that I sit down at the keyboard Tuesday evening with no notion what my next post ought to be about. What astonishes me is that the muse has always come through, though there are times I can almost see her distractedly pulling down random volumes from the bookshelves of Parnassus, looking for scraps to toss me.

Very often, though, it's her more improbable tidbits that bring the most unexpected insights. I can think of no other excuse for this week's post, for the idea at its core came out of a moment of mental collision hard to describe in any other way. That moment arrived on the weekend just past, when I looked up from a paperback copy of Giambattista Vico's New Science to the surreal skyline of Las Vegas at night.

Now it's probably worth saying up front that of all the cities I've ever visited, Las Vegas is my least favorite: a garish urban cancer that apparently exists for the sole purpose of proving that it's possible to take a barren, scorpion-infested wasteland and make it into something even worse. I was there for a conference that took advantage of the cheap rates offered by a third-rate casino hotel, and would not have gone there otherwise. What made Vegas an unlikely source of inspiration that evening, I think, is that it takes modern industrial society's least laudable features to their furthest extreme; its utter disconnection from nature, its insatiable appetite for resources, and its promotion of distraction and greed as the highest goals of human life mirror the worst features of the world three centuries of industrialism have built.

That made Vico a particularly apposite commentator. Giambattista Vico lived from 1668 to 1744; he spent his career as a teacher of rhetoric at the University of Naples, and devoted his off hours to one of the great intellectual projects of his time. His masterpiece, Principles of a New Science Concerning the Common Nature of Nations, appeared in three editions of increasing complexity, the last one after his death, and was almost completely ignored for most of a century thereafter. When it finally found its audience in the mid-19th century, its influence was profound, and continues to this day.

The New Science, as the work is generally known, was nothing less than the first modern attempt to make sense of the laws governing history. Vico was perhaps the first modern Western thinker to recognize the parallel historical trajectories of his own society and that of classical Greece and Rome; using those as his two test cases, he attempted to sketch out "the course the nations run," the process by which a society rises from barbarism to civilization and falls back to barbarism again. With only two examples to work from, Vico inevitably jumped to many conclusions that don't always hold up well in the light of a broader view of world history, but some of his ideas are astonishingly prescient, and his basic intuition—that societies go through broadly similar stages on the way from their initial rise to their final collapse—remains central to any attempt to make sense of history on the grand scale.

Vico's argument is complex and difficult to summarize, but one of its core themes — the one whose relevance to the present struck me most forcefully that night in Las Vegas — is the role of abstraction. A wide range of social phenomena, Vico pointed out, focus entirely on specific concrete realities in the early days of a culture, and evolve toward abstraction over the lifespan of the culture. Law codes start out as lists of rules for specific cases, and broaden into statements of principles covering infinite variation in practice; words leave behind concrete meanings — how many people nowadays recall that the verb "understand" once meant literally "to stand under," in the sense of upholding or supporting something? — and take on ever more nuanced meanings; religion begins in the shattering impact of the numinous on individual lives, and diffuses into elegant theological notions disconnected from the realities of human experience.

So, too, economics. Vico barely mentions the economic sphere — as a scholar of rhetoric and law, his interests lay else-where — but the economic history of the Western world fits his scheme precisely. The cultures that clawed their way back up from the bitter dark ages that followed the fall of Rome knew only one form of real wealth, agricultural land — a habit of thought that still survives in the phrasing that calls land, and only land, "real property." The warrior aristocracies that threw back the last barbarian invasions from Europe and imposed a tenuous peace on their battered societies defined themselves by their landholdings; possession of a "knight's fee" — enough land to support a single armored horseman — was the one requirement of noble status in those days. Money existed in the form of coinage, but most people went from one year to the next without ever seeing any; nearly all goods and services moved through customary patterns of exchange in which market forces had no place.

The waning of the Middle Ages saw the gradual replacement of these customary economies with a new economics of precious-metal currency. Feudal tenure, by which farmers held the right to their land in exchange for specific duties defined by tradition, gave way to cash rents, and a significant part of the population moved away from the land to proto-industrial wage labor in the newly expanding cities. This was a step toward abstraction; gold and silver coins replaced fields of grain as the basic definition of wealth, and made way for concentrations of economic power far more extreme than anything the Middle Ages had seen.

Further abstractions followed. By the 17th century, banks began to issue paper receipts for gold and silver in their vaults, and these receipts could be exchanged like the coinage that backed them. The invention of the banknote was followed promptly by the practice of printing more banknotes than a bank's gold and silver reserves would cover, on the assumption that most of the notes would never be cashed in for metal; when word of this practice spread, the first bank runs followed. In the same way, companies found they could bring in capital by selling shares of their future earnings; the purchasers of these shares then found that their prices could be bid up or down, and stock speculation was born.

Fast forward a few more centuries, and we arrive at today's global economy, which consists primarily of the buying and selling of abstractions. The concept of wealth, which was once limited to the immediate means of production, and then shifted to mean the precious metal markers used to denominate the value of production, has now mutated into arbitrary numbers that can be wished into existence by a few keystrokes. When the US government announced a few days ago that it was investing $250 billion in the nation's banks, for example, that money did not have to be pulled out of some imaginary bank account in the national treasury, much less extracted from the dwindling productive capacities of America's remaining factories and farms; it was conjured into being by government fiat, in order to replace some even vaster sum of abstract wealth that more or less dissolved into twinkle dust over the preceding weeks.

What makes this pursuit of the abstract so dangerous, of course, is that abstract value is not the same thing as the concrete realities it once represented: green fields and grain in storehouses; strong muscles and the work they accomplish; or for that matter, factories, the resources that keep them running, and the products that come from them. These are real wealth; the layers of economic abstraction piled atop them are simply complex social games that determine who gets access to how much of this real wealth—and those games can become so complex., and so dysfunctional, that they get in the way of the production of real wealth. The flight into abstraction can proceed so far, in other words, that the abstractions interfere with the concrete realities underlying them.

This possibility became appallingly real in the week or so immediately preceding my trip to Las Vegas. The overnight interbank loan market—an economic abstraction so arcane that not even economists seem to be able to explain its function in ordinary English—froze up, and as a result stock markets worldwide panicked and crashed, erasing trillions of dollars in paper wealth in a single week. Desperation moves by the world's central banks bought a few days of respite, but today's trading brought another disastrous slump. (Connoiseurs of irony may find it worth noting that today was the birthday of economist John Kenneth Galbraith, whose The Great Crash 1929 anatomized exactly those speculative delusions that were rehashed in the last two decades and caused the current debacle.)

A stock market crash, it bears remembering, does not cause crop failures, labor shortages, or the destruction of industrial machinery. Its impact is purely on the fabric of economic abstractions built atop the real wealth of land, labor, and industrial plant. Yet that impact can be devastating; in the depths of the last Great Depression, the production of goods shrank to a small fraction of what it had been before the 1929 crash. There was still plenty of land, plenty of laborers, and plenty of machines, not to mention millions of families whose breadwinners would have liked nothing so much as a chance to earn money and buy products; the only thing that could not be made to work was the market where abstractions were bought and sold, and without its help, the real economy ground to a halt.

We are facing the same situation now, and official attempts to stabilize the economy are failing because they focus on the abstractions rather than the realities underlying them. The $250 billion just poured down a Wall Street rathole, for example, could have been used instead to pay for the rebuilding of America's rail network, with dramatic positive effects that would have resonated throughout the economy. Any such project would hire hundreds of thousands of workers across the spectrum of skilled and unskilled trades; locomotives and rolling stock would have had to be built, countless miles of track laid and upgraded, stations repaired or built from scratch, and every dollar spent on all these things would ripple outward through the economy, supporting businesses of every kind and refinancing local banks with deposits rather than loans. Projects of the same kind played a large role in helping many countries in the 1930s begin to pull themselves out of the morass of the last Great Depression.

Instead, the $250 billion has been assigned the task of making up for a portion of the largely imaginary wealth that has already evaporated from the balance sheets of banks. Abstraction has triumphed over economic realities, and the multiple impacts of that failure of imagination will be with us for a long time to come.

108: THE TYRANNY OF THE IMMEDIATE
(Originally published 22 October 2008)

One of the great challenges that has to be faced in any attempt to make sense of history while it's happening is the misleading impact of short-term trends. While the late housing bubble was still inflating, for example, soaring real estate values made it easy for most people to fool themselves into believing that it made sense to sink their net worth, and then some, into houses priced at even the most delusional levels. They had seen prices march steadily upwards, month after month and year after year, and that experience made it seem likely that the same steady march would continue for the foreseeable future.

The same mistake on an even more grandiose financial scale underlies the implosion of much of the world's banking system in recent months. The first generation of derivatives, credit default swaps, and equally exotic financial livestock netted huge profits for their original breeders; so did the next generation, and the next, and before long these dubious securities—valued with an optimism usefully summed up in the phrase "mark to make-believe"—accounted for a very large proportion of the paper assets held by banks, hedge funds, and the like. Because the financial community's recent experience with such things had been so positive, all too few investors glanced further back and saw what happened every time in the past that financial paper unlinked to sources of real wealth had been allowed to breed beyond the carrying capacity of the market.

The difficulty, as I've suggested in previous posts, is that historical change happens at a pace much more leisurely than textbook summaries suggest. Most people who didn't live through the opening years of the last Great Depression leave school with the notion that when the stock market crashed in the fall of 1929, the economy reached a full stop by the time investors stopped plummeting from Wall Street windows. In reality, it took more than three years for the economy to finish contracting, and scenery en route included a dramatic stock market rally in 1930 and some of the best days of rising prices, in percentage terms, that Wall Street has ever seen. At every point along the course of contraction, furthermore, financial pundits drew false conclusions from short-term changes. The resulting headlines have more than a little similarity to the ones that clutter the financial press today.

This habit of reading too much into short-term conditions has shown itself more than once in the recent economic convulsions, and guesses about the future price of oil — a subject of interest to many peak oil researchers — have been particularly affected. Earlier this year, as the price of oil soared to $143 a barrel, a great many people argued that it would keep on climbing to $200 or $250 a barrel in the near future. Now that the price of oil has slumped below $70 a barrel, the tide of opinion has turned, and some pundits are now predicting a continued slump to $50 or even $35 a barrel. These predictions seem quite plausible at the moment they're uttered, but then so did the idea that shares in dot-com startups would keep on climbing in value all through 2000.

The problem with linear projections of oil prices is that several factors unrelated to ordinary issues of supply and demand dominate the price of petroleum just now. One of the most important comes out of the crucial but rarely remembered fact that, while oil is priced in US dollars, most of the oil in the world these days is produced and used in countries where the US dollar is not the local currency. Since the value of the US dollar has been anything but stable of late, the price of these transactions in dollars has changed dramatically, while the price in any other terms has remained much more stable.

A barrel of oil for which a Japanese refinery pays 7500 yen, say, would cost US$75 if the dollar buys 100 yen and a bit over US$65 a few months later if the dollar rose to 115 yen. Has oil dropped in price? Only on paper, since the refinery's bank account changes by the same amount each time. Check out exchange rates, and you'll find that the period when oil spiked to $143 a barrel was also a period when the value of the US dollar dropped steeply against other currencies, while the plunge in the price of oil since then has paralleled a steady rise in the relative value of the dollar.

Even more dramatic, though, has been the effect of commodity speculation on the price of oil. Those economists who still insist that a completely free market will manage production and price with perfect rationality have apparently done their best to ignore the multiple monkey wrenches speculation throws into the market's machinery. The crucial point to realize is that the results of speculation, unlike most other economic phenomena, are radically asymmetric over time. It's worth taking a moment to understand how this works.

Consider a poker game in a tavern back room. Like speculation, poker is not a productive economic activity; instead, it is a means of exchange by which money passes from one person to another on the basis of differences in skill and luck. The results of a poker game, however, are symmetric — that is, in each game, the winnings of the winners are equal to the losses of the losers. You'll never see a poker game in which all the players win and nobody loses, or vice versa.

Yet this is more or less what takes place in the successive phases of a speculative bubble. While the bubble is inflating, nearly everyone wins; the difference between one tulip bulb, internet stock, or condominium and another during the first phase of their respective bubbles was simply how much money you would make from it, not whether you would gain or luse. Once the bubble bursts, by contrast, nearly everyone loses; if you bought tulip bulbs at the peak of the Dutch tulip mania, internet stocks in 2000, or real estate last year, the question a year or two later was not whether you lost money or not, but simply how much of your wealth was gone.

This is what makes unrestrained speculation so serious a threat to the functioning of market societies: it amplifies the extremes of the business cycle out of all proportion. On the way up, it boosts the funds available for investment as well as speculation, and encourages overinvestment in productive capital by fostering unsustainable levels of consumption; on the way down, it slashes the availability of investment funds, helping to drive the vicious circle of contraction and disinvestment that feeds a recession and can turn it into a depression. Still, damaging as these effects are, they are temporary; sooner or later, every boom turns into a bust; sooner or later, every bust bottoms out and yields to the first stirrings of recovery.

This is exactly the dynamic traced by the price of petroleum over the last two years or so. The price spike to $143 a barrel was driven by many factors, including the first stirrings of a decline in the world's production of conventional petroleum, but speculation played a massive role. For well over a year beforehand, financial pundits had been touting petroleum and other commodities as surefire investment vehicles, and those who got in early often made a great deal of money as oil prices climbed through 2007. This laid the foundations for a dramatic speculative bubble in the first half of 2008. Not that many years before, the idea that oil might break $100 a barrel was unthinkable to most people, and those who argued for it couched the idea in terms of a "superspike" driven by some international crisis like a US assault on Iran; what happened instead was a classic speculative bubble that zoomed far beyond anything the facts would justify, and then inevitably crashed.

The inevitable crash brought the price of a barrel of oil down more than 50% from its all-time high. It's crucial to remember, though, that the bust phase of the speculative boom-and-bust cycle is just as exaggerated as the boom. Generally speaking, speculative busts in the past have tended to drop proportionally as far below the long-term trend line as the preceding boom rose above it, and then revert to the mean. If, as seems likely right now, petroleum is nearing a bottom somewhere around $60 a barrel, the proportional mean between peak and trough—and thus the rough current location of the mean toward which oil prices will tend to revert—is a little above $90 a barrel. Under normal circumstances, this would be the price toward which oil prices would tend to return over the months to come.

The problem, of course, is that these are not normal circumstances. While the US dollar gains in value against other currencies, as mentioned above, the price of oil will dip accordingly; if the dollar begins sliding again, on the other hand, we can expect price increases. Furthermore, not all oil fields are created equal; some of the production brought on line over the last two years or so pays for itself only when oil is well above current prices, and the likelihood that some of these will be shut down or abandoned — to say nothing of the likely impact of the unfolding credit crunch on drilling and production — make a mockery of any attempt at exact prediction.

The governmental response to the credit crunch and the near-implosion of the speculative end of the economy has its own implications, and these also push the situation away from normal. In a truly free market, the bust would have erased most of the capital that had been available for speculation, and destroyed so many businesses that the survivors would be likely to flee the more exotic realms of finance for a generation to come; this is exactly what happened in the 1930s, for instance. In the present case, though, governments around the world have propped up investment banks and speculative markets with huge inflows of cash, preventing the wave of bankruptcies that would normally end a speculative boom as wild as the one just finished. One very likely possibility is that the investment banks will attempt to launch another round of speculative excess in order to improve their balance sheets before the political consensus that supports them comes unglued; if this happens, commodities are a likely target, and could soar upwards again.

Looming over all these factors is the arrival of peak oil. Since 2005, world production of petroleum has been locked into a narrow plateau that not even a 300% increase in prices could breach, and the most believable estimates suggest that by 2010, that plateau will turn into a slow and irrevocable decline. Many of the official figures for oil production lump biofuels and tar sand extractives in with conventional petroleum; since these latter are produced using large amounts of oil and other fossil fuels, there's a real sense in which some of today's petroleum production is being counted twice, hiding any early signs of the approaching contraction. The credit crunch and the low price of oil, furthermore have placed additional challenges in the way of the already difficult struggle to replace the world's rapidly depleting oil fields.

The obvious implication of peak oil is that the mean price of peak oil is likely to trend upward over time. The less obvious implication is that changes in the mean price may well be hard to extract from the chaotic data provided by an economy in disarray. Thus when peak oil advocates came to believe that the price of oil would soar upwards from $143 a barrel, they were running ahead of the date; when, as now, some of them are predicting a continuing decline in the price of oil for years to come, they are very likely doing the same thing. The tyranny of the immediate makes these short-term phenomena seem much more significant than they are.

My guess, based on historical examples, is that the price of petroleum and other commodities will find a bottom within the next month or two, stay there for a while, and then begin a ragged upward movement as renewed speculation cuts in sometime in the first half of 2009. Radical changes in the relative value of the US dollar could change that forecast, though the trends I've outlined might well still be visible if the price of oil is tracked in other currencies; a concerted attempt to reflate the economy by engineering a new commodities boom, that would have an even more dramatic effect, though the impact of rising commodities prices on a crippled economy could be dire enough that the boom might collapse of its own weight in short order. Over the long run, though, investments in energy conservation and less energy-extravagant infrastructure are likely to pay off in a big way—and the long term is what most needs to be kept in mind just now.

109: ARGUMENTS FROM IGNORANCE

(Originally published 29 October 2008)

For some time now I've been wondering how to bring up a certain habit of thought that, as I see it, forms one of the taproots feeding the contemporary crisis of industrial civilization. That it had to be discussed here on The Archdruid Report I never doubted, but in the midst of a cascade of dramatic current events, that discussion can seem very nearly beside the point. When the system of hallucinatory finance that propped up the illusion of American prosperity for a quarter century may be going to pieces around us, panic selling in commodity markets by speculators hit with margin calls is sending fossil fuel prices to lows just as unsustainable as their recent highs, and the wheels are coming off America's global empire, I find myself wondering, is it really a good time to go wandering off in pursuit of intangibles?

Then perspective returns, and I remember that it's precisely the intangibles, the states of mind and attitudes toward the world that form a culture's collective discourse, that define what it can and cannot accomplish as the age of oil comesto an end. As I've commented before, it's not technical issues that make our present predicament so difficult; it's the failure of collective will that keeps even the most grudging acknowledgment of our predicament, and even the most modest response to it, completely off the radar screens of mainstream politics in every nation in the industrial world. Until the "mind-forg'd manacles" of dysfunctional thinking are unlocked and tossed aside, constructive plans for the world after peak oil on anything past an individual level are wasted effort, since they will not be implemented by societies that cannot grasp the need for them.

I had a cogent reminder of this over the past week, when three efforts of mine to spark collective discussion about these issues — my book The Long Descent, a reading and booksigning at a local bookstore here in southern Oregon, and the most recent post here — fielded three responses that used very different arguments to make a common claim. A reader of my book emailed me to tell me he thought I was refusing to give proper weight to the possibility that new technology would save our civilization from the impact of peak oil; a serious young man who attended the reading came up afterwards to ask me what I thought about the possibility that the current crisis would drive humanity to achieve a new stage of spiritual evolution, after which we will easily replace fossil fuels with currently unimaginable resources; a new reader of this blog sent in a comment insisting that peak oil was an illusion manufactured by sinister elites who were suppressing inventions that would allow everyone to have all the energy they wanted.

Mind you, I'd encountered every one of these assertions before. Ever since this blog first started suggesting that the end of the age of cheap abundant energy was the natural and inevitable result of a human ecology hopelessly out of step with the realities of life on a finite planet, I've fielded a great many emails and comments insisting, basically, that it just ain't so — that one way or another, for one reason or another, humanity could have its abundant energy resources and burn them too, and can reasonably expect more of the same forever. The three responses I've just cited by no means exhaust the full spectrum of arguments advanced to back this curious claim, but they're good representative samples of the type.

Now it's possible to dispute each of these claims on their own terms, and I've done that more than once on this blog and elsewhere, but there's a very real extent to which this is a waste of breath. Each of them is what the old logicians used to call an argument from ignorance. They insist on the presence of a factor that can't be proved or disproved — a technological advance that hasn't happened yet, an allegedly imminent spiritual transformation that has to be taken on blind faith, or a conspiracy so secret and pervasive that it can manipulate everything we think we know about the world — to insist that we don't actually have to do anything about peak oil.

Such arguments prove nothing, of course; their only virtue is that they're impossible to disprove. I've come to think that this last detail is why they're so popular. It's a very charming social habit, dating back to the 18th century Enlightenment, to profess the belief that people come to decisions about the world by sitting down with the relevant facts, assessing them calmly, and then making a decision on that basis. I think most of us are aware, though, that few decisions are actually made this way; much more often, people start from the conclusion that appeals to their emotions and intuition, and then go looking for logical reasons to support the belief they've already chosen.

Most of the time, this is actually a good thing. Left to itself, the reasoning mind tends to run to extremes; it's because most human decisions obey the nonrational promptings of emotional patterns laid down in childhood that our lives have any continuity at all. This same process, averaged out over the millions who inhabit a nation, provides a sense of stability and identity essential to our collective life. Still, the emotions' habit of projecting the past onto the blank screen of the future can become a ghastly liability when the future no longer resembles the past in some crucial sense.

That's the situation we're facing now. Between 1980 and 2005, political gimmickry and the reckless overproduction of the North Slope and North Sea oil fields crashed the price of oil to right around US$10 a barrel — corrected for inflation, the cheapest price in history. During that quarter century of unsustainable excess, energy was so cheap that the cost no longer mattered; it seemed to make perfect sense to live in rural Oregon and commute daily by jet to San Francisco or Seattle, or to arbitrage wage costs by manufacturing consumer goods for the American market in Third World sweatshops and shipping them halfway around the world to their customers, or to build internet server farms, thousands of them, each one drawing as much electricity from the grid as a medium-sized town.

That world of unlimited free energy is the world in which nearly all of us in the industrial world lived until very recently, and it's the only world people who are under the age of 35 or so can remember at all. Thus it's not surprising that when people are faced with the claim that the future will be very, very different, they tend to reject the notion out of hand, and if the only reasons they can find to justify that rejection are arguments from ignorance like the ones I cited above, then arguments from ignorance are what they'll cite.

The problem is that at this point we don't have time to wait for hypothetical solutions to show up and save us. The Hirsch Report pointed out in 2005 that, to avoid severe economic disruption, any effective response to peak oil had to get started at least twenty years before the beginning of petroleum production declines. Any less than that, and the result is damage to the economy; the shorter the lead time, the worse the damage, and waiting until production declines actually begin is a recipe for crippling economic impacts that could make it impossible to respond to the crisis effectively at all.

This is dire news, because we no longer have the twenty years Hirsch specified; we most likely have only two years left. By most calculations, in fact, conventional petroleum production actually peaked the same year the Hirsch Report was published; apparent increases since then have happened because biofuels, tar sand extractives, and other alternative fuels that require high energy inputs have been lumped together with conventional oil; and the best estimates suggest that even with the alternatives factored in, production will face serious declines beginning around 2010. That gives us desperately little time to respond, and no time to spare for arguments that insist some unknown phenomenon will pop out of the woodwork just in time to save us.

There are times late at night when I find myself wondering if similar reasonings could have been heard in the Yucatan lowlands as the Terminal Classic period of Mayan history arrived. and the paired jaws of declining soil fertility and catastrophic drought clamped around the throat of Lowland Maya civilization. There were plenty of potential responses as the corn harvests began to fail, centering on a transition from corn culture to less valued foods such as ramon nuts, but ideological factors made such a transition difficult for the ahauob, "divine lords" of the Maya city-states, to contemplate; abundant corn harvests filled the same role in their culture as abundant fossil fuel supplies have in ours.

Thus, instead of facing the crisis, the ahauob responded by hoping that something would provide them with a way out of it. Some of them, anticipating America's recent neoconservative movement, went to war with other city-states to seize their corn supplies, while others offered up human sacrifices and built ever more grandiose temples in the hopes that the gods would take the crisis away. None of this helped, and much of it probably made the situation worse; one way or another, the result was a "rolling collapse" that, over a century and a half, turned the thriving Maya cities of the lowlands to crumbling, overgrown ruins inhabited by a scattering of survivors.

The idea that the cities of contemporary North America could meet the same fate is quite literally unthinkable to most people today, but then the Maya, the Romans, and the people of other collapsed civilizations all probably found their historical destiny just as unthinkable before it happened. There may be little reason to hope that anything like a majority can be helped to think the unthinkable in time to make a difference, but the effort seems worth making, and challenging the sort of arguments from ignorance I've described above might be a good first step.

110: HISTORY AND HOPE
(Originally published 5 November 2008)

I'd meant to talk in this week's Archdruid Report post about the peak oil conference I attended last weekend in suburban Detroit. Still, that will have to wait for next time, as last night's election results deserve a comment of their own.

Mind you, I intend to leave the political implications for others to discuss. The separation of church and state has been denounced by far too many people, on the left as well as the right, who have forgotten that it was originally put there to protect churches from political interference, not vice versa. It is nonetheless one of the essential foundations of the religious liberty that enables me to practice my Druid faith; one of the lessons I draw from this is that, as the head of a religious organization, I have the civic duty to keep my mouth shut about matters of partisan politics. There will no doubt be a banquet of political discussion in the months ahead of us lavish enough to satisfy even the most eager palate.

What I want to discuss just now, though, has less to do with the candidates in the presidential election now ended, than with the millions of ordinary people who filed into polling places yesterday and decided between them. All through the last two years or so, since Barack Obama began what seemed at the time like an improbable quest for the US presidency, one concern expressed repeatedly by the media and ordinary people alike was the possibility that the election would end up being about the issue of race. In a certain sense, that was indeed what happened — but in a very unexpected sense.

Some four decades after the assassination of Martin Luther King, the American people had the chance to judge an African-American candidate, in King's words, not by the color of his skin but by the content of his character—and by and large, they rose to that not inconsiderable challenge. There may well have been some who voted for Obama because of his ethnic background, just as there were doubtless some who voted against him for that reason; but even among those who voted for his opponent, there were many who did so not because of Obama's race, but simply because they disagreed with his policy proposals, just as if he were any other candidate.

That is an achievement of immense scope. It may just turn out that this nation has at long last begun to heal the old wound of racial hatred that has riven America right down to its core since the first days of European settlement. So deep a wound will not close at once; as Wendell Berry pointed out some years ago in a book too rarely read, the scar tissue of the racial divide reaches all through our national psyche, on all sides of the various color lines that still wall us away from each other—and from ourselves. Still, it's no little thing that a majority of voters in Virginia, the heart of the old Confederacy; in Indiana, where a quarter of all adult males belonged to the Ku Klux Klan a mere seventy years ago; and in this nation as a whole, voted for the first time in history to send a black man to the White House.

We have no way of knowing in advance what kind of president Barack Obama will turn out to be, or how history will regard his tenure. He's proven himself in a difficult campaign to be resourceful, energetic, thoughtful, and almost superhumanly cool under pressure, but many people have arrived at 1600 Pennsylvania Avenue with abilities like these, and some of them have crashed and burned. Many of the cards in the hand he'll have to play will be dealt him by decisions made months and years beforehand, or by circumstances nobody can control.

Still, a door has been opened, and I can't help but think that America will be better off from the simple fact that the highest levels of its political system are no longer exclusively reserved to the fraction of its population that happens to be white. Nor is yesterday's impact limited to issues of race; I think it almost certain that America's first woman president will be inaugurated within a decade, and it's even odds which of the two major parties will nominate her.

The broadening of the pool of potential talent this implies will be desperately needed in the years to come. It's unfortunate, though it was probably inevitable, that the major issues of this moment in history were barely mentioned by any party, major or minor, in the presidential campaign. Over the next decade or so, the United States will have to work out a way to stand down from a global military-economic empire it can no longer afford to maintain; it will have to find the money and the means to replace a mostly fictive economy based on the manipulation of baroque financial instruments with a real economy based on the production of goods and services for people; it will have to make good on decades of malign neglect inflicted on the national infrastructure on nearly every level, even as it struggles to convert a suburban landcape viable only in an age of cheap abundant fossil fuels to something that makes sense in the world of scarce and expensive energy ahead of us.

Few of the changes that will be imposed by these necessities will be popular. Many, in fact, will be bitterly resented, and none of them will come cheaply. We have wasted so many opportunities and poured so many of our once-abundant resources into a decades-long joyride that the next few years will almost certainly impose one wrenching challenge after another on a society that the recent past has left very poorly equipped to face them. Our history is among the heaviest burdens we face, because the habits we learned during America's imperial zenith are among the things that are most necessary to unlearn in the new and far more multipolar world dawning around us.

Still, I find myself feeling a bit more hopeful than before, for the burden of racial hatred was also profoundly rooted in American history and identity, and the verdict of last night's election suggests that it has turned out to be subject to change. I think of the difference forty years has made, from 1968, when an assassin's bullet cut down Martin Luther King and inner cities across America exploded in violence, to 2008, when a nation's ballot sent Barack Obama to the presidency and many of those same inner cities celebrated straight through the night. We live in a different country now, and the possibility that Americans might be able to rise to the massive challenge of the deindustrial transition has become just slightly harder for me to dismiss out of hand. Still, that turn of history's wheel is still ahead of us, and we will have to wait and see.

111: FACING PEAK OIL IN MOTOWN

(Originally published 12 November 2008)

The weekend before the election, as I mentioned in last week's post here, I went to Michigan to attend a peak oil conference: the Fifth Annual Conference on Peak Oil and Community Solutions, to give it its full moniker. In more ways than one, it provided me with a wide-angle snapshot of one end of the peak oil movement; since the peak oil story is as much about human responses to geological realities as it is about the realities themselves, the trip — and it was a trip, in several senses of the word — may be worth recounting here.

Archdruids are a bit thin on the ground these days, and so the five years since my election to that office have made air travel a larger part of my life than I'd prefer. (My carbon offset consists of not owning a car.) The drill is almost second nature at this point: pack light and fast, reach the tiny local airport well before sunrise, down a cup of tea and try to ignore the blaring television in the lobby while people going elsewhere file out onto the tarmac and head for turboprops and small jets. For entertainment, I had a volume of Gregory Bateson to read and a volume of thirteenth-century Latin sorcery to translate — in case you were wondering, yes, there are indeed species of geek other than the computer variety, and I plead guilty.

I spent the flight staring out the window at half a continent's worth of scenery while trying to fit my head around Bateson's take on systems theory or the tangled syntax of some scrap of atrocious medieval Latin, and spent the ride from the airport to the hotel in suburban Auburn Hills taking in glimpses of Detroit: long-abandoned factory buildings in ruins, gritty slums with colorfully named churches and every third house boarded up, posh suburban neighborhoods with ostentatious yards, huge office buildings breaking the skyline, and then the huge mass of Chrysler's headquarters complex looming up beside the freeway like a pharaoh's tomb. I half-expected to see an inscription out of Shelley's "Ozymandias" there:

> My name is Iacocca, CEO of CEOs;
> Look on my works, ye bankers, and despair!

Then we arrived in Auburn Hills. It was the sort of suburb built for cars rather than people, where strip malls crouch back from six-lane boulevards as though hoping that their vast parking lots will shield them from the traffic, city hall looks like one more corporate office building, and reader boards on the same restaurants you'd find a thousand miles away struggle to project a pallid imitation of bonhomie into empty space. The sidewalks—where there were sidewalks—had been there long enough that grass poked up here and there through cracks in the edges, but I never saw anyone using them but me. Drivers on their way into parking lots gave me goggle-eyed looks, as though they'd thought pedestrians were as mythical as hippogriffs. It was a strange place for a peak oil conference; given the equally surreal luxury-hotel setting of this year's ASPO-USA conference, I started to wonder if some hidden cosmic law requires the biggest possible contrast between the subjects of these conferences and their physical setting.

Still, Oakland University, where the conference actually took place, was pleasant enough, with buildings in late 20th century academic brickwork separated by wide grassy lawns that will make good vegetable gardens in another decade or two. By Friday lunchtime, attendees had started to gather, conversations sprang up, and a curious sort of temporary community took shape, centered on the challenges and possibilities of a world that doesn't exist yet: the world on the far side of peak oil.

If I recall correctly, it was Randy Udall who pointed out some time ago that the peak oil community divides along a fault line between "suits" and "sandals"—that is, the people who come to peak oil from a background in business, government, and the academy, on the one hand, and the people who come to it from a background in activism and alternative culture, on the other. The annual ASPO conferences are for the suits, while the Peak Oil and Community Solutions conference caters to the sandals; at the latter, community organizers, permaculture designers, and ecovillage residents greatly outnumbered university professors, petroleum engineers, and investment advisers.

One of the things I took away from the conference, oddly enough, is that the divide is a source of strength rather than a sign of weakness. None of the presentations at either conference would have been well suited to the other, which meant that between them, the conferences offered a much broader image of the state of the world's energy predicament and the options for dealing with it. In the space between the number crunching of the geologists and the visions and strategies of the activists, something useful takes shape. I think the peak oil movement needs both, for much the same reasons that vertebrates have two eyes instead of just one.

By nearly any calculation, though, archdruids fall well into sandal territory, and so it will probably not surprise any of my readers that I found the weekend in Michigan more congenial than that earlier weekend in Sacramento. High points included Dmitry Orlov's progress report, delivered with his trademark dry wit, on the stages of collapse; a slide show by Shane Snell on ecovillages he'd visited while touring North America in a biodiesel-powered camper; lively conversations with a couple of solar energy techs at the Green Living expo; and three trips to local green hotspots—a charter school's environmental classroom, a sustainable restaurant in a nearby town, and the Upland Hills Ecological Awareness Center, one of those classic Seventies earth-bermed passive solar structures with big round PV cells above the flat-plate collectors and a wind turbine turning lazily overhead.

This last was particularly welcome, because I came of age in the years when this latter sort of structure counted as cutting-edge tech, and I still have the same sort of nostalgic regard for it other people have for their high school football team or the music that was playing on the radio during their first date. If our society had made the right collective choices at the end of the Seventies, buildings and programs like Upland Hills might be as common as, well, shuttered car plants in Michigan are today; even after the mistakes of the last thirty years, the survivors of the species still have quite a bit to teach.

I don't propose to claim that all the presentations at the conference were useful or all the speakers inspiring; there were inevitably some slow moments and some ground familiar to everyone present rehashed for the dozenth time, and a few glaring false notes — in particular, a presentation on the Transition Town movement that was as glib and pushy as a pyramid scheme sales pitch, and succeeded mostly in replacing my generally positive take on that movement with hard questions I haven't yet been able to resolve to my own satisfaction. Still, questions are at least as worth taking home as answers, and often more so.

The night after the conference closed, as I packed for the flight home, I certainly had plenty of questions to take with me. Some of them — the next moves in oil production, the outcome of the upcoming election, the future course of the financial crisis on Wall Street and Main Street — had been buzzing through the conference all weekend. I'm not sure that others got asked at all, but they were implicit in everything we had been doing. From beginnings in a handful of internet sites and email lists a decade ago, the peak oil movement has grown and diversified dramatically, and has begun to find an audience beyond the small circles of worried professionals, green activists, and eccentrics who formed its backbone for so many of its formative years.

At this point nearly all the near-term predictions central to the movement in its early years have proved themselves, while the conventional wisdom that dismissed those predictions out of hand is much the worse for wear. As peak oil proponents claimed, petroleum production worldwide hit a plateau in the first few years of the century, and has never been able to break above it; oil prices have spiked well up into three digits; and the raw impact of energy costs has been implicated by more than one scholar as a trigger for the financial unraveling still going on around the world. The words "peak oil" are starting to find their way more and more often into the mainstream media and the wider public dialogue about our future.

The possibility of opening a window of opportunity for significant change, the theme of my main talk at the conference, can't be rejected out of hand any more. The question that I couldn't shake that night is whether any part of the peak oil movement—suits, sandals, or any combination thereof—is ready to deal with the possibilities and problems that will have to be faced if that happens. That question, too, I have not yet been able to answer to my own satisfaction. I hope other peak oil proponents are thinking about it too, because we may all have to confront its implications in the fairly near future.

112: PREMATURE TRIUMPHALISM

(Originally published 19 November 2008)

In last week's post, I mentioned in passing that a presentation at the 5th Annual Peak Oil and Community Solutions Conference at the beginning of the month had left me with hard questions about the Transition Town movement. A good fraction of the comments I received in response to that post centered on that one brief reference. This probably shouldn't have surprised me; these days, the Transition Town movement has become one of the more popular responses to the emerging crisis of the industrial world, and its spread has generated both a great deal of enthusiasm and a rather smaller amount of criticism.

I think both of those are merited. So far, at least, the Transition Town movement has done more and gotten further than most other responses to the crisis of the industrial age, and by any measure, some of its achievements are worth celebrating. The core idea of the movement is that a small geographical area — a town, a village, an urban neighborhood, or the like — can make the transition to a postpetroleum world by harnessing the ideas and efforts of local people. The plan, now available in book form, starts with a small steering group of activists who raise public awareness, forge alliances with local activists and governmental bodies, manage the process of putting together a consensus vision for a sustainable future, and finally midwife the birth of a plan, modeled on that vision, that can be adopted by the community and put to work.

It's an engaging project; still, two things give me pause. The first, frankly, was the presentation I watched, a slick sales pitch that started by proclaiming its subject "the most inspiring movement in the world" and went on from there. If you've seen talks put on by well-funded activist groups any time in the last few decades, you know how this one went: the global problem painted in black and white, the implied failure of all other responses, the inspiring story, the appealingly described plan, the clever double binds that give it emotional conviction, and the slow drift toward hard sell at the end. I'd been reading Gregory Bateson on the flight out, so the double binds were hard to miss — "The Transition Town process doesn't tell you what to do, and we're telling you to do the Transition Town process" was one of the better examples.

For all that, the presentation did what it was supposed to do. The presenter had a crowd of people around him after the lights went up, though there were also plenty who left shaking their heads, and I heard blistering comments in the back of the meeting room and in conversations out in the lobby. Still, it's one thing to generate enthusiasm and harness it, and quite another to be sure that the resulting energy is going somewhere useful. The Transition Town movement seems to have done a fine job of the first; it's the latter that concerns me, and informs the second of my two concerns about the movement.

That concern unfolds from the basic assumption underlying the project: that a contemporary community can imagine a better future and then successfully plan out the route there in advance. That's a popular assumption nowadays, and of course it's been basic to most ways of thinking about social change since the heyday of the Enlightenment more than two centuries ago. Most of the French philosophes whose ideas lit the fuse of the French Revolution claimed that a better world could be planned out in advance and then put in place by the collective will. Note, though, that this isn't how things turned out; what replaced Louis XVI's feeble monarchy was not the happy republic of reason so many people expected, but rather a parade of tumbrils hauling victims to Madame Guillotine and the cannon and musketry of the Napoleonic Wars.

To judge by recent history, we are no better at guessing the future than the philosophes were. We do know a few things about the most likely future ahead of us. We have good reason to think that the decades to come will bring sharp decreases in the energy per capita available to people in the industrial world, and in all the products and services provided by energy—which, in an industrial economy, means every product and service there is. We have good reason to think that the current human population is more than the world can support once fossil fuels run short. We have some reason to think—at least this is the point of view that makes sense to me—that these processes will bring the decline and fall of industrial civilization, along a trajectory like those of other civilizations that outran their resource bases. How these broad patterns will work out in the microhistory of a town or a region, though, is anyone's guess, and history seems to take an impish delight in frustrating our expectations.

Planning for the future becomes especially risky when, rather than starting from present realities and trying to figure out what can be done, it starts from a vision of a desirable future and tries to figure out how to get there. The gap between the futures we imagine and the realities that replace them, after all, tends to be embarrassingly vast. Many of my readers may recall, as I do, what the year 2000 was supposed to be like, according to accounts in the 1960s: manned bases on the Moon, undersea cities dotting the continental shelf, fusion plants turning out limitless cheap power, geodesic domes everywhere, and commuters traveling by helicopter instead of by car. One forward-thinking builder in Seattle during those years topped his new parking garage with a helipad and control tower in hopes of getting a jump on the competition. As far as I know, no helicopter ever landed there, and the garage with its forlorn tower was torn down to make room for condos a few years ago. How many of today's plans will face the same sort of disappointment? I doubt the number will be small.

Proponents of the Transition Town movement are gambling that their case is different—that this time, at least, it's possible to for a community to imagine a desirable future, put together a plan to get there, and have the plan succeed in what promises to be an uncommonly difficult historical period. An old proverb reminds us that a camel is a tiger designed by a committee, but Transition

Town proponents are again gambling that their case is different — that the sort of group process that usually fosters bland compromises based on conventional wisdom will manage this time to pick strategies that will cope successfully with the turmoil of a challenging future. They are also gambling, of course, that the effort put into making Transition Plans will create something more useful than the dozens of progressive energy plans that were adopted by American municipalities in the 1970s, and have been sedulously ignored ever since.

Is that gamble worthwhile? In many cases, actually, I think it is. Even if the broader agenda of the movement fails, some of its elements — such as encouraging people to relearn practical skills, and fostering local food production — will likely prove helpful in almost any future we're likely to encounter. What's crucial, though, is that the gamble be recognized as a gamble: as a venture into unknown territory that carries no guarantee of success. The value of the movement can't be known for sure until we see how Transition Towns weather the end of the industrial age. Since that process promises to unfold over decades or even centuries, any conclusions based on today's experiences are tentative at best, and it also needs to be remembered that a monoculture of paradigms is just as deadening as any other kind.

Back in the heyday of the New Left, seasoned radicals used to warn their juniors of the dangers of "premature triumphalism" — the notion, as popular as it was mistaken, that revolution was right around the corner and we would all soon be eating strawberries and cream in the people's paradise. The temptation of premature triumphalism seems to afflict any movement that attempts to bring about social change; the neoconservatives who are now stumbling toward the exit doors of American public life had a thumping case of it and, in the usual way, got thumped. Like so many others, they are finding out that announcing victory too soon is a great way to gain followers in the short term, and an even better way to lose them all in the longer term when events don't live up to artificially heightened expectations.

I hope the Transition Town movement manages to dodge that bullet. People in that movement have put together a toolkit that may well have broad uses as we get ready for the end of the industrial age; they are conducting an intriguing experiment, and early results look promising; they are understandably enthusiastic about their project. All this is welcome, but I'm still reminded of the old shopman's rule that you don't actually know how to use a tool until you are ready to name at least three ways it can be abused and at least three situations where it's the wrong tool for the job.

113: LOOKING FOR ROONG THISDARA

(Originally published 26 November 2008)

There have been many times, during the two and a half years I've been writing posts for The Archdruid Report, when I've found myself staring at a blank computer screen of a Wednesday morning, wondering what on Earth I can say that my readers might find even remotely interesting. Happily, such times have been scarce this November. A passing reference, in my post two weeks ago, to my dissatisfaction with a presentation on the Transition Town movement brought a flurry of comments asking me to say more about that; I did so last week, and fielded another flurry of comments as well as some lively critiques on other blogs.

The core argument of last week's post centered on the possibility of building a better future by deliberate planning, and many of the comments and critiques took issue with my suggestion that this is not only impossible but counterproductive. While most of these latter noted that they were participants in the Transition Town movement, the ideas they expressed in that context are anything but unique to that movement; rather, it expresses a consensus that extends through most of the peak oil scene, and indeed, most of contemporary society. Despite its popularity, though, this confidence in our ability to plan the future seems woefully misplaced to me, and the reasons that have forced me to dissent from the consensus may be worth discussing here.

Trying to plan a way out of the crisis of industrial society is an old habit. Back in the 1970s, when the challenge posed by the limits to growth was first showing up on the radar screens of our collective discourse, a great deal of discussion centered on how global planning could back humanity away from the brink; since then, similar plans on various scales—local, regional, national, global—have appeared at regular intervals. The durable Lester Brown, to name only one of these would-be planners, released the original version of his Plan B in 2003; he's now on version 3.0, and further versions will no doubt be forthcoming in due time.

A double helping of irony surrounds all this flurry of planning. If the crisis we face could be met by making plans, we'd have little to worry about; the difficulty is that making plans is the easy part. Go digging in the archives of most American municipalities and you'll find an energy plan drafted and adopted, after extensive citizen input, in the 1970s, calling for exactly the changes that would have made matters today much less dire: conservation standards, public transit projects, zoning changes to reduce the need for cars, and so on. You'll have to brush a quarter inch of dust off the plan to read it, though, since nobody has looked at it since the Reagan years, and not one of its recommendations was still functioning when the housing boom began in the early 1990s. A certain skepticism toward another round of plans may thus be in order.

Yet there's a second dimension to the irony, because the recurrent gap between plan and implementation is not the only difficulty that has to be faced. The assumption common to all these plans is that it's possible to anticipate the process of transition to a deindustrial society in enough detail to make planning meaningful. I suggest that this assumption is badly in need of a hard second look.

There are two widely held beliefs these days about how we can deal with the end of the age of petroleum. The first claims that we simply need to find another energy source as cheap, abundant, and concentrated as petroleum, and run our society on that instead. The second claims that we simply need to replace those parts of our society that depend on cheap, abundant, concentrated energy with others that lack that dependence, and run our society with them instead. Most people in the peak oil scene, I think, have caught onto the problem with the first belief: there is no other energy source available to us that is as cheap, abundant, and concentrated as petroleum; the fact that we want one does not oblige the universe to provide us with one, and so we might as well plan to power our society by harnessing unicorns to treadmills.

The problem with the second belief is of the same order, but it's much less widely recognized. Toss aside the parts of our society that depend on cheap, abundant, concentrated energy, and there's nothing left. Nor are the components needed for a new low-energy society sitting on a shelf somewhere, waiting to be used; we've got some things that worked tolerably well in simpler agrarian societies, and some promising new developments that have been tested on a very small scale and seem to work so far, but we have nothing like a complete kit. Thus we can't simply swap out a few parts and keep going; everything has to change, and we have no way of knowing in advance what changes will be required.

This last point is often missed. One of the people who commented on last week's post, a software designer by trade, pointed out that he starts work on a project by envisioning what the new software is going to do, and then figures out a way to do it; he argued that it makes just as much sense to do the same thing with human society. A software designer, though, knows the capabilities of the computers, operating systems, and computer languages his programs will use; he also knows how similar tasks have been done by other designers in the past. We don't have any of those advantages in trying to envision a sustainable future society.

Rather, we're in the position of a hapless engineer tasked in 1947 with drafting a plan to develop word processing software. At that time, nobody knew whether digital or analog computers were the wave of the future; the handful of experimental computer prototypes that existed then used relays, mechanical linkages, vacuum tubes, and other soon-to-be-outmoded technologies, while the devices that would actually make it possible to build computers that could handle word processing had not yet been invented, or even imagined. Under those conditions, the only plan that would have yielded any results would consist of a single sentence: "Invest heavily in basic research, and see what you can do with the results." Any other plan would have been wasted breath, and the more detailed the plan, the more useless it would have been.

The difficulty faced by our imaginary engineer is that meaningful planning can only take place when the basic outlines of the solution are already known. A different metaphor may help clarify how this works. Imagine that you suddenly wake up in a hotel room in Edinburgh. A mysterious woman tells you that you have been drugged and brought there secretly, it's now December 30, and you have to get a message to someone you will meet beneath the statue of Nelson in Trafalgar Square in London at midnight on New Year's Eve. If you succeed, Earth will be saved and you will get 100 million Euros. Since you know where you are, where you have to be, and how much time you have—the clock by the bed says 10 am—you can easily make plans and carry them out.

Now imagine the same scenario, except that the hotel room could be anywhere and you have no idea what day or time it is. Until you know where you are and how much time you have, planning is impossible. When the mysterious woman leaves, rather than heading for the door, the first thing you might logically do is to throw open the curtains. The results determine your next step. If you see the familiar skyline of Edinburgh, you can proceed at once to make and implement plans; if the vista before you is the clutter and bustle of an industrial town in Asia, you may need to learn more before planning becomes possible; if you see two moons setting in a pink sky above a cityscape of glittering domes, and the beings walking alongside the canal nearby have pointed ears and green skin, the one thing you know for certain is that the trip to Trafalgar Square is going to be interesting!

Now imagine the same scenario, except that the landscape outside has the pink sky, two moons, and alien promenaders, and the mysterious woman tells you that you have to get to the local equivalent of Trafalgar Square by the local equivalent of New Year's Eve. All hope of planning has just gone out the window. Your only option is to improvise as you go, try as many options as possible, collect tidbits of information, and attempt to piece together what you learn into a workable mental model. Nor will you have any way of knowing whether your model is right or wrong until you fling yourself out of an ornate airboat, sprint up to the giant bas-relief of Gresh the Omnivorous at Roong Thisdara right at the purple of the high red of twelfth Isbil past Eshrey of the rising calendar, and find the person you need to meet waiting there for you.

Conventional ideas of planning tend to assume situations like the first scenario I've just outlined, where the problem and the potential solutions are both clearly visible and the only issue is how to connect them. More innovative ideas of planning—and it's to the credit of the peak oil scene that these latter have been very well represented there—tend to assume situations like the second scenario, where investigation must precede planning, and then follow along the planning process to keep it on track, rather like a herdsman's dog trotting alongside a flock of sheep. As I see it, though, the situation we face at the end of the petroleum age most resembles the third scenario, where all we have to go on is a relatively vague idea of what a solution might be like, success or failure can be known only in retrospect, and improvisation is the order of the day.

The core fact of the matter, after all, is that what we are trying to invent here—a society that can support some approximation of modern technology on a sustainable basis—has never existed on Earth. We have no working models to go by; all we have, again, is a mix of agrarian practices that seem to have been sustainable, on the one hand, and some experiments that seem to be working so far on a very small scale, on the other. Our job is to piece something together using these, and other things that don't exist yet, to cope with future challenges we can only foresee in the most general terms. That leaves us, in terms of the metaphor, looking for Roong Thisdara when the only thing we know about it is that it's roughly equivalent to Trafalgar Square.

Now of course it's quite possible to imagine post-industrial communities and societies in a fair amount of detail, and several imagined futures of this sort have found enthusiastic followings. The fact that something can be imagined, though, does nothing to prove that it will work. It's not too hard to envisage a perpetual motion machine, say, or an investment that keeps on gaining value forever, and as we've seen, it's quite possible to build a substantial social movement around belief in the latter, only to find out the hard way that attractive visions and passionate beliefs can rest on foundations of empty air. I recognize that many people find belief in such visions a powerful source of hope in a difficult time, and I sympathize with their feelings, but if we allow the desire for emotional comfort to trump the need to face unwelcome realities, we are in very deep trouble indeed.

There is actually a third irony to all this. As mentioned above, the last round of energy crises in the 1970s saw a great deal of energy go into making plans. A great deal of energy also went into improvisation, in a wide range of fields — notably alternative agriculture, renewable energy, and home design and construction. The plans have been forgotten; I don't know of a single one that was still in force a decade down the road. The improvisations, on the other hand, have not; they include today's organic intensive gardening, permaculture, most of today's arsenal of solar energy methods, a range of alternative homebuilding methods, and much more.

Nobody drew up plans to develop these things, after all; the developers simply developed them, working things out as circumstances demanded, and shared what they learned with others as they went. Thus nearly all the ingredients being inserted into the current crop of plans for the deindustrial future were themselves the product of improvisation. It might be worth suggesting on this basis that our best option would be to skip the plans altogether and get to work on more improvisations.

All the points made here can be phrased in another way: a society is more like an organism than an artifact, and while artifacts can be planned and manufactured, organisms must evolve. This last point, though, presupposes an understanding of the difference between evolution and the ideologies that have sometimes been dressed up in evolution's cast-off clothing — an issue that will be central to next week's post.

114: TAKING EVOLUTION SERIOUSLY
(Originally published 3 December 2008)

Back in 1904, sociologist Max Weber proposed that the modern period was witnessing "the disenchantment of the world"—a process which traditional mythic ideas that wove meaning into human experience were being replaced by the alienating and dehumanizing worldview of materialist science. There's some truth to Weber's thesis, but I'm not sure he anticipated the inevitable backlash: the Procrustean stretching and lopping of scientific ideas in the popular imagination that has turned many of them into substitute myths.

One example that has been much on my mind of late is the way the theory of evolution has been manhandled into a surrogate mythology. The reason it's been on my mind is simple enough: whenever I discuss peak oil at a lecture, book signing, or some other public setting, it's a safe bet that someone will raise a hand and ask what I think about the possibility that the approaching crisis is part of our transition to a new evolutionary level. I am always left wondering what to say in response, because this sort of question is almost always rooted in the notion that evolution is a linear movement that leads onward and upward through a series of distinct stages or levels—and this notion is a pretty fair misstatement of the way evolution takes place in nature.

Few things in the history of ideas are quite so interesting as the way that new discoveries get harnessed in the service of old obsessions. When X-rays were first detected in 1895, for example, one of the first results was panic over the possibility that the new rays might make it possible to see through clothing; the New Jersey state legislature actually debated a bill to ban the use of X-rays in opera glasses. Wildly inaccurate as it was, this notion was root-ed in profound fears about sexuality, and so it took many decades to dispell — when I was a child, ads in comic books still claimed to sell "X-ray glasses" that would let you see people naked.

Something not that different happened to the theory of evo-lution, and thus nearly all of today's popular notions about evolution are shrapnel from the head-on collision between Dar-win's theory and the obsessions of the era in which that theory emerged. Social class rather than sex was the driving force here; as religious justifications for the English caste system faltered, the manufacture of scientific justifications for social hierarchy became a growth industry, and by the time the ink was dry on the first copies of "The Origin of Species," evolution was already being drafted into service in this dubious cause. The resulting belief sys-tem was very nearly a parody of George Orwell's "Animal Farm" in advance — all living things evolve, but some are more evolved than others.

Now of course this is nonsense. A human being, a gecko, a dandelion, and a single-celled blue-green alga are all equally evolved — that is, they have all been shaped to the same degree by the pressures of their environment, and their ancestors have all undergone an equal amount of natural selection. We think of humans as "more evolved" than blue-green alga because Victori-an Social Darwinists such as Herbert Spencer engaged in concep-tual sleight of hand, transforming the amorphous outward surge of life toward available niches into a ladder of social status, with English gentlemen at the top level and everybody and everything else slotted into place further down. The concept of evolutionary stages or levels was essential to this conjurer's act, since it allowed social barriers between classes to be mapped onto the biological world.

In nature, though, evolution has no levels, it just has adapta-tions. There is no straight line of progress along which living things can be ranked. Instead, evolutionary lineages splay outward like the branches of an unruly shrub. Sometimes those branches take unexpected turns, but these evolutionary breakthroughs can no more be ranked in an ascending hierarchy than organisms can.

They move outward into new niches, rather than upward to some imagined goal. There are any number of examples from nature; the one I want to use here is the evolution of bats.

The ancestors of the first bats were shrewlike, insect-eating nocturnal mammals, related to early primates, who scampered through the forest canopies of the Eocene around 60 million years ago. For animals that live in trees, the risk of falling is a constant source of evolutionary pressure, and adaptations that will help manage that danger will likely spread through a population; that's how sloths got their claws, New World monkeys got prehensile tails, and many animals of past and present got extra skin that functions as a parachute. If the extra skin bridges the gap between forelegs and the hindlegs, the most common adaptation, you get the ability to glide, like flying squirrels, colugoes, and the like; you've got a viable adaptation, and there you stop.

If the extra skin is mostly on and around the forelimbs, though, you've just jumped through the door into a new world, because you can control your glide much more precisely, and you can put muscle into the movements—in other words, you can begin to fly. Once you can do better than a controlled fall, furthermore, the trillions of tasty insects flitting through the forest air are on your menu, and the better you can fly, the more you can catch. The result is ferocious evolutionary pressure toward improved flight skills, and in a few hundred thousand generations, you've got agile flyers. That's what happened to bats, as it happened some 200 million years earlier to the ancestors of the pterodactyls.

By 55 million years ago, bats almost identical to today's insect-eating bats were darting through the Eocene skies. Sonar seems to have taken a while to evolve, and some offshoots of the family—the big fruit bats and flying foxes, for example—took even longer, but the basic adaptations were set and, to the discomfiture of countless generations of mosquitoes and moths, have remained ever since. As evolutionary breakthroughs go, the leap into flight was a massive success; bats are the second most numerous of mammal orders, exceeded only by the rodents, but it's impossible to fit the breakthrough that created them into any linear scheme.

Applying an ecological concept to human social systems always takes tinkering, but there are good reasons to accept the idea that societies are capable of evolution; like populations of other living things, human communities face pressures from their environments, and adapt or perish in response. Here again, though, the evolutionary process moves outward in all directions rather than ascending an imaginary hierarchy of levels. Hunter-gatherer systems seem to have been the original form of human society, but other forms branched off as adaptations opened doors to possibilities that were likely as appealing at the time as the bug-filled night sky must have been to the first clumsily flapping proto-bats.

Where large herbivores could be tamed, therefore, nomadic herding societies came into being; where many food plants could be raised in intensive gardens, tribal horticultural societies were born; where extensive fields of seed-bearing grasses offered the best option for survival, agrarian societies took shape. As it turned out, grains could be bred to yield large surpluses that could be transported and stored, and so the agrarian system opened the door to large-scale divisions of labor and the rise of cities. These in turn made complex material culture possible, and ultimately drove the creation of the machines that broke into the Earth's stockpiles of fossil carbon and gave the modern world its three centuries of exuberance.

Thus industrial society is not "more evolved" than other societies, for for that matter "less evolved." It was simply the most successful adaptation to the evolutionary pressures that opened up once fossil fuel energy had been tapped, and it outcompeted other systems in something of the same way that an invasive exotic outcompetes less robust native organisms. As fossil fuels deplete and climate change unfolds, the balance of evolutionary pressures is shifting, and as the new reality of limits takes hold, selection will favor those systems that are better adapted to the new ecological constraints of global climate instability, energy scarcity, and resource shortage.

The fact that those new systems are better adapted to new realities, however, does not free them from the human condition. This is where the rubber meets the road, because the people who ask me about the prospects of a new evolutionary level are rarely asking whether the societies of the future will be better adapted to an environment of resource scarcity. They are generally asking whether societies on the other side of an imagined evolutionary leap will be free from problems such as poverty, war, and environmental destruction.

The best way to assess this, it seems to me, is to consider what happened the last time human social evolution yielded a breakthrough to a new way of living in the world: that is, the rise of industrial societies beginning around 1750. Agrarian societies suffered from poverty, war, and environmental destruction, and so did all the other "evolutionary levels" or, rather, adaptations, right back to the hunter-gatherers. Many hunter-gatherers among the First Nations in North America, for example, had sharp social inequalities, a busy slave trade, and a long history of fierce tribal wars. Their ecological relationships were less problematic, since those native societies that failed to find a balance with nature, such as the Mound Builders and the people of Chaco Canyon, collapsed long before 1492.

Just as bats faced the same experiences of hunger, social squabbles, and the unfriendly attentions of predators as their ancestors, the societies that took up industrialism experienced poverty, war, and environmental destruction just like earlier societies, and it's hard to think of a good reason why the new societies that emerge in response to the evolutionary pressures of the deindustrial age should be exempt from the same troubles. Evolutionary adaptations can make things easier for living things — plenty of predators in the Eocene must have been discomfited when bats evolved the ability to flutter away to safety — but no living thing is exempt from the balances of the natural world. It's a mistake, in other words, to see evolution as a movement toward Utopia.

When I've tried to explain any of the above in public, though, someone — and it's not always the same someone who asked the original question — usually insists that this may be how biological evolution works, but spiritual evolution is different. Some of my readers just now may have come up with the same objection. All I can say in response is I know of none of the world's great spiritual traditions that would approve the claim that people living extravagant lifestyles of wealth and privilege—this is, after all, a fair description of life in modern industrial societies from the standpoint of the rest of human experience—can expect a sudden leap to an even more comfortable and convenient life, just because they happen to want it, and would find it a useful way to avoid dealing with the consequences of their own shortsighted choices.

This may seem unduly harsh. Still, the notion that an evolutionary leap will extract us from the mess we've made for ourselves is as much a distortion of the realities of the evolutionary process as any Social Darwinist screed. If people want to believe that a miracle will rescue them from the predicament of industrial society, they have every right to their faith, but it would confuse communication a little less to call it a miracle, instead of trying to wrap it in the borrowed prestige of Darwin's theory. Perhaps it's the bias instilled by my own Druid faith, furthermore, but it seems to me that if we are going to use evolution as a metaphor, we need to start by taking evolution seriously, rather than imposing our own fantasies on the very different stories that nature is telling us.

115: DISSENSUS AND ORGANIC PROCESS

(Originally published 10 December 2008)

In bringing up the vexed relationship between evolution as it happens in nature, on the one hand, and the ways the concept of evolution has been redefined in current ideologies on the other, last week's Archdruid Report post dipped a tentative toe into some very deep and murky waters. Over a century or more, ideas and metaphors from the natural sciences have become potent factors in the public life of the western world; terms such as "natural," "organic," and, yes, "evolution" have been caught up by any number of players in the scrimmage of contemporary culture, and more often than not have come out much the worse for wear.

There's no shortage of ingenious ways to misuse concepts such as these, but one in particular has had a pervasive presence in our collective dialogue. Perhaps the best way to show it at work is to track the use of natural concepts in one of the towering creative minds of the twentieth century, American architect Frank Lloyd Wright.

Full disclosure probably requires me to admit up front that I'm a fan of Wright's work, and not only because he was one of the handful of first-rate creative talents to have been influenced by the modern Druid tradition. In his quest for an organic architecture—notice the concept lifted from the life sciences—he reshaped the vocabulary of space and form in ways that are still being explored by architects today, and he also produced rather more than his share of stunningly beautiful buildings.

Still, there are few geniuses whose works are without flaws, and Wright was not one of them. Stewart Brand of Whole Earth Catalog fame has set out the case for the prosecution in his useful book How Buildings Learn. To begin with, Brand points out, all Wright's roofs leak. This may seem like a small thing, but since the basic purpose of shelter is to keep weather out, and it's not actually that difficult to design a watertight roof, Wright's failure to accomplish this fundamental requirement is not a good sign.

More generally, Wright paid close attention to the esthetic qualities of building materials, but not always to their structural strength; the results included a fair number of splendid buildings that could not hold up to normal wear and tear, or in some cases, the simple force of gravity. Thus a great many Wright buildings have had to be torn down since his time, and others linger on as museums, struggling to raise the money to meet their huge maintenance costs. Similar concerns run through every aspect of his work; the chairs he designed were beautiful, for instance, but many of them are acutely uncomfortable to sit in.

The problem with Wright's work, essentially, is that he applied his core concept of organic architecture in too one-sided a way. The way he structured space resonates intensely with the nature of the site, the purpose of the building, and the esthetic of the materials he used; so far, so good. The difficulties arose because he handled at least two other aspects of the building process in a profoundly inorganic way. The first of these, as mentioned already, was his cavalier attitude toward the structural qualities of materials, and more generally to the "substance" side of Aristotle's famous form/substance dichotomy. The rain that leaked through Wright's roofs, and the dampness that pervaded his famous house Fallingwater—it had a stream running through the middle of it, complete with waterfall—and made its first owner refer to it as "Rising Mildew," are substances as relevant to the architect as the material forming the beams that support the floors. An architecture that embraced substance in an organic way would arguably shape form according to the physical potentials and weaknesses of the relevant substances, just as Wright's forms were shaped by the esthetics of the substances he used.

The second aspect is subtler, and the book by Stewart Brand mentioned above is perhaps the best guide to it. A building is a pattern in space and in substance, but it is also a pattern in time, following its own trajectory from the first work on the site to the last swing of the wrecking ball. Successful buildings adapt to the people who live in them or use them, just as the people adapt to the buildings; Brand argues that in this sense, buildings "learn." Many of Wright's buildings—though there were important exceptions—were distinctly slow learners, and some proved to be wholly unteachable. Admittedly, in Wright's day as now, the architect's job mostly ended when the blueprints were handed over to the builder; additionally, of course, creative minds in his milieu were expected to be prima donnas, and his income and reputation depended at least in part on playing that role. Most of today's fashionable architects suffer from the same fixation on form over substance and process, without the benefit of Wright's sure esthetic touch.

All this may seem far removed from the questions that have become central to this blog—the twilight of the industrial age and the birthing of constructive responses to its end—but the same three dimensions just considered—form, substance, process—apply to design in any context, from a mud hut to an alternative currency. Mud huts aside, most modern design that tries to be organic focuses, as Wright did, on organic form, and much of it neglects substance and process. Thus, for example, you get plans for "renewable" energy systems that may use sun or wind, but can't be made or maintained without petroleum products and massive energy inputs, and power equally unsustainable machines or lifestyles.

These same concerns apply even more stringently to plans for social change. Plenty of proposals for allegedly "natural" or "ecological" societies, communities, and institutions have been floated over the last three decades or so, and most of them are natural in the same sense that Wright's architecture is organic: they represent one person's best shot at grasping the natural potentials of a situation. Very often, though, these proposals fail to address issues of substance or process. Substance in a social context refers, among other things, to the people who will presumably take up the new social system, but who inevitably bring to it attitudes and behavior patterns from other social contexts and the evolution of our species; it's notorious, and also true, that most Utopian schemes would work wondrously well if human beings could just stop behaving like human beings.

Process in a social context, in turn, refers to the way that the new system is to be designed, set in motion, and adapted to meet changing needs, but there is another dimension as well: how the new system is to deal with competition from other social systems. When this has been addressed at all, it has too often been phrased in simplistic and stereotyped terms, as by insisting that lifeboat communities have plenty of guns so they can fight off the marauding hordes that feature so largely in contemporary survivalist fantasy. The history of Utopian communities in North America offers a useful corrective; most of the successful communes of the nineteenth century, for example, went under once the founding generation died off and the younger generations found communal life less appealing than the seductions of mainstream culture. The same thing could easily happen in a generation or so to any number of the communities being planned so eagerly today, since a future in which the inhabitants of such communities have no other options is probably the least likely of all the possibilities before us.

I've critiqued the Transition Town movement in these essays, but the value of organic process is one thing that this movement has grasped at least as well as anybody in the peak oil movement just now. Those who are still trying to impose plans based on some ideology or other on the fluid potentials of the future might learn a few things from this source. Still, it's possible and, I think, useful, to go further still in the same direction. One potentially valuable way of doing so is the process of dissensus.

I've borrowed that term from postmodern theorist Ewa Ziarek, who introduced it in a book on ethical theory in 2001. As most of my readers likely guessed at first glance, dissensus is the opposite of consensus, and it comes into play when consensus, for one reason or another, is either impossible or a bad idea: when, that is, irreducible differences make it impossible to find any common ground for agreement on the points that matter, or when settling on any common decision would be premature.

This latter, I suggest, is a fair description of where we stand as we face the future that will follow the end of the industrial age. There's an interesting dichotomy in our knowledge of the future: history can give us a fair idea of the type of events that we will encounter, but neither it nor anything else can give us the details. When housing prices started zooming upwards a few years back, quite a number of people compared that to other speculative bubbles and correctly predicted that an enormous crash would shake the world economy when the bubble popped—but neither they nor anyone else could have known in advance when the crash would come or what the details of its downward course would be.

The twilight of the industrial age puts us in a similar place. Looking at what's happened to previous civilizations that overshot the limits of their resource base, it's not hard to recognize the parallels and predict the onset of the familiar process of decline and fall. That process has some constant features, and it's probably safe to predict that those will occur this time too: for example, mass migration is a very common consequence of the fall of civilizations, and recent warnings about tidal flows of environmental refugees in the not too distant future suggest that it may be a safe bet to assume that the same thing will happen in our future. What nobody can anticipate are the details: what will set any particular migration in motion, what its scale, route, and final destination will be, and above all what the timing will be.

Lacking those details, a consensus plan is not a good idea. If you knew today, let's say, that the region containing your ecovillage was going to have much less rain in the future, you would make one set of choices; if you knew that the same region was going to have much more rain in the future, you would make another, and so on. If you knew that a million refugees from climate change will be coming through your town, your plans would be very different from the ones you would make if you knew that your town would be far from the migration routes. Since these things can't be known in advance, though, whatever consensus you reach has a very real chance of being exactly the wrong choice. This is where dissensus comes to the rescue. In a situation of uncertainty, encouraging people to pursue different and even opposed options increases the likelihood that somebody will happen on the right answer.

Dissensus, it deserves to be said, is not simply a lack of consensus. Like consensus itself, it has its own methods and process, its own values and style; the Thelonious Monk CD playing in my study as I type these words might also serve as a reminder that where dissensus is encouraged, and individuals pursue their own visions rather than submitting to a socially based consensus, the results can include dazzling creativity. Frank Lloyd Wright, with whom I began this essay, was a master of dissensus; great artists usually are. Yet the greatest master of dissensus is arguably Nature itself.

Those first inch-long vertebrates who darted about in shallow seas half a billion years ago, after all, did not come to some sort of genetic consensus about where evolution was going to take them, nor did the evolutionary process itself push them in one direction. Some of their offspring became fish, some amphibians, some reptiles, some birds, and some mammals, and a few of the latter are either typing this essay or reading it. Evolution is dissensus in action, the outward pressure of genetic diversification running up against the limits of environment and, now and then, pushing through to some new adaptation: the wings of bats, the opposable thumbs of primates, the cultural evolution of human beings. As we enter a future of new limits and unpredictable opportunities, this is arguably the kind of organic process we need most.

116: WHY DISSENSUS MATTERS
(Originally published 17 December 2008)

During the last month or so, these essays have tried to present an extended critique of the very common notion that we can collectively plan for, and achieve, the future that we decide we want. By now, though, that point has been pushed about as far as it will go. Those of my readers who are going to get my point have gotten it, and are likely more than ready to go on to something else, while those who continue to believe they can order up a future to go will continue to believe that no matter what gets said here.

Still, that discussion leads on to a further question, one that can't reasonably be avoided here. Given that I don't think much of the prospects of planning a desirable future and then making it happen, what am I suggesting instead? That's a harder question to answer than to ask, because the only answer I have to offer presupposes certain things about what we can know about the future, and those have to be clarified first. The same thing is true, to be sure, about the attempts to plan the future I've critiqued. If we could know where history is headed and what influence our actions could have on it, making firm plans for the future would be a safe bet. Equally, if it's impossible for us to know anything at all about the future, then all bets are off, no course of action is more likely to succeed than any other, and the only option left would be moment-by-moment improvisation.

Still, it seems to me that neither of these extremes fits our situation. There are certainly things ahead that we will never expect until they show up on the doorstep, but not everything about the future falls into this category. An interesting distinction also lies between many of the things we can know about and many of the things we can't: very often, we have no way of knowing what will happen, but we can predict very accurately that certain things won't happen, and we can also accurately predict the kinds of things that will happen.

A specific example may help show how this works. Some years ago, when the late housing bubble was shifting into overdrive, quite a number of people—I was among them, though I didn't have a public platform for my predictions in those days—noted the acceleration in housing prices and drew two conclusions. The first was that those who insisted real estate could increase in value forever were wrong: not just a little bit wrong, but utterly, catastrophically wrong. The second was that if real estate kept zooming up, there was going to be a massive crash. (Those who see this as 20/20 hindsight may visit the Housing Panic blog, one place where these predictions appeared.)

Both predictions, it's worth noting, were based on the evidence of history. Ever since market economies evolved the capacity to support speculative bubbles, people have lost their senses at intervals over some investment or other: tulips, stock, real estate, precious metals, commodities, you name it. The infallible sign that this has happened is the claim that the investment in question is exempt from supply and demand and will just keep increasing in value. I think most of us remember when exactly these things were said about tech stocks, and it's been rather les than a year since many people insisted that the same things were true about petroleum: wrong in both cases, and in every other case in human history. Thus we can know something about the future: we can accurately predict that no speculative investment will rise in value indefinitely.

The second prediction followed on the heels of the first. Because millions of people were climbing aboard the real estate bandwagon, and prices were zooming upwards, it was a safe bet that eventually prices would slump, people would sell off their investments, and the result would be a crash; that's the way every speculative bubble in history has ended. Thus the bloggers on Housing Panic knew the kind of thing the future would hold: a collapse in real estate prices in which a great many people would lose a huge amount of money. Those who noticed that banks were loaning money recklessly to speculators also knew that many banks would go under; again, that's the kind of thing that happens when greed trumps caution and banks forget that money should only be loaned to people who can pay it back.

What nobody knew was when the crash would come, what would trigger it, and how it would play out. This is the difference between knowing what kind of thing will happen and knowing what will happen. Nothing is more difficult than timing a bubble. Isaac Newton, arguably one of the brightest human beings who ever lived, tried to time the market during the South Sea Bubble and lost most of his money. (Any of my readers who consider themselves smarter than Newton are invited to try to predict the turning point of the current bubble in US treasury bills. Since the bursting of that bubble will probably put what's left of the global economy into cardiac arrest, this is by no means a purely academic exercise.)

These same considerations apply to any attempt to predict the future, and in particular to the central theme of this blog, the twilight of industrial civilization and the long descent into a new dark age. Civilizations, like speculative bubbles, have promoters who insist they can keep on going forever; just as with bubbles, announcements of that sort have historically been a clear sign that serious trouble is not too far off. It's a safe bet, in any case, that every bubble will pop and every civilization will decline and fall. Those who are heavily invested in a particular bubble or civilization will of course insist that it's different this time, just as their predecessors did; those claims have been wrong so far, and the evidence isn't favoring them this time, either.

It's quite possible, in turn, to predict the kind of things that will happen as industrial civilization lurches down the uneven slope of decline. Plenty of civilizations have done that before, and the common features stand out clearly from history; some of these features are already visible in the present case — it's educational to page through Spengler or Toynbee and note how many features of a declining civilization had not yet appeared in their time, but have shown up on schedule in ours. What nobody can know in advance is just how these trends will work out in detail.

This is the perspective on the future that frames the proposals I've made here and elsewhere for coping with the long descent ahead of us. It's certainly possible to know in advance some of the things that won't happen. For example, declining civilizations always seem to get prophets who insist that some vast and improbable transformation will suddenly replace their civilization with the kind of society they would rather inhabit. They are always wrong, and such prophecies should be seen as signs of the times rather than knowledge about what will actually happen.

Set such fantasies aside, and it's not that difficult to predict the kind of things that will happen as our civilization runs down. Mass migrations, for example, usually take place when civilizations collapse; the tidal force of migrant workers and refugees streaming across today's borders is already making headlines, so it's a safe bet this process will shift into high gear in the future. On the other hand, it's anyone's guess how those migrations will affect individuals and communities in any given corner of the world. I've suggested in these essays, for instance, that the western shores of North America may end up receiving some millions of refugees by sea from Japan. The Japanese islands can only support a small fraction of their current population on local resources; the northern Pacific currents go the right direction, and Japan has a huge and capable merchant marine and fishing fleet, so means, motive, and opportunity are present.

None of this makes the arrival of the first rusting container ship full of refugees on an Oregon beach a certainty. For all we know, Japan might purchase eastern Siberia from a disintegrating Russia thirty years from now, and settle its extra population there; it might go to war with China and suffer losses so drastic that the point becomes moot; or some other unexpected turn of events might set history in motion down a different path. What we do know is that as fossil fuels run short and importing food becomes a strategy without a future, a large fraction of the population of Japan will either relocate or die, what they do about that bitter choice is less predictable.

Thus the knowledge we can get provides no basis for making a future to order, but potentially allows room for something beyond improvisation. Since a miracle is not going to bail us out from the results of our collective mistakes, we need not waste time waiting for one, and can get to work in more practical ways. Since the kind of things that happen early in a civilization's decline are tolerably well documented, we can assess trends already at work in the areas where we live, and guess at the near-term challenges we are likely to face. Since the endpoint of the process of decline is also fairly well documented, we can try to anticipate what things, readily available now, will be scarce and useful to our descendants, and do what we can to see that those things get passed down the chain of years to the waiting hands of the future.

Now it's true, of course, that none of these options are foolproof. Even with the guidance of history, it's possible to misjudge the shape of the future disastrously, and even those who guess the future in advance may not be able to avoid its dangers. This is why the concept of dissensus, introduced last week, is vital just now: as any ecologist can tell you, in the face of unpredictable change, the wider the range of variation in a species, the more likely that some of them will have what it takes to adapt. A monoculture of ideas, organizational styles, or paradigms is just as vulnerable as a monoculture of living things, and so our best option just now is to encourage disagreement, so as to foster as many different approaches to the future as possible.

The need for dissensus, it should be stressed, does not simply cover the technologies different individuals and groups might decide to pursue, the organizations they might choose to make or support, or the survival strategies that might seem most promising to them. It also reaches into the realm of ends. I have said this several times in recent posts, but it bears repeating: we have no idea what kind of society is best suited to a world after industrialism. It's far more likely than not, in fact, that such a society will have little in common with the notions that middle-class intellectuals in the industrial world today might have of it. This doesn't mean that we shouldn't try to imagine such a society; it does mean that attempts to push diverse visions into a single consensus are as unproductive as they are futile.

Diversity in the realm of ends, finally, also applies to the most basic decisions about the way the predicament of our time is framed. For some people, the most meaningful challenge focuses on rebuilding communities to help them and their residents get through the end of the age of abundance. For others, it focuses on building new societies they hope will replace the one we have now. For still others, it focuses on developing new technologies, or rescuing old ones, to replace those that will stop working when today's lavish energy supplies run out. There are those for whom raw survival is the most important thing, and there are those who have come to terms with the inevitability of death and are pursuing other goals.

Which of these choices is the best? Wrong question. All of them, and more, are necessary parts of a dissensus-based approach to the crisis of industrial civilization. As you read these words, members of a city council in a Midwestern college town may be mulling over a project that will pull their community through hard times, while activists one town over, with the best intentions in the world, devise a similar program that will fail and take their town's future with it. One ecovillage in Ohio may be inventing social forms that will evolve into the neotribal societies of the 22nd century, while another attempt on similar lines sparks quarrels that tear a community to shreds. One hobbyist in Montana, staring at pictures of a 19th century solar steam engine, may start making the prototype of a machine that will become the prime energy source of the ecotechnic age, while others miss the necessary insight and waste their lives on dead ends.

What adds spice to the irony is that we have no way of knowing in advance which is which. All any of us can do is pursue the work that calls to us individually, cooperate with others who share the same commitment, take the measures to weather the crisis that seem to make sense from where we are, and remember that those who disagree with us most heartily may be assembling their own piece of a puzzle that is, ultimately, bigger than any of us.

117: HISTORY'S ARROW

(Originally published 24 December 2008)

One of the advantages of being a Druid is that you get to open your holiday presents four days early. Last Sunday's winter solstice was pleasant, with a scattering of snow on the ground outside and candles burning indoors as we celebrated the rebirth of the sun. As one hinge of the year's cycle, the solstice is a good time to ponder the shape of time: on the small scale, with hopes for the year to come and memories of the one now passing; the middle scale, as I think back on past holidays and the uncertain number that still lie ahead; and the large scale, with which this blog is mostly concerned. In keeping with that seasonal theme, I want to talk a bit about history on the large scale, and the ideas our culture uses to frame the idea of history.

One of the things that has interested me most about the reactions to the ideas about the shape of the future I've presented here on The Archdruid Report is the extent to which so many of them presuppose one particular way of thinking about history. Like the character in one of Moliére's plays who was astonished to find that he had been speaking prose all his life, a great many people these days have embraced a distinctive philosophy of history, but seem never quite to have noticed that fact.

This is hardly a new thing. One of the ironies of the history of ideas is the way that so many cultural themes, surfacing first in avant-garde intellectual circles, are dismissed out of hand by the grandparents of those who will one day treat them as obvious facts. Modern nationalism, to cite one example out of many, began with the romantic visions of a few European poets, spilled out into the world largely through music and the arts, and turned into a massive political force that shredded the political maps of four continents. To some extent, this is the intellectuals' revenge on an unreflective society: the men of affairs who treat the arts as amenities and dismiss philosophy as worthless abstraction spend their workdays unknowingly mouthing the words of dead philosophers and acting out the poems they never read on the stage of current events.

The way of thinking about history I have in mind today follows the same pattern. Karl Popper, who devoted much of his career to critiquing it, called it historicism. This is the belief that history as a whole moves inevitably in a single direction that can be known in advance by human beings. Exactly what that single direction is supposed to be varies from one historicist to another; choose any point along the spectrum of cultural politics, and you can find a version of historicism that treats the popular ideals and moral concerns common to that viewpoint as the linchpin of the historical process. The details differ; the basic assumption remains the same.

That same assumption has also spread to infect nearly every contemporary discussion of change over time. After my post "Taking Evolution Seriously" appeared a few weeks back, for example, one of my longtime readers forwarded me comments from a discussion on an email list, whose members took me to task in no uncertain terms for my discussion on the evolutionary process. When I said that no organism is "more evolved" than any other and that evolution has no particular direction or goal, they insisted, I was simply wrong; evolution progresses in the direction of increased complexity over time, one person claimed, and another suggested that I would be better informed if I read more of the writings of the late Stephen Jay Gould.

Now I have no objection to reading more of Gould's work, as I've already enjoyed many of his books. For that matter, I've read a fair amount of evolutionary theory, beginning with Darwin and continuing through some of the most recent theorists, and also took college courses in evolutionary ecology and several related branches of environmental science. One thing this taught me is that attempts are always being made to stuff evolution into a historicist straitjacket. Another thing I learned is that these attempts are rejected by the great majority of evolutionary biologists, because the evidence simply doesn't fit.

Some evolutionary lineages have moved from more simple to more complex forms over time, but others have gone in the other direction, and the vast majority of living things on Earth today belong to phyla that have not added any noticeable complexity since the Paleozoic. Nor has the Earth's biosphere as a whole become more complex; the entire Cenozoic era—the 65 million years between the last dinosaurs and us—has been less biologically rich than the Mesozoic era that preceded it, and the global cooling of the last fifteen million years or so has seen a decrease in the world's biological complexity, as ecosystems have adapted to the more rigorous conditions that have spread over much of the world.

The facts on the ground, then, simply don't support any claim that evolution moves toward greater complexity. No other version of historicism fares any better when applied to evolution, either. Yet ninety-nine times out of a hundred, when you hear people outside of a university biology department talking about evolution, what they have in mind is a linear process leading in a particular direction. They are, in other words, talking historicism.

Trace these ideas back along their own evolutionary lineage and a fascinating history emerges. The founder of the current of thought that gave rise to today's historicism was an Italian monk named Joachim of Flores, who lived from 1145 to 1202 and spent most of the latter half of his life writing abstruse books on theology. Most Christian theologians before his time accepted Augustine of Hippo's famous distinction between the City of God and the City of Man, and assigned all secular history to the latter category, one more transitory irrelevance to be set aside by the soul in search of salvation. Joachim's innovation was the claim that the plan of salvation works through secular history. He argued that all human history, secular as well as sacred, was divided into three ages, the age of Law under the Old Testament, the age of Love under the New, and the age of Liberty that was about to begin.

Some of his theories were formally condemned by church

councils, but his core theory proved unstoppable. Every generation of church reformers from the thirteenth century to the eighteenth seized on his ideas and claimed that their own arrival marked the coming of the age of Liberty; every generation of church conservatives stood Joachim on his head, insisted that the three ages marked the progressive loss of divine guidance, and portrayed the arrival of the latest crop of reformers as Satan's final offensive. As secular thought elbowed theology aside, in turn, Joachim's notion of history as the working out of a divine plan got reworked into secular theories of humanity's grand destiny.

Notable among these was the theory argued by the Marquis de Condorcet in Sketch for a Historical Picture of the Progress of the Human Spirit in 1794. A rich historical irony surrounds this work; Condorcet had been a strong supporter of the French Revolution, and hoped that the end of the monarchy would usher in a republic of reason; instead, he was condemned to death by the new government and wrote his Sketch while he was on the run from the guillotine. He nonetheless described human history as an inevitable rise from barbarism to a future of reason and progress in which all of human life would undergo endless improvement.

Condorcet's faith in perpetual progress found many listeners, but a more influential voice was already waiting in the wings: Georg Wilhelm Friedrich Hegel, who managed the rare feat of becoming both the most influential and the most unreadable philosopher of modern times. In his Philosophy of History, which was published shortly after his death in 1831, he argued that history was the process by which human freedom (which, for him, was not quite the freedom of the individual; he idolized Napoleon and the government of Prussia) was maximized in time. In Hegel's mind, Joachim's threefold rhythm of history was reworked into the three phases of thesis, antithesis, and synthesis, by which every opposition was resolved into a higher unity.

Hegel's view of history became enormously influential, less through his own work—I challenge any of my readers to plow through the Philosophy of History and come out the other side with anything but a headache—than through the writings of those influenced by him. Political radicals at both ends of the spectrum jumped on Hegel's ideas; on the left, Karl Marx used Hegelian ideas as the foundation for his philosophy of class warfare and Communist revolution; on the right, Giovanni Gentile, the pet philosopher of Mussolini's Fascist regime, was a rigorous Hegelian. For that matter, Francis Fukuyama, who played a role much like Gentile's for the neoconservative movement, drew his theory of an end to history from Hegel.

Still, the spread of Hegel's ideas isn't limited to the radical fringes, or even to those who know who Hegel was. I think most people who have been following the issue of peak oil for more than a few months have noticed, when the subject comes up for discussion in public, one of the most common responses is "Oh, they'll think of something." Ask the person who says this to explain, and odds are you'll be told that every time the world runs out of some resource, "they" find something new, and the result is more progress. This is Hegel reframed in terms of economics; shortage is the thesis, ingenuity the antithesis, and progress the synthesis; the insistence that the process is inevitable puts the icing on the Hegelian cake. More generally, the logic of historicism governs the entire narrative: history's arrow points in the direction of progress, and so whatever happens, the result will be more progress.

Examples could be added by the page, but I hope the point has been made. Still, it's crucial to realize just how deeply historicism has become entrenched in all modern thinking. If, dear reader, you think yourself untouched by it, I encourage you to try a thought experiment. The average species, paleontologists tell us, lasts around ten million years. Imagine that by some means—a visit from a time machine, say, that leaves you holding a history of humanity written by an intelligent species descended from chipmunks—you find out that this is how long we have. We won't achieve godhood, or reach the stars, or destroy the planet, or enter Utopia; instead, the nine million years we've got left will be like recorded history so far. Civilizations will rise and fall; our species will create great art and literature, interpret the universe in various ways, explore many modes of living on the Earth; finally, millions of years from now, it will slowly lose the struggle for survival, dwindle to small populations in isolated areas, and go extinct.

If that turns out to be humanity's future, would you be satisfied with it? Or would you feel that some goal has been missed, some destiny betrayed? If the latter, what makes you think that?

Now of course it may be a waste of breath to contend with ideas as pervasive and deeply rooted as historicism, but the effort has to be made, if only because historicism has a dismally bad track record as a basis for prophecy. Name a historicist belief system that's been around more than a few years, right back to Joachim of Flores himself, and you'll find a trail of failed predictions of the imminent arrival of the goal of history. (Joachim himself apparently believed that the age of Liberty would arrive in 1260; no such luck.) If we are to have any useful sense of the future ahead of us, historicist belief systems are among the worst sources of guidance available to us.

Fortunately there are other choices. In next week's post, I plan on talking about some of those. In the meantime, best holiday wishes to all my readers — whatever holidays you celebrate at this time of year.

118: HISTORY'S MEANING, HISTORY'S CHOICES

(Originally published 31 December 2008)

The end of one year and the beginning of another has been a time for celebration and reflection since around the time calendars were invented, and even though the date has been kicked around the yearly cycle pretty comprehensively by history's boot—it hasn't been that long, all things considered, since the civil year in the English-speaking world began in late April—there's a point to the custom. Our individual lives have their turning points, and so does the collective life of communities and cultures; the hinge of time when one year changes to another provides a useful reminder of such things. It's in this spirit that I want to wrap up one of the threads of discussion that's shaped my posts on The Archdruid Report for several weeks now.

Several times now in these essays, I've brought up the names of some of the major theorists of cyclic history—Giambattista Vico, Oswald Spengler, Arnold Toynbee—and talked a little about how their ideas illuminate the current crisis of industrial civilization. For the last three centuries, the tradition these authors and their works embody has challenged the historicist faith discussed in last week's post: the belief that history has an arrow with the words "this way only" painted on it somewhere; that, in other words, it has a direction, a purpose and a goal. If a meaningful sense of history is a tool worth having as we face the predicament of our time, and historicism does not provide such a sense—and to my mind, at least, both these assertions are far more true than not—the vision of cyclic history is one place where something more useful might be found.

Mind you, cyclic and historicist views of history are both out of fashion these days; there is no shortage of scholars who lump them together as "metanarratives," and insist that they should be banned from serious history. The problem with this insistence is that human beings think in stories as inevitably as they walk with feet. Attempting to chase metanarratives out of history simply results in assaults on those metanarratives unpopular enough to be noticed, while those that are accepted unthinkingly slip past the sentries with ease. The statement "history follows no pattern," after all, is itself a metanarrative: a narrative about historical narratives that embodies a particular approach to historical knowledge. Thus attempts to talk about the shape of history should not be dismissed out of hand; the question that needs to be asked of them is simply whether they help to make sense of the course of historical events.

Yet this question itself can be read in more than one way. Historicist and cyclic theories of history both try to make sense of history, but they try to make different kinds of sense; they get different answers because they ask fundamentally different questions. At the core of historicism is the intuition that history has a meaning, while at the core of the cyclic vision is the intuition that history has a pattern—and "meaning" and "pattern" are by no means interchangeable terms. Most historicist theories, mind you, find pattern as well as meaning in history. Most cyclic theories, by contrast, leave questions of the meaning of history entirely open, and some—Oswald Spengler was particularly outspoken in this regard—reject the idea that history as a whole has any meaning or purpose with as much vehemence as any positivist.

Spengler's reasons for this rejection are worth examining, because his rejection of historicism went deeper than just about any other thinker I can name. He argued that history can have no overall meaning, because it's impossible to talk of meaning at all except within the worldview of a given culture; each culture evolves its own distinct way of experiencing human life in the universe, and the only meaning humans can know is embodied in these distinctive worldviews. No culture's worldview is more or less true than any other, nor are the worldviews of cultures that arise later on in history an improvement in any sense on the ones that came before; each culture defines reality uniquely through its own dialogue with the inscrutable patterns of nature and the human experience. Interestingly, Spengler applied this logic to his own work as well; he offered his theory not as an objective truth about historical cycles, but simply as the best account of historical cycles that could be given from within the perspective of modern Western — in his terms, Faustian — humanity.

When it got past superficialities, much of the criticism that has been directed at Spengler's work over the last nine decades took aim squarely at his insistence that every culture's worldview is equally valid, and that humanity therefore does not progress. What makes his resolute rejection of our culture's superiority unacceptable to so many people, though, is precisely that it offends against the pervasive historicism of our age. Only the belief that history is headed somewhere in particular, with our civilization presumably in the lead, makes his thesis in any way problematic.

For what it's worth, I think that Spengler was right in principle but wrong on a minor but important detail. He was certainly right to point out that trying to rank worldviews of different cultures according to some scheme of progress or other yields self-serving nonsense. Ancient Egyptians understood the universe in one way, and modern Americans understand it in another, not because Americans are right and Egyptians were wrong — or vice versa! — but because the two cultures were not talking about the same things, nor were they using the same symbolic language for the discussion. A worldview based on explorations of the metaphysics of human life in the language of myth cannot meaningfully be judged by the standards of a worldview that takes analysis of the physical world in the language of mathematics as its starting point.

To say that the industrial world's technological progress proves the superiority of its worldview merely begs the question, since the Egyptians did not value technological progress. They valued cultural stability and they achieved it, maintaining cultural continuity for well over 3000 years — a feat our own civilization is not likely to equal. By their standards, for that matter, our society's ephemeral fashions, ceaseless cultural turmoil, and incoherent metaphysics would have branded it as an abject failure at the most basic tasks of human social life.

As I see it, though, Spengler undervalued the process by which certain kinds of technique invented by one culture can enrich later cultures. A very relevant example is classical logic, among the supreme achievements of the Apollonian culture, which was inherited in turn by the Indian, Syrian-Byzantine-Arabic (in Spengler's language, Magian), and Faustian cultures. No two of these cultures did the same thing with that inheritance; a toolkit Greeks devised to pick apart spoken language was used in India to analyze the structures of consciousness, in the Levant to contemplate the glories of God, and in Europe and the European diaspora to unravel the mysteries of matter. Without Greek logic, though, some of the greatest creations of all three inheritor cultures — the rich philosophical dimensions of Hinduism and Buddhism, the great theological syntheses of Islam and Christianity, or the fusion of logic with experience that gave rise to the modern scientific method — certainly could not have been done as easily, and quite possibly might not have happened at all.

What this implies is that, while history is not directional, it can be cumulative. Nothing in the history of cultures older than Greece suggests that the emergence of logic was inevitable, just as nothing in the subsequent history of logic justifies the claim that logic is developing toward some goal or other. Still, the toolkit of logic, absent before the Greeks, enriched a series of cultures that flourished after them. There are countless examples, and they span the full range of human cultural creations; for a small but telling example, consider how the practice of counting prayers on a string of beads, which originated in India, has spread through most of the world's religions. For another, consider the way that forty centuries of East Asian intensive agriculture inspired the emergence of organic growing methods that are probably our best bet for tomorrow's food supply. Every person who finds spiritual solace in prayer or meditation with a rosary, or is planning a backyard organic garden to help put food on the table next year, has good reasons to be grateful for the slow accumulation of technique over time.

Thus there's a fine irony in the insistence by so many people these days that evolution will shortly relieve us of the necessity to deal with the consequences of our own mistakes, and get history back on track to their imagined goal. They're right that the historical changes under way now are evolutionary in nature; their mistake lies in thinking, to put the matter perhaps a bit too harshly, that evolution is some sort of cosmic tooth fairy who can be counted on to leave a shiny new future under the modern world's pillow to replace one rotted away by three centuries of extravagant living. Instead, the historical development of cultures parallels the way that evolution actually works in nature. Cultures, like species, tend to collect those adaptations that meet their needs, and discard the ones that don't. Thus those techniques that happen to meet the needs of more than one culture tend to survive more often than those that don't, just as those cultures that are able to make use of a suitable range of inherited techniques are more likely to thrive than those that do not.

I trust none of my readers are drowsy enough by this point to think that I am suggesting that the accumulation of useful techniques is the meaning, purpose, or goal of history. From my point of view, for whatever that may be worth, meanings, purposes, and goals are not to be found in any objective sense in the brute facts of existence; they are always and only attributes applied creatively to existence by conscious persons, and the emergence of meanings, purposes and goals common to more than one person depends on the relation between the person proposing these things and those who choose to accept or reject them. (Atheists may read this statement in one sense, and religious people in quite another; interestingly enough, the logic works either way.)

Like biological evolution, though, the cultural evolution I am proposing here is in no way inevitable. The crises that surround the decline and fall of civilizations, in particular, very often become massive choke points at which many valuable things are lost. One reasoned response to the approach of such a choke point in our own time thus might well be a deliberate effort to help the legacy of the present reach the waiting hands of the future. The same logic that leads the ecologically literate to do what they can to keep threatened species alive through the twilight of the industrial age, so that biological evolution has as wide a palette of raw materials as possible in the age that follows, applies just as well to cultural evolution.

Thus it may not be out of place to imagine a list of endangered knowledge to go along with today's list of endangered species, and to take broadly equivalent steps to preserve both. There are certainly other meanings, purposes and goals that can be found in, or more precisely applied to, either the inkblot patterns of history as a whole or the specific challenges we face right now, in the early stages of industrial civilization's decline and fall. We can decide as individuals whether to build on the heritage of our culture, to explore the legacies have been handed down to us from other cultures, or to scrap the lot and try to break new ground, knowing all the while that other individuals will make their own choices and the relative success of the results, rather than any preference of ours, will determine which of them plays the largest role in shaping the future.

My own choice centers on the preservation of those parts of the modern world's heritage that I find most valuable, and most promising, as tools for the futures that seem most likely to me. If that way of putting things seems uncomfortably subjective, personal, and even arbitrary, dear reader, you're beginning to get the point of the last month or two of *Archdruid Report* posts. Our own subjective, personal, and arbitrary perceptions are the only things we have to go on, and the results tend to be much less problematic when we accept this fact, rather than trying to cast the shadows of our desires onto history's arc and stare at them in the fond delusion that we're staring destiny in the face.

One way or another, we all have choices to make as the new year dawns. Some of us will face the harsh decisions that come with unemployment, foreclosure, and bankruptcy; others will encounter the moral challenges that face those who have wealth while others go hungry; still others will have other choices. Not everyone will be at liberty to take the deindustrial future into account as they make their choices, but I hope some will do so, and whatever you choose in this regard — whether or not it corresponds to any of the things I've discussed here—it might be wise to take action on the basis of your decisions sooner rather than later. A year, after all, is not the only thing that's ending around us just now.

ABOUT THE AUTHOR

Born in the gritty Navy town of Bremerton, Washington, and raised in the wastelands of mid-twentieth century suburbia, John Michael Greer has been writing since about ten minutes after he figured out how to hold a pencil. He is the author of more than fifty books on a range of subjects from the future of industrial society to Druid nature spirituality, and currently blogs at www.ecosophia.net. He lives in Rhode Island with his wife Sara.